Facades

Design, Construction & Technology

BRAUN

Facades

Lara Menzel

Design, Construction & Technology

BRAUN

CONTENTS

8 Preface

Culture/Public

12 **Zenith Music Hall**
Massimiliano and Doriana Fuksas

14 **LaM – Lille Museum of Modern,
Contemporary and Outsider Art**
Manuelle Gautrand Architecture

16 **Medical Library Oasis**
HPP Architects

20 **Carl-Henning Pedersen & Else-Alfelt Museum**
C. F. Møller Architects

21 **House of Prayers in Černošice**
Fránek Architects

22 **Rhine Falls Visitor Center**
Leuppi & Schafroth Architekten

24 **Moderna Museet**
Tham & Videgård Arkitekter

26 **City Hall Zaanstad**
Soeters Van Eldonk architecten

27 **MAS | Museum aan de Stroom**
Neutelings Riedijk Architects

28 **Mora River Aquarium**
Promontorio

30 **Parish Center in Rivas-Vaciamadrid**
Vicens + Ramos

32 **ABC Museum**
Aranguren & Gallegos

36 **Harpa Reykjavik Concert Hall and
Conference Center**
Henning Larsen Architects

40 **Red Sun Pavilion**
Ateliers Jean Nouvel

42 **Ordos Museum**
MAD

44 **Festival Hall Plauen**
CODE UNIQUE Architekten

46 **Forum Schönblick**
Klaiber+Oettle

48 **Örsta Gallery**
Claesson Koivisto Rune Architects

49 **2010 Taipei Flora Exhibition – Far Eastern EcoArk**
Miniwiz

50 **NO99 Straw Theater**
SALTO architects

52 **Pantheon Nube**
Clavel Arquitectos

54 **White Chapel**
Jun Aoki & Associates

56 **Pavilion 21 MINI Opera Space**
Coop Himmelb(l)au

Education/Research/Health

58 **Center for Sustainable Energy Technologies**
Mario Cucinella Architects

62 **Adaptonic Transfer Center**
JSWD Architekten

64 **Käthe Kollwitz School**
Schmucker und Partner Planungsgesellschaft

66 **Villaverde Health Care Center**
estudio.entresitio

68 **Kekec Kindergarten**
Arhitektura Jure Kotnik

70 **ASU Walter Cronkite School of Journalism &
Mass Communication**
Ehrlich Architects

72 **Martinet Primary School**
Mestura Architects

74 **Kindergarten Ajda 2**
Arhitektura Jure Kotnik

75 **Nursery in the Park**
Santiago Carroquino architects and
Gravalos Di Monte architects

76 **Santa Isabel Kindergarten**
Santiago Carroquino architects

78 **Center for Dialysis**
Nickl & Partner

80 **Cib – Biomedical Research Center**
Vaíllo & Irigaray + Galar

82 **Smarties**
Architectenbureau Marlies Rohmer

84 **Institute for Ornithology**
adam architekten

88 **TU Chemie Graz**
Zinterl Architekten

90 **Secondary School**
4a architekten

92 **Lecture Hall and Department of Real Estate Business**
Ferdinand Heide Architekt

94 **BioMedizinZentrum Bochum**
hammeskrause architekten

96 **ZET – Sustainability Lab**
knerer und lang

100 **Public Secondary School**
Schulz & Schulz Architekten

102 **Oslo International School**
Jarmund/Vigsnæs AS Architects

104 **Center for Pediatric Medicine Angelika-Lautenschläger-Klinik**
Nickl & Partner

Industrial

108 **Floodwater Pumping Station**
Dirk Melzer landscape architecture + v-architekten

110 **Booster Station South**
Group A

111 **Primary Substation – 2012 Olympics**
NORD

112 **CUSWC – Central Urban Solid Waste Collection**
Vaíllo & Irigaray + Galar

Living/Hotel

114 **Residential Complex Granatniy 6**
SPEECH Tchoban & Kuznetsov

116 **Aloft London Excel**
Jestico + Whiles

120 **Suites Avenue Aparthotel**
Toyo Ito & Associates, Architects, UDA Arquitectos

122 **Residential Multi-familiy Home**
Halle 58 Architekten

124 **Hotel Quai de Seine**
Chaix & Morel et Associés | JSWD Architekten

126 **The Integral House**
Shim-Sutcliffe Architects

127 **Jurčkova**
Enota

128 **2C Houses**
Vaíllo & Irigaray + Eguinoa

132 **House 77**
dIONISO LAB

134 **W London Leicester Square**
Jestico + Whiles

135 **Chrome Hotel**
SANJAY PURI ARCHITECTS

136 **Apartment House in Chelsea**
Ateliers Jean Nouvel

138 **House p**
fischer berkhan architekten

140 **Town Hall Hotel**
RARE Architecture

144 **Trojan House**
Jackson Clements Burrows Architects

145 **House on Henry's Meadow**
Shim-Sutcliffe Architects

146 **Hotel Courtyard by Marriott**
Zechner & Zechner

148 **Block 16**
René van Zuuk Architekten

150 **Sotelia**
Enota

152 **Town Villas Siesmayerstraße**
Jo. Franzke Architekten

154 **Residential Suites Linienstrasse**
Gewers & Pudewill architects designers engineers

158 **Duplex House**
Arndt Geiger Herrmann Zurich

Mixed-Use

160 **Kraton 230**
Mei architecten en stedenbouwers

162 **Mixed-Use Affordable Housing**
Patrick T I G H E Architecture

164 **Hotel + Office Tower**
Vaíllo & Irigaray + Eguinoa

166 **Netherlands Institute for Sound and Vision**
Neutelings Riedijk Architects

167 **8 House**
BIG – Bjarke Ingels Group

168 **Rose am Lend**
INNOCAD Architektur

CONTENTS

170 **Residential and Commercial Building**
GKS Architekten+Partner

172 **"The Wave"**
Hon.Prof. Johanne Nalbach,
Nalbach + Nalbach Architekten

174 **Le Monolithe**
MVRDV

176 **Revitalization WestendGate**
Just/Burgeff Architekten with a₃lab

180 **Mixed-Use Development**
Renzo Piano Building Workshop

182 **Airspace Tokyo**
Faulders Studio

Office

184 **The Orange Cube**
Jakob + MacFarlane Architects

188 **Office Building**
SPEECH Tchoban & Kuznetsov

190 **Fin House**
Thomas Pink | Petzinka Pink Architekten

194 **S11 "Steckelhörn 11"**
J. MAYER H. Architects

196 **Euro Space Center**
Philippe Samyn and Partners,
architects & engineers

198 **German Embassy, Warsaw**
Holger Kleine Architekten

202 **Four Elements**
Thomas Pink | Petzinka Pink Architekten

206 **Origami Office Building**
Manuelle Gautrand Architecture

208 **Office Block**
Philippe Samyn and Partners,
architects & engineers

210 **Galilée**
Studio Bellecour Architects

214 **IBA DOCK**
Prof. Han Slawik

216 **Lighthouse**
Thomas Pink | Petzinka Pink Architekten

218 **Kontor 19 in the Rheinauhafen**
GATERMANN + SCHOSSIG

222 **Cinetic Office Building**
Valode & Pistre architectes

224 **spectr[a]um**
LAb[au], laboratory for architecture and urbanism

225 **Reiss Headquarter**
Squire and Partners

226 **The Crystal**
schmidt hammer lassen architects

230 **Q1 in the ThyssenKrupp Quarter**
JSWD Architekten | Chaix & Morel et Associés

234 **Transoceanica Headquarters**
+ arquitectos

235 **weather.tower**
LAb[au], laboratory for architecture and urbanism

236 **Capricorn House**
GATERMANN + SCHOSSIG

238 **Conference and Finance Center of the VW Bank**
Architekten BKSP Grabau Leiber Obermann
and Partners

242 **ADA 1 – Office Building "An der Alster 1"**
J. MAYER H. Architects

244 **Im Zollhafen 22, Rheinauhafen**
GATERMANN + SCHOSSIG

248 **Commercial Center Punto Bregaglia**
Renato & Reto Maurizio

250 **The New York Times Building**
Renzo Piano Building Workshop
with FXFowle Architects

254 **Kuggen**
Wingårdh Arkitektkontor

Retail/Showroom

256 **New Façade of Galeria Kaufhof**
ANGELIS & PARTNER

258 **John Lewis Department Store and Cineplex**
Foreign Office Architects

262 **Zeilgalerie – Façade Redesign**
3deluxe in/exterior

264 **Placebo Pharmacy**
klab Architecture

266 **Grukšovje**
Enota

268 **"Nowy Swiat" Shopping Center**
Progress Eco

270 **Leonardo Glass Cube**
3deluxe in/exterior

274 **Hard Rock Cafe**
Architectkidd

276 **Star Place**
Ben van Berkel / UNStudio

278 **Sportalm Flagship Store**
Baar-Baarenfels Architekten

280 **Eurospar Vorkloster**
Dietrich | Untertrifaller Architekten

282 **Breuninger Fabric Façade**
DITTEL | ARCHITEKTEN

284 **Showroom Kiefer Technic**
Ernst Giselbrecht + Partner

288 **Galleria Centercity**
Ben van Berkel / UNStudio

Sports/Leisure

290 **Greenpix Zero Energy Wall**
Simone Giostra & Partners

294 **Temporary Bar**
LIKEarchitects

295 **New Holmenkollen Ski Jump**
JDS/Julien De Smedt Architects

Traffic

296 **Car Park Two at Chesapeake**
Elliott + Associates Architects

298 **Santa Monica Civic Center Parking Structure**
Moore Ruble Yudell Architects & Planners

300 **Parking Garage**
Inbo

302 **Car Park One at Chesapeake**
Elliott + Associates Architects

304 **HTCE Parking Lot**
Inbo

306 **Gnome Garage Almere**
Mei architecten en stedenbouwers

308 Architects Index

319 Picture Credit

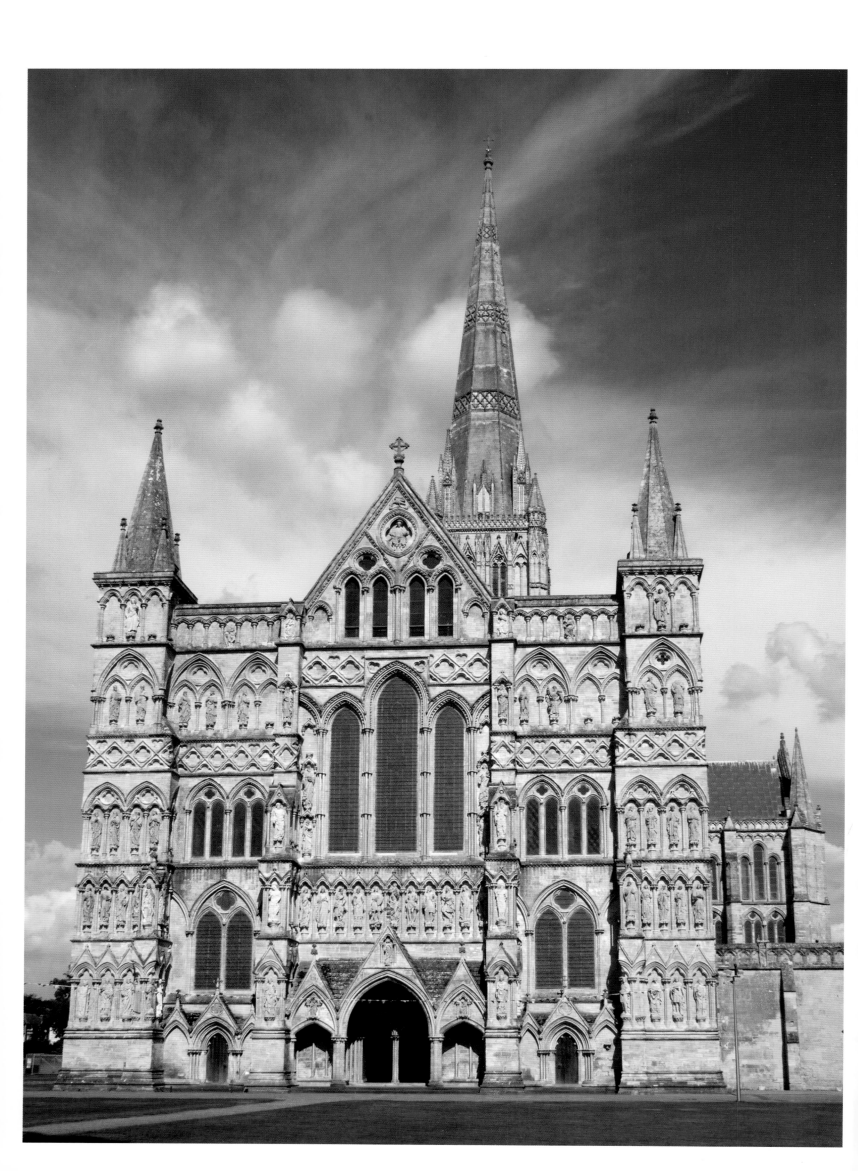

Facing the Front

by Chris van Uffelen

The word façade is derived from the Latin term "facies", or outward appearance. It connotes the outwardly visible surface structure of buildings – in a narrower sense only the appearance of the front side of a building even. This is usually the side of the main entrance, in Christian churches, for example, mostly the western side. In highly visible locations, for example on a hill overlooking a city, a different side can also serve as the front side. However, the main façades with the main entrance generally face public urban sites (city, square) and dominate the appearance of the building. Nevertheless, side façades such as those of Gothic naves or Baroque palace gardens can be designed as elaborately as the main façade with its dominating building structure. The other sides of buildings were usually designed more simply, even though architectural history includes examples of all-round prestigiously designed buildings, the most famous example being the Villa La Rotonda (1571) by Andrea Palladio.

Today's architecture differentiates less among the different façades – many buildings have a different appearance on all sides and often only the entrance indicates the main façade of the entire building's skin. Contrary to the concept of the outer wall, the term façade primarily denotes an architectural and not a constructional principle. It refers to the outermost building layer and the ones behind, if they are visible. The outer wall denotes the constructive unit, while the façade describes the visual surface of the building's skin.

The differentiation between the outer wall and the façade is especially crucial in situations where they are separated from each other. The façade can become an independent structure that completely obscures the look of the building behind it by exhibiting a completely different structure. While most Romanesque era façades immediately revealed the structure of the building's architectural parts, or narthexes and westworks served as independent entrance structures, the double-tower façade of St. Etienne in Caen initiated the development of Gothic façades as independently structured front sides. In the Gothic era, screen façades also evolved, which were placed as thin layers in front of the actual buildings (Salisbury Cathedral). Veneered façades (Palais Bourbon, Paris) provided new looks to hide outdated old buildings. Façades

did not completely cover the building behind them only in rare cases, such as Leon Battista Alberti's Sant'Andrea in Mantua. This building is a particular vivid example of the façade's design and proportion – a combination of a triumphal arch and a temple front – dominating the dimension of the building situated behind it. During the Renaissance era, the conceptualization of façades had a key significance. The shapes and proportions of antiquity were used as models to be emulated. The horizontal division into a plinth section, main section and terminal top section became canonical and had to be brought in sync with the functions, while the vertical division of the main section had to also fit in harmoniously. Andrea Palladio devised the 'giant order' as prototype solution to the latter requirement in his monumental design of the Palazzo Valmarana-Braga in Vicenza. With his design of the façade of Il Gesù in Rome during the early Baroque era, Giacomo della Porta was even able to establish a façade style that became binding for the entire Jesuit order. The church building by Giacomo Vignola located behind it was the initial building of the Baroque. Baroque façades often feature an unprecedented three-dimensional quality. Convex and concave elements simulated movement in the building fronts and had a much more powerful effect on the urban space than the comparatively planar façades of the previous eras with their orthogonal projections and bays. In this era and the subsequent Rococo the colorfulness of façades also reached a vividness that had not been seen

↖↖ | **West front Salisbury Cathedral,** England, 1258.
↖ | **Villa Rotonda,** Italy, 1571.

since Antiquity. The subsequent Neoclassicism required a new appearance based on the assumption that antique temples were bright white and the return to traditional façade proportions.

Due to the very strict shape codex of the Neoclassicism era, there were particularly frequent clashes between the desired look and functionalities, which is clearly apparent on numerous churches where the Christian tower dominates the heathen temple (Allan Dreghorn's St Andrew in Glasgow). After Historicism and Eclecticism had utilized the entire scope of previous elements during the 19th century, the question of the relationship between the outer wall and the façade suddenly took on a whole new dimension: for the Monadnock Building in Chicago, Burnham and Root had to render the ground floor walls almost 2 meters thick to enable them to carry the weight of the 16 floors. However, the suitable solution was already present at the time: Iron (Joseph Paxton's Crystal Palace in London 1851) and steel lattice formwork (Jules Saulnier's Menier factory in Noisiel 1871) were thin and resilient. Louis H. Sullivan, who established the new dimensions of Chicago's steel frame construction high-rises by adjusting the plinth, main part and terminal section, uttered the far reaching statement "form follows function." In conjunction with the honesty discussions of 100 years earlier, Adolf Loos' "Ornament and Crime", and Le Corbusiers "Five points of architecture" (including ribbon windows and free façades), this led to the sober façades of Classical Modernity. Nevertheless, these façades were far from being as free of "intentional shapes" as they claimed to be. The whitewashing itself was already a deliberate style feature, often hiding the rather outdated building methods (Erich Mendelsohn's Einstein Tower made of brick).

At around this time the media façade was born – creating a second appearance with nightly neon signs and illumination, and – much more consequential – the curtain wall. Initially created for factories (1903 Steiff toy factory in

Giengen; 1911 Walter Gropius' Fagus factories), this type of façade that was no longer bearing but resting on the bearing structure conquered the whole world through the Dessau-based Bauhaus movement and remains to this day among the most popular façade types, in addition to the continuously used punctuated façade (solid construction with openings) and million and transom (half-timbered) styles. Ludwig Mies van der Rohe conceived a perfect curtain wall design for the Seagram Building in New York, resolving the corner conflict between the static system and the façade rhythm, which was already a concern during Greek Antiquity. The curtain façade and other element and system façades (Egon Eiermann's honeycomb tiles for the Horten department stores of the 1960s) dominated the post-war era. The self-supporting concrete shell (Felix Candela) was also given a new impetus, resulting in three-dimensional external expressions of engineering architecture the likes of which had not been seen since the Baroque era. Today, the glazed curtain façade, the most popular kind of this façade type, competes with structural glazing for the greatest possible transparency. In this process, the glass panes are glued, giving the impression of a vast pane without fixtures. The continuously popular exterior insulation finishing system (EIFS), however, has often resulted in an unattractive uniformity of building's outward appearance.

The design of the Centre Pompidou in Paris (by Renzo Piano, Richard Rogers and Gianfranco Franchini, 1977), opposed the uniformity and technical perfection of the post-war façades by placing the supply technology on the outside, while the post-modern style (also of the 1970s) revived the decorative façade elements known since Antiquity (tympanum, attached column) in an abstracted and often ironic fashion. In 1987, Jean Nouvel's Institut du Monde Arabe caused a stir by integrating blinds into glass façade elements to shade the interior, promoting the development of façade modules with integrated functions.

The latest architecture focuses on technical consideration in an unprecedented way: the design is affected by necessity and awareness and currently also by the economic viability of ecological construction. The double-skin façade creates a climatic buffer between an interior and a frequently glazed exterior façade layer that at the same time allows natural ventilation even of large high-rises. Vertical gardens (Patrick Blanc) not only visually enliven the urban landscape, but also improve the structural physical properties and the local climate by hydrating the air and reducing dust. Essentially, the suspended, rear ventilated façades are a return to the "apron architecture" that Classical Modernity sought to eliminate – albeit due to functional and ecological considerations. The double-skin façade is contracted to the closest possible distance, and the exterior layer takes on the representative and protective function, while the insulation and the static function are handled by the "interior exterior wall". However, technology is excellently accounted for in the current style of second modernity, which can be described as new elegance. Following the architectural historical tradition of Mies van der Rohe (Barcelona Pavilion), architects are seeking high-quality surface materials and unconventional patterns that provide the buildings with an exclusive look, creating a prestigious exterior without the traditional façade elements of Post-Modernity. Almost all buildings of this book can be seen in this context, even though the variety of applied materials and shapes are not found anywhere in architectural history.

↗↗ | **Centre Pompidou**, Paris, France, 1977.
→ | **Façade of Institut du monde arabe,**
Paris, France, 1987.
→→ | **Openings create an ornamental play of light and shadow.**

Massimiliano and
Doriana Fuksas

↑ | Detail façade

Zenith Music Hall

Strasbourg

This building is an autonomous sculpture. Situated in an undeveloped area outside the city of Strasbourg, the Zenith Music Hall can accommodate up to 12,000 people. Shaped like an asymmetric oval, the steel and concrete structure is enveloped in an orange-colored fabric, composed of glass fiber with silicone spread across two sides. This sculpture, with distinctive non-parallel ring-shaped folds, is opaque at daytime and almost transparent at night time. At night it turns into a magical lamp that makes the hall stand out from its surroundings. The inner experience is transmitted to the outside through the transparent skin – the building becomes a "light sculpture".

CONSTRUCTION FACTS

Structure: new building. **Construction type:** steel and concrete structure. **Material:** fabric composed of glass fiber with silicone spread. **Fixing:** fabric wrapped around metal structure. **Special functions:** backlit textile façade.

Address: 67034 Strasbourg, France. **Client:** Communauté Urbaine de Strasbourg. **Completion:** 2008. **Building type:** music hall. **Other creatives:** Betom (structural engineering), Pixelum (illumination engineering), Altia (acoustics), Architecture et Technique (scenography). **Construction engineer façade:** Form TL (textile structure), Canobbio (wrapping and laying), Interglas (production fabric and façade wrapping).

↑ | Interior view construction
↓ | Longitudinal section
↓↓ | Cross section

↑ | Detail textile façade

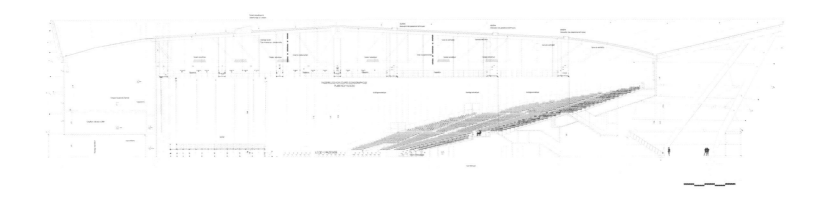

Manuelle Gautrand
Architecture

↑ | Lit façade at night

LaM – Lille Museum of Modern, Contemporary and Outsider Art

Villeneuve

The project involved the refurbishment and extension of the Lille Modern Art Museum, which is on the historic monuments list. While leaving a distance, the architect also created a contact between the extension and the existing buildings. The extension wraps around the north and east sides of the building in a fanned splay of long fluid and organic volumes. On one side, the fan ribs stretch in close folds to shelter a café-restaurant opening to the central patio. On the other, the ribs are more widely spaced to form the five galleries for the Art brut collection. The façade consists of smooth untreated concrete, with moldings and openwork screens to protect the bays from too much daylight. The slight color tint of the surface concrete varies according to the intensity of light.

CONSTRUCTION FACTS

Structure: new construction, in context. **Construction type:** concrete façade, curtain wall (extremities). **Material:** precast concrete for the "moucharaby" panels. **Fixing:** punctuated fixing. **Insulation:** thermal insulation, sun screen. **Special functions:** several layers protect the art pieces.

Address: Alleé des Musées, Villeneuve d'Ascq, France. **Client:** Lille Métropole Communauté urbaine. **Completion:** 2010. **Building type:** museum. **Other creatives:** Renaud Pierard (museography). **Construction engineer façade:** Khephren (structure).

↑ | Detail "moucharaby"

↑ | Fragmented daylight inside

↓ | South elevation

↓↓ | Patio

HPP Architects

↑ | Library on campus
→ | Exterior view

Medical Library Oasis

Dusseldorf

The plans for the new medical library of the Dusseldorf University Hospital focused on the theme of "The library experience." On a total of ten levels, the new 38-meter high building contains library facilities, a cafeteria, as well as recreation and event areas. The building is crowned by a roof terrace offering an unobstructed view of the university campus. The façade design of the library is inspired by a capillary system, a concept that was effectively implemented on the smooth white façade skin. Organically shaped glass sections extend across the slim cube, creating attractive points of interaction between the inside and the outside. The result is an animated building with a unique identity and great recognition value.

CONSTRUCTION FACTS
Structure: new building, solitaire on campus.
Construction type: rear ventilated curtain wall. **Material:** solar protection glazing, glass mosaic tiles. **Fixing:** punctuated fixing.
Insulation: R-value: 0.48 W/(m²K).

Address: Universitätsstraße 1, 40225 Dusseldorf, Germany. **Client:** Universitätsklinikum Düsseldorf A.d.ö.R.. **Completion:** 2011. **Building type:** library and learning center. **Other creatives:** Bollinger + Grohmann Ingenieure (structural engineering), Winter Ingenieure (HVAC), ARGE Silvia Pappa/UKW (interior design). **Construction engineer façade:** Bollinger + Grohmann, IFP Fassadenplanung.

↑ | **Organically shaped glass elements with glass mosaic tiles**
↓ | **Detail sections façade**

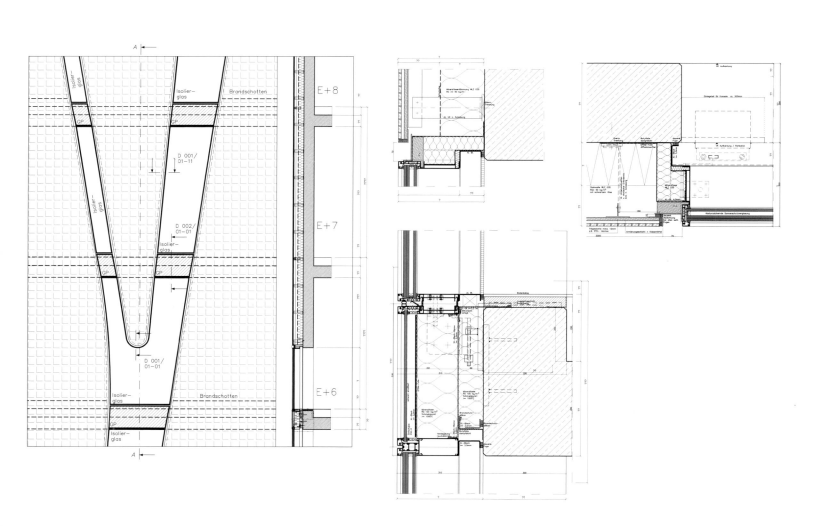

↑ | Entrance area
← | Detail interior façade

C. F. Møller Architects

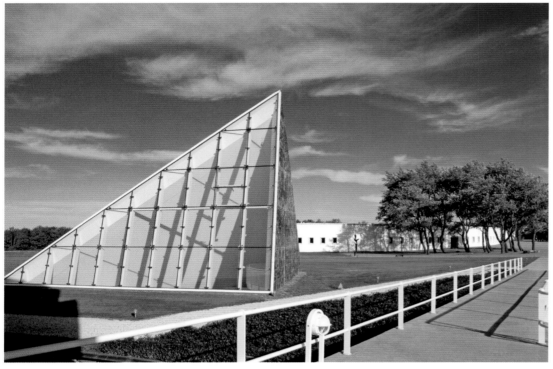

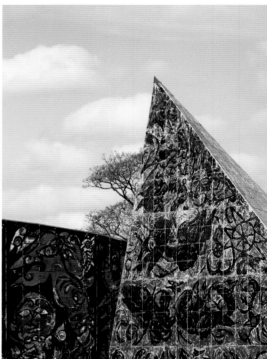

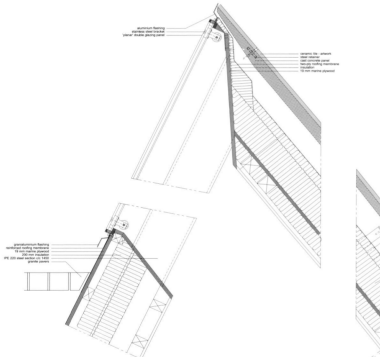

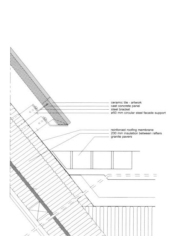

↖↖ | Pyramidal skylight prism
↑↑ | Façade with ceramic tiles
↖ | Vertical section of skylight prism
↑ | Detail colorful tiles

Carl-Henning Pedersen & Else Alfelt Museum

Herning

The 1976 Carl-Henning Pedersen & Else Alfelt Museum contains works by the Danish artists Carl-Henning Pedersen and Else Alfelt, who were both active in the Cobra movement. The museum is characterized by the unity of art and architecture in the sculptural form. The façade is clad with ceramic tiles and decorated with Carl-Henning Pedersen's colorful mythical beasts. In 1993, the museum was expanded to provide more space for the arts collection. Another geometrical shape, the extension forms a prism and has an underground square that connects to the existing collection. It was designed in close co-operation with Carl-Henning Pedersen.

PROJECT FACTS
Address: Birk Centerpark 1, 7400 Herning, Denmark. **Client:** Herning Municipality and The Carl-Henning Pedersen & Else Alfelt Museum. **Completion:** 2007. **Building type:** museum. **Other creatives:** Carl-Henning Pedersen, Else Alfelt (artists). **Construction engineer façade:** MidtConsult A/S.

CONSTRUCTION FACTS
Structure: new building, extension. **Construction type:** rear ventilated curtain wall. **Material:** handmade artwork on cast concrete panels, laminated glazing panels. **Fixing:** punctuated fixing.

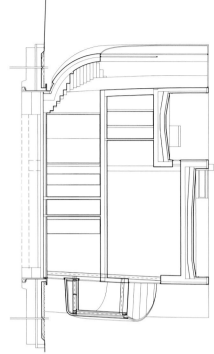

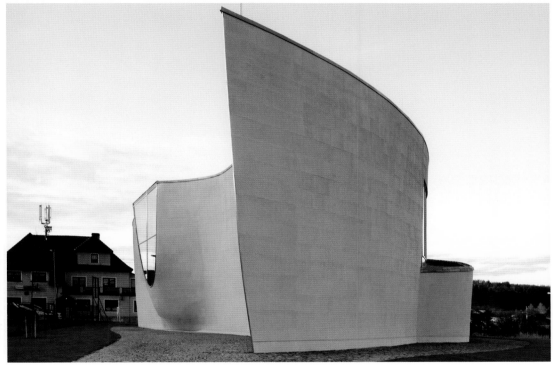

↑↑ | **East view**
↑ | **View from north**
↗↗ | **Cross section**
↗ | **Southeast view**

House of Prayers in Černošice

Černošice

CONSTRUCTION FACTS

Structure: new building, solitaire. **Construction type:** brick arched walls with ETICS, partly concrete. **Material:** silicate plaster, relief designed. **Fixing:** combination of mechanical fixing and patching. **Insulation:** R-value: 0.27 W/(m²K).

The House of Prayer in Černošice is made of bricks with a gently waving shape. The concrete parts of the building have been left visible and the façade is continuously afluted to highlight its plasticity. The architects use the term plasticity to describe the adaptation of a building to the environment. It is a flexible reaction to the nature of the location where it is situated. The building aims to serve the religious and social life of the community, which is the investor. It also includes the preacher's apartment on the second floor. Both houses were built for half of the original budget.

PROJECT FACTS

Address: Hradecká 2192, Černošice - Vráž, Czech Republic. **Client:** Brethren Church in. **Completion:** 2010. **Building type:** ecclesiastical. **Other creatives:** Federico Díaz (artist).

Leuppi & Schafroth
Architekten

↑ | South-west view

Rhine Falls Visitor Center

Laufen-Uhwiesen

Located in Canton Zurich, the Rhine Falls visitor center integrates a souvenir shop, a bistro, public toilet facilities and a multipurpose hall into an existing staff house. The difficult task of transforming the nondescript house into a public building was achieved by extending the pitched roof and developing a new skin that wraps the entire structure. The new façade, made of weatherproof steel plates, forms a suit of armor that unifies the building into a single primary form. On the ground level, folded canopies reveal a second layer with entries, display cases and a ticket counter. The perforated steel elements on the upper level filter sunlight into the multipurpose hall.

CONSTRUCTION FACTS
Structure: renovation and extension.
Construction type: curtain wall distanced from existing façade. **Material:** 8 mm weatherproof steel plates, solid and laser-perforated. **Fixing:** bolted to steel frame. **Insulation:** thermal insulation. **Special function:** sun screen and visual filter.

PROJECT FACTS

Address: Areal Schloss Laufen, Laufen-Uhwiesen, Switzerland. **Client:** Canton Zurich Dept. of Property Management represented by the Building Dept. of Canton Zurich. **Completion:** 2010. **Building type:** public.

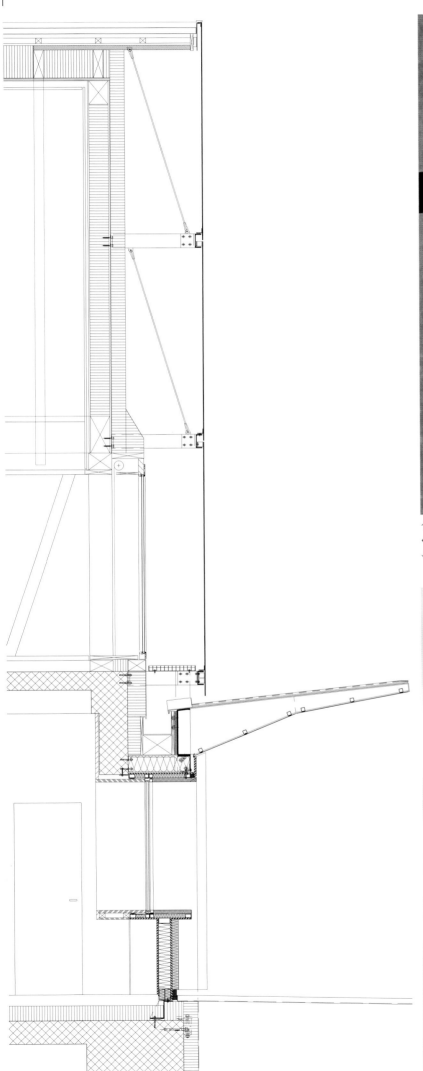

↑ | Detail façade corner
← | Section south façade
↓ | View from south

↑ | Preserved portal and new façade

Moderna Museet

Malmö

This museum is housed in a former industrial building. To comply with security standards for art exhibitions, a building within a building had to be created. An extension of the existing building provides a new entrance and reception space, as well as a cafeteria and new upper gallery. Its perforated orange façade relates to the existing brick architecture and introduces a contemporary element to the neighborhood. The perforated surface gives the façade a visual depth, which is animated by the dynamic shadow patterns that it creates. The ground floor is fully glazed allowing sunlight to enter through the perforated façade.

CONSTRUCTION FACTS

Structure: extension of an existing building. **Construction type:** solid construction. **Material:** perforated (lasercut) metalsheets. **Fixing:** suspended perforated metal. **Insulation:** glare shield. **Special functions:** integrated logotype.

Address: Gasverksgatan 22, 21129 Malmö, Sweden. **Client:** Stadsfastigheter, Malmö. **Completion:** 2009.
Building type: museum.

↑ | Façade extension
↓ | Detail section façade

↑ | Café behind façade
↓ | Concept diagram

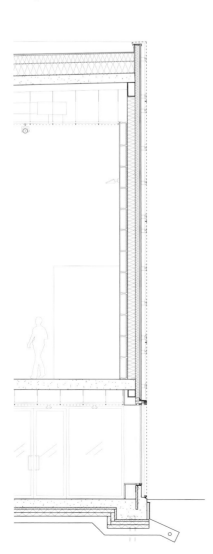

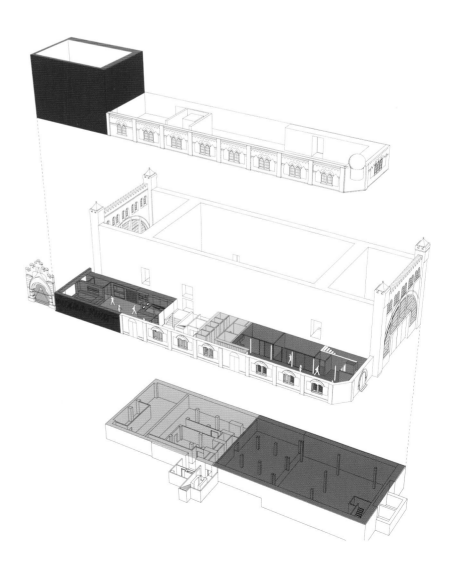

Soeters Van Eldonk
architecten

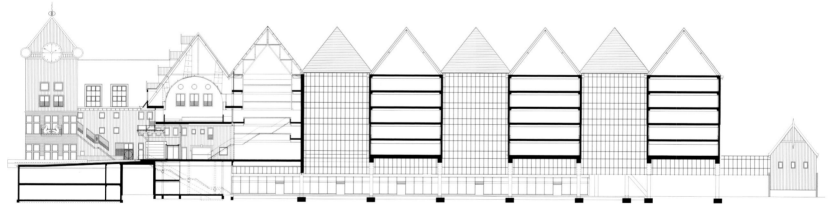

↑↑ | **East façade**
↑ | **Longitudinal section**

City Hall Zaanstad

Zaandam

Zaandam houses like the new municipality city hall are famous for their typical façade architecture – very flat wooden façades painted in all shades of green, with an architectural style that is reinforced by the use of white cornices, windows, and scrolls. Another characteristic of Zaandam houses is their eclecticism with elements borrowed from a variety of styles and periods. These characteristics were implemented in this building as well. Just as Zaandam houses and their façades are often interpretations of world-famous architecture from Italy or France, internationally renowned architects such as Rossi, Venturi, Piano, Pei, and Natalini are paraphrased in the façades of the city hall.

CONSTRUCTION FACTS
Structure: new building. **Construction type:** post-and-beam construction. **Material:** fiber cement siding. **Fixing:** adhesive and screws. **Insulation:** thermal insulation.

PROJECT FACTS
Address: Stadhuisplein 100, 1506 MZ Zaandam, The Netherlands. **Client:** NS Poort, Utrecht.
Completion: 2011. **Building type:** public. **Other creatives:** Studio Erik Gutter, Blaricum (interior). **Construction engineer façade:** VM Bouw, Dongen.

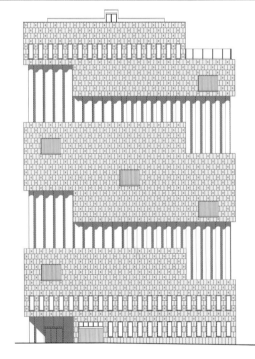

↑ | View from east
↗↗ | View from across the dock
↗ | Elevation

MAS | Museum aan de Stroom

Antwerp

CONSTRUCTION FACTS
Structure: new building. Construction type: curtain wall. Material: hand-cut red Indian sandstone, corrugated glass. Fixing: stone anchors. Insulation: thermal insulation.

Façades, floors, walls, and ceilings of the tower are entirely covered with large panels of hand-cut red Indian sandstone, evoking the image of a monumental stone sculpture. The four-color variation of the natural stone panels is computer-generated and can be found all over the façade. The spiral gallery is finished with a gigantic curtain of corrugated glass. Its play of light and shadow, of transparency, and translucence turns this corrugated glass façade into a light counterweight to the heavy stone sculpture.

PROJECT FACTS
Address: Hanzestedenplaats, 2000 Antwerp, Belgium. Client: City of Antwerp in cooperation with AG Vespa. Completion: 2010. Building type: museum. Other creatives: Bureau Bouwtechniek (structural design). Construction engineer façade: Bureau Bouwtechniek (stone façade), ABT (glass façade).

↑ | View over the lake

Mora River Aquarium

Cabeção-Mora

Echoing the rural barns of the Évora district in the Alentejo region of Portugal, this building was conceived as a single and monolithic pitched roof shed of white pre-cast concrete trusses with single spans of 33 meters. Inside, this elusive hut shelters a complex sanctuary of water moving through diverse fresh water habitats with more than 500 specimens of sea life. This project was implemented in collaboration with the Boston-based architectural and marine biology firm cosestudi, a studio with whom Promontorio has teamed up for various international aquarium proposals.

CONSTRUCTION FACTS
Structure: new building. **Construction type:** pre-cast concrete porticos. **Material:** light concrete, glass. **Fixing:** self-supporting. **Special functions:** solar gain reduction.

Address: Parque Ecológico do Gameiro, Ap.35 7490-909 Cabeção-Mora, Portugal. **Client:** Municipality of Mora. **Completion:** 2006. **Building type:** aquarium.

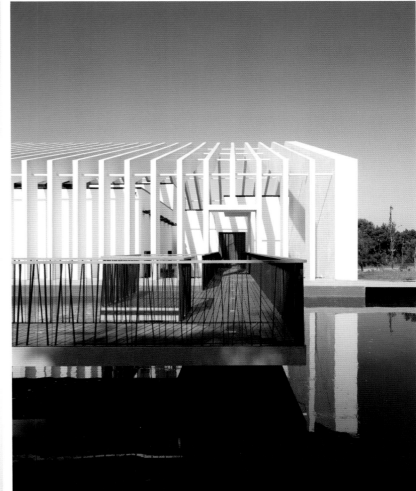

↑ | **Pitched shelter**
↓ | **Vertical section**

↑ | **Entrance**
↘ | **Detail walkway and façade**

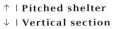

Vicens + Ramos

↑ | **View from backyard**

Parish Center in Rivas-Vaciamadrid

Madrid

The Church of Santa Monica at Rivas Vaciamadrid is defined by its longitudinal floor-plan. Its shape is that of a wedge turned sideways with one of its sides curving along the street. Starting from a mere edge and becoming thicker, it appears to "explode" at the north end and send forth its lights into the urban neighborhood and sky. The façade is made of Corten steel. The building houses the chapel for daily worship as well as private quarters for priests and office space for the management.

CONSTRUCTION FACTS

Structure: new building. **Construction type:** building construction. **Material:** flake-cut corten steel. **Fixing:** gas metal arc welding. **Insulation:** R-value: 0.57 W/(m²K).

Address: Calle Jazmín c/v Calle Clavel, Rivas-Vaciamadrid, Madrid, Spain. **Client:** Obispado de Alcalá de Henares. **Completion:** 2008. **Building type:** ecclesiastical. **Other creatives:** Andrés Rubio (structural engineering), 3i (installations).

↑ | **North view**
↓ | **East elevation**

↑ | **Façade curving along the street**
↓ | **East view**

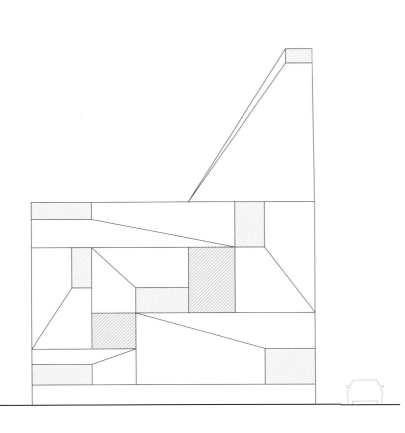

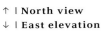

↑ | Façade with night lighting
→ | Façade and internal patio

ABC MUSEUM

Madrid

The new Drawing and Illustration Center of ABC provides access from two streets, connecting them by an internal patio. The internal patio is used for access to and as an atrium for the building, allowing it to express its contemporary and modern character. The architectural mechanism used for support is the creation of a "tensioned vacuum", a "spatial dihedron" formed by the horizontal plane of the floor of the patio and the vertical plane of the internal façade of the old factory. Both planes are made of the same material – blue annealed steel in a matt grey shade – and both present similar triangular gaps for the light to enter the interior. This generates the "weightlessness" between that which is real, imaginary and symbolic.

CONSTRUCTION FACTS

Structure: redevelopment and extension.
Construction type: post-and-beam construction, perforated façade. **Material:** steel and laminated safety glass, anodized aluminum, brick. **Fixing:** punctuated fixing.
Special functions: light effects.

Address: Calle de Amaniel 29–31. Madrid, Spain. **Client:** Grupo Vocento. **Completion:** 2010. **Building type:** museum.

↑ | **Internal patio with view towards the museum's café**
↓ | **Elevation new façade**

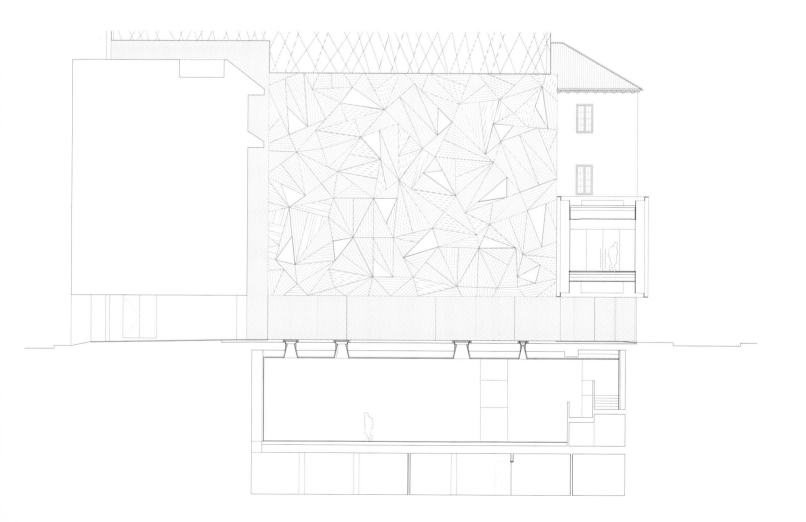

↑ | View from inside
← | Façade from the street

↑ | View of entrance
→ | Interior view foyer and staircase

Harpa Reykjavik Concert Hall and Conference Center

Reykjavik

The Concert Hall of 28,000 square meters features a façade made of glass and steel to which it owes a kaleidoscopic play of colors, reflected in the more than 1,000 quasi-bricks composing the southern façade. Light and transparency are key elements in the building. The crystalline structure created by the geometric figures of the façade captures and reflects the light, promoting the dialogue between the building, the city, and surrounding landscape. The façade changes according to the viewing angle and thereby responds to the surrounding city lights, ocean, and sky. With the continuously changing scenery, the building displays an endless array of colors.

CONSTRUCTION FACTS

Structure: new building. **Construction type:** structural glazed curtain wall (base), non-standard grid façades with add-on steel system (east, west, north façades), three-dimensional self-supporting steel frame (south façade). **Material:** laminated dichromatic glass. **Fixing:** structural glazing. **Insulation:** thermal insulation.

Address: Austurbakki 2, 101 Reykjavik, Iceland. **Client:** Austurhofn. **Completion:** 2011. **Building type:** concert hall. **Other creatives:** Batteriid Architects (local architects), Olafur Eliasson (artist).

↑ | Detail south façade
↓ | Elevation north façade

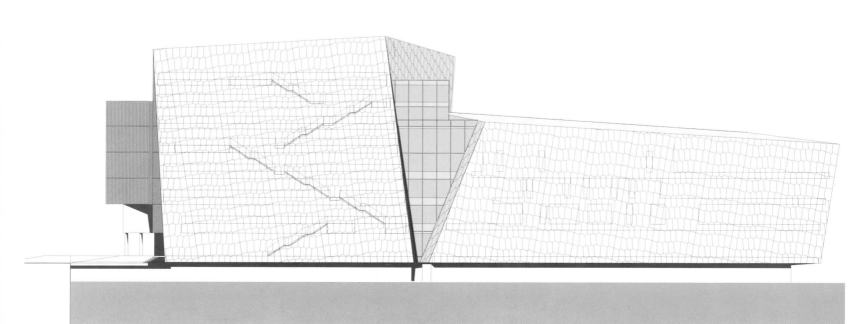

↑ | South façade
← | View from inside

Ateliers Jean Nouvel

↑ | Red pavilion stands out in the park

Red Sun Pavilion

London

The 2010 pavilion for the Serpentine Gallery in London was designed by renowned architect Jean Nouvel in Hyde Park. The building's geometric forms are clad with varied materials – glass, polycarbonate and fabric. The exterior and interior spaces are designed in a flexible manner to accompany different numbers of guests and adapt to the changing summer weather. The red color stands in stark contrast to the green park surroundings and reminds the viewer of the iconic double-decker busses, phone booths, and mail boxes of London. The pavilion features retractable awnings and a freestanding wall. It consists of a glass, polycarbonate, and fabric structure.

CONSTRUCTION FACTS
Structure: new building, temporary. **Material:** glass, polycarbonate, fabric.

Address: Serpentine Gallery, Kensington Gardens, London, United Kingdom. **Client:** Serpentine Gallery. **Completion:** 2010. **Building type:** public. **Other creatives:** ARUP London (structural engineering).

↑ | **Detail screen from red transparend polycarbonate**

↓ | **East elevation**

↑ | **View from inside**

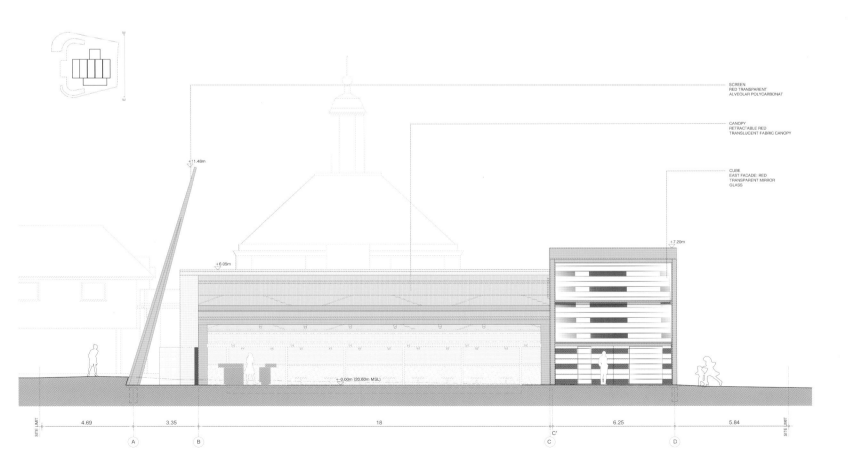

↑ | Exterior, view towards entrance

Ordos Museum

Ordos

The Art and City Museum in Ordos constitutes a futuristic shell to protect the cultural history of the region and counterbalance the rational new city outside. Encapsulated by a sinuous fa-çade, the museum sits upon sloping hills – a gesture to the recent desert past and now a favor-ite gathering place for local children and families. Upon entering the atrium, a brighter, more complex world unfolds. A canyon-like corridor connects the eastern and western entrances, allowing the space to become an open extension of the outer urban space. Visitors meander through the space as if through the future of the eternal Gobi desert.

CONSTRUCTION FACTS

Structure: new building. Construction type: steel structure and steel space frame. Material: coated aluminum panels. Insulation: thermal insulation.

Address: Ordos, China. **Completion:** 2011. **Building type:** museum. **Other creatives:** China Institute of Building (BIAD) (associate engineer). **Consultants façade:** SuP Ingenieure GmbH, Zhuhai King Glass Engineering Co. Ltd, Melendez & Dickinson Architects.

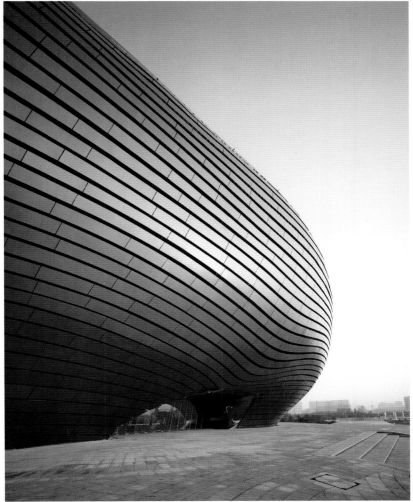

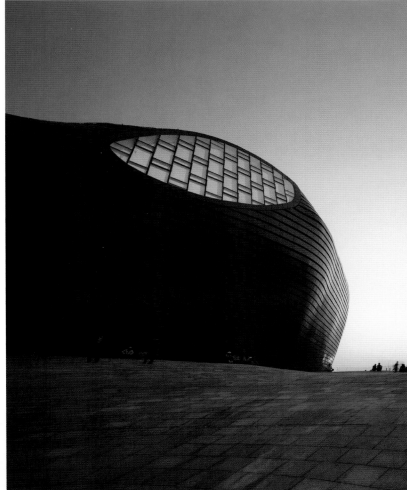

↑ | **Entrance area**
↓ | **Sections**

↑ | **View at night**
↓ | **Futuristic shell**

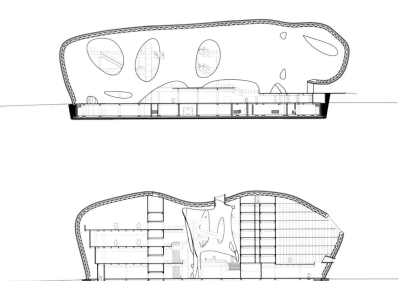

CODE UNIQUE Architekten

↑ | View at night

Festival Hall Plauen

Plauen

The multipurpose hall for the city of Plauen was constructed in 1989. The addition of a small hall increased its capacity. The new building contains the foyer area expanded across two floors, which separated the entrance area with the cloak room and bathroom from the hall level with the lounge and bar. The glazed façade gave the hall a new "face". It makes the structures and divisions of the newly section visible from the outside. The foyer façade is a mullion and transom design, whose solid profile bears the load of the roof's steel trusses. Protruding from the façade, the body of the smaller hall has a double façade. The clearance between the two layers is accessible and contains the sun screen. The outer glazing is printed with a pattern of historic Plauen lace.

CONSTRUCTION FACTS
Structure: reconstruction and extension.
Construction type: post-and-beam construction (foyer), double-skin façade (smaller hall). **Material:** steel, aluminum, insulation glazing. **Fixing:** point mounting (smaller hall). **Insulation:** R-value: 1.2 W/(m²K). **Special functions:** integrated sun screen.

PROJECT FACTS

Address: Äußere Reichenbacher Straße 4, 08529 Plauen, Germany. **Client:** City of Plauen. **Completion:** 2007. **Building type:** culture. **Other creatives:** Volker Giezek, Martin Boden, Lutz Schneider, Steffen Burucker, Lutz Anke, Steffen Barnikol, Gerald Schumann.

↑ | Detail view printed glazing
↓ | Detailed drawing façade

↑ | View towards entrance

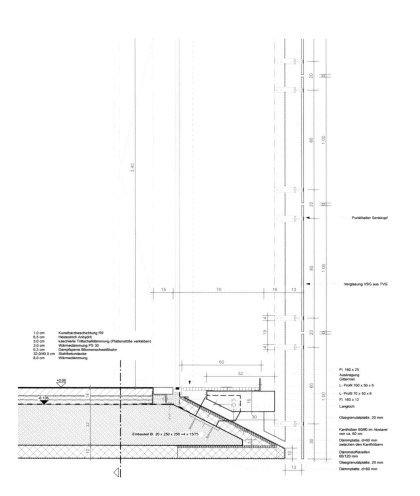

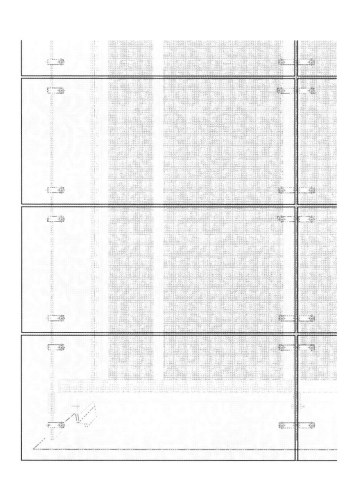

Klaiber+Oettle

↑ | South side

Forum Schönblick

Schwäbisch Gmünd

The newly built "Forum Schönblick" is embedded in a park landscape. The hall structure consists of a closed volume to the north, covered in a pre-patinated copper façade. For fire safety reasons, the substructure is a metal construction with profiled sheeting. The natural copper color changes throughout the day. Towards the south, the building opens up towards the extensive landscape. The glass façade is a light mullion and transom structure. The steel profile substructure is minimized to ensure maximum transparency. The glazing in combination with the sun screen control ensures maximum energy gain, while also preventing overheating in the summer.

CONSTRUCTION FACTS
Structure: new building, in context. **Construction type:** rear ventilated curtain wall. **Material:** aeruginous copper. **Fixing:** on metal substructure. **Insulation:** R-value: 0.20 W/(m²K).

Address: Willy-Schenk-Straße 9, 73527 Schwäbisch Gmünd, Germany. Client: Christliches Gäste-zentrum Württemberg. Completion: 2006. Building type: cultural. Construction engineer façade: Ohligschläger und Ribarek.

↑ | Detail copper façade
↓ | Section façade

↑ | Interior facade
↓ | View from north
↓↓ | Main elevation

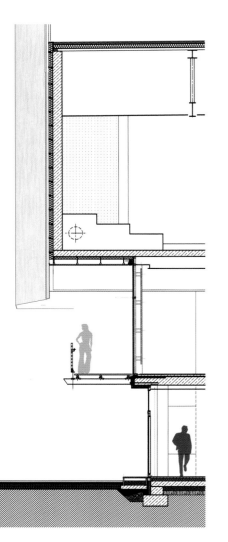

Claesson Koivisto Rune
Architects

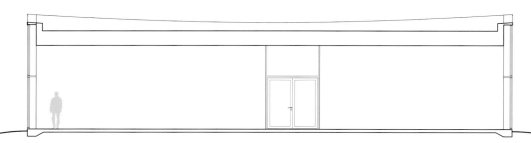

↖↑ | Exterior view at night
↑↑ | Detail façade
↖↖ | Section
↖ | Lit façade at night
↑ | Entrance at night

Örsta Gallery

Kumla

Sited atop an artificial hill, the building's base follows the hill's topology. The resulting series of curves, combined with mirroring roofline curves, make the planar façades seem curved too. Furthermore, the narrow façade openings make the scale of the 6.7-meter tall building difficult to judge from a distance. The interior, divided into four differently sized galleries, has both central cross access and complete side circulation. The white-painted façades are coated with three tons of special reflective glass beads that are similar to the reflective components of zebra crossings. Viewed from the same angle as the incident light source, it glows as if lit from within. The artificial red night-lighting effect, "Husfenomen", is a site-specific art work by Mikael Pauli.

CONSTRUCTION FACTS
Structure: new building. **Construction type:** light-weight concrete block masonry walls, stucco. **Material:** al fresco miniature glass beads. **Fixing:** solid construction. **Insulation:** thermal insulation. **Special functions:** reflective components glow as if lit from inside.

PROJECT FACTS
Address: Örsta 511, 692 72 Kumla, Sweden. **Client:** Anders and Birgitta Fasth. **Completion:** 2010. **Building type:** gallery. **Other creatives:** Mikael Pauli, artist/inventor of façade application.

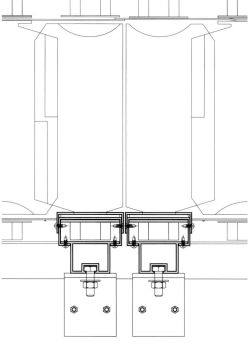

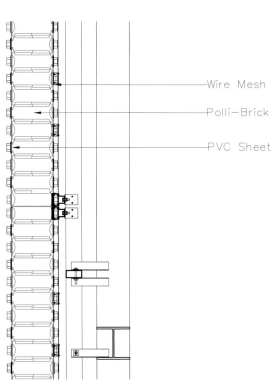

Wire Mesh

Polli–Brick

PVC Sheet

↑↑ | Exterior at night
↑↗ | Detail PET wall
↑ | Detail façade
↗ | General view
↗↗ | Section façade

2010 Taipei Flora Exhibition – Far Eastern EcoArk

Taipei

CONSTRUCTION FACTS

Structure: new building. **Construction type:** curtain wall. **Material:** polli-brick. **Fixing:** punctuated fixing. **Insulation:** thermal insulation. **Special functions:** generation of light.

The EcoARK Pavilion in Taipei is the world's first fully functional public structure made of 1.5 million recycled plastic bottles. The building owes its comfortable internal environment to natural ventilation, an exterior waterfall that bathes the structure in water collected from rain, as well as the bottles' high insulation properties. Embedded solar power captured during the day runs EcoARK's LED lighting systems at night. It weighs 50 percent less than a conventional building, yet is strong enough to withstand the forces of nature, including fire! The EcoARK Pavilion will be disassembled and distributed to schools all over Taiwan to teach children about the importance of recycling.

PROJECT FACTS

Address: Zhongshan N.Rd., Taipei, Taiwan. **Client:** Far Eastern Group. **Completion:** 2010. **Building type:** exhibition pavilion. **Other creatives:** Far Eastern Genenral Construction Inc..

SALTO architects

↑ | Entrance area

NO99 Straw Theater

Tallinn

The dramatic appeal of the building stems from its contextual setting on its particular site and its black, uncompromisingly mute main volume, which contrasts with a descending "tail" with an articulate angular roof. The façade consists of uncovered straw that has been painted black. This is unique in such a large public building. For reinforcement purposes, the straw walls have been secured with trusses, which is a type of construction that has not been used before. As the building is temporary, it has not been insulated the way a normal straw construction would require but has been kept open to experience the raw tactile qualities of the material and accentuate the symbolic level of the life cycle of this sustainable material.

CONSTRUCTION FACTS
Structure: new building, solitaire in context. **Construction type:** post-and-beam construction. **Material:** straw bales. **Fixing:** part of the solid construction. **Special functions:** bird nesting, topsoil.

Address: Rannamäe tee 11, Tallinn, Estonia. **Client:** theatre NO99. **Completion:** 2011. **Building type:** temporary theater.

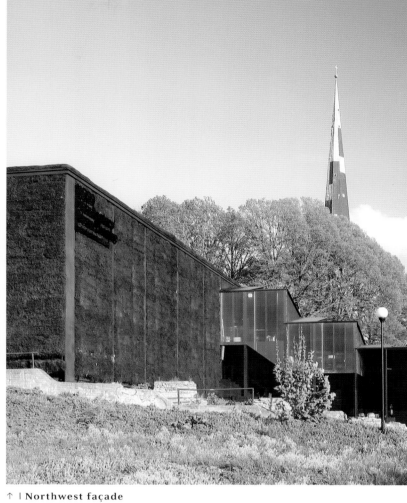

↑ | **Living façade**
↓ | **View on site**

↑ | **Northwest façade**
↓↓ | **Section**

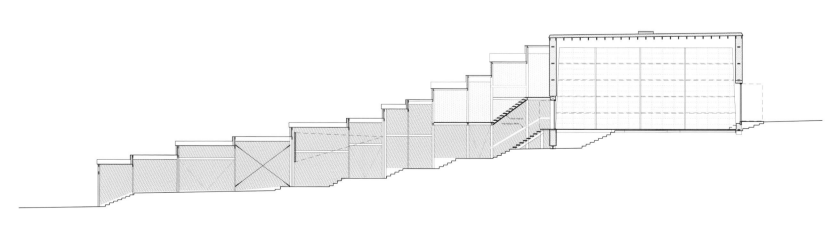

Clavel Arquitectos

↑ | Closed tomb

Pantheon Nube

Murcia

The entrance doors of this tomb are modeled on medieval winged altars. They form a closed wall with no handles, which serves to underline the belief that tombs should be sealed and must never be opened. Inside, an abstract cloud structure is crossed by sunbeams, effecting spiritual stimulation. The moment crystallizes in the abstraction of the white cloud, the end of a path that starts from the basement, ascends to the intermediate platform and continues to the cloud's space where the sight gets lost in the abstract and unreal atmosphere that fills the area. The back wall is made from a combination of laminated glass and onyx, giving it a certain degree of transparency.

CONSTRUCTION FACTS
Structure: new building. **Construction type:** double-sided curtain wall. **Material:** laminated safety glass with polyvinyl butyral film of translucent white. **Fixing:** bonding.

Address: Cemetery 'Nuestro Padre Jesús' in Espinardo, Murcia, Spain. **Client:** Private. **Completion:** 2010. **Building type:** tomb. **Construction engineer façade:** Intersa (construction company).

↑ | **Opened tomb in context**
↓ | **Longitudinal section main façade**
↘ | **Detail back wall**

↓ | **Open doors at night**

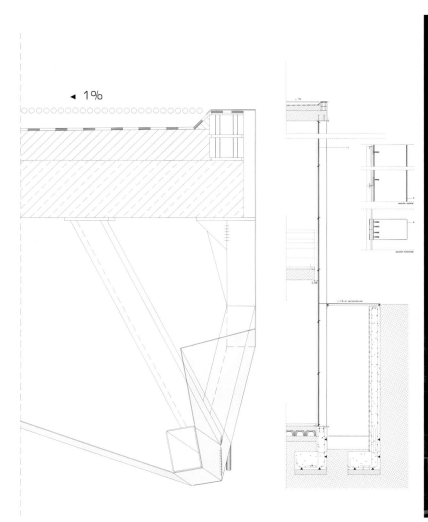

◄ 1%

Jun Aoki & Associates

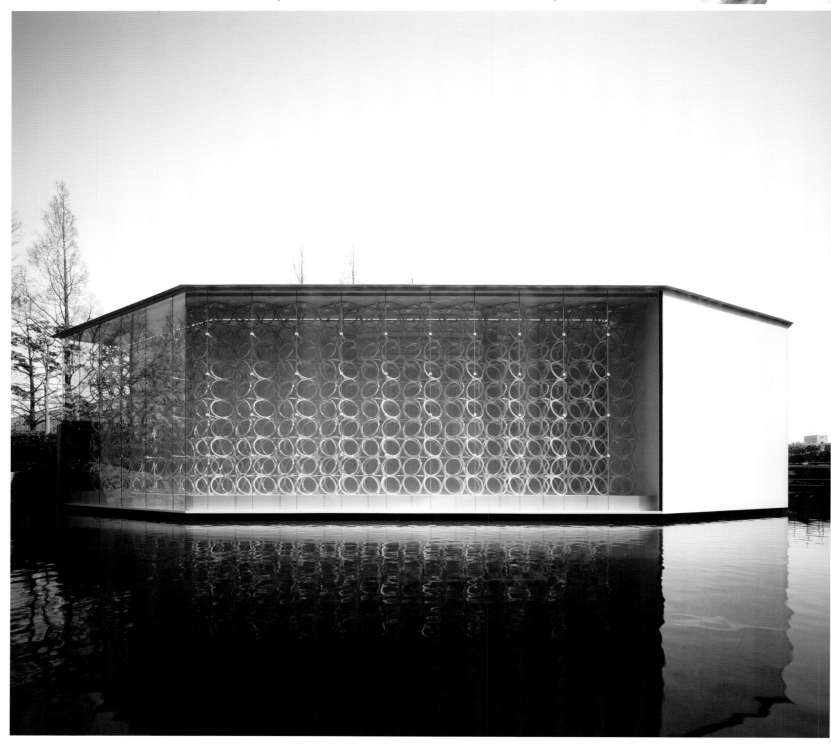

↑ | Chapel in beautiful setting

White Chapel

Osaka

White Chapel is a small chapel within the premises of the Hyatt Regency Osaka. It is used for wedding ceremonies and accommodates 80 people. The structure consists of steel rings arranged in squares 60 centimeters in diameter, with sides of 25 millimeters, which are interlocked three-dimensionally. The ring components were inspired by the shape of a tetrahedron. Its flat planes were replaced with rings, connected at their edges. The three-dimensional layout of the rings corresponds to the array of the circle formed by the 4 regular hexagons within the unit. The steel rings are welded together into a foam-like three-dimensional grid that mainly consists of voids. This not only supports the roof but also assists the glass exterior as an MPG System. A double-layered woven screen of white organdy is hung inside the grid.

CONSTRUCTION FACTS
Structure: new building. **Construction type:** metal point glazing system supported by ring truss structure. **Material:** square steel rings which are interlocked three-dimensionally. **Fixing:** punctuated fixing.

Address: 1-13-11 Nanko-Kita, Suminoe-Ku, Osaka, Japan 559-0034. **Client:** Obayashi Corporation. **Completion:** 2006. **Building type:** wedding chapel. **Other creatives:** Space&Structure Engineering Workshop Inc. (structure), ITL Co., Ltd. (lighting), NUNO Corporation (fabric). **Construction engineer façade:** Naigai Technos Corporation.

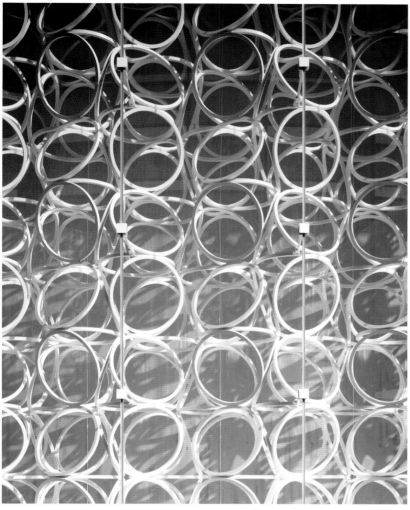

↑ | Detail façade
↓ | Details rings

↑ | View from inside
↓ | Interior wall

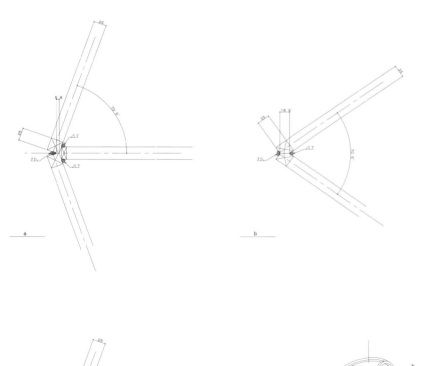

Coop Himmelb(l)au

↑ | **Exterior view at night**

Pavilion 21 MINI Opera Space

Munich

The pavilion of the Bavarian State Opera for experimental performances contains 300 seats and 700 temporary standing places and can be dismantled and transported. Although a light-weight construction, it meets the high acoustic requirements of a concert hall. This is achieved through "soundscaping" – pyramid-like shapes reflect and absorb the sound by incorporating the spatial transformation of sound sequences. The interior wall and ceiling surfaces were fitted with a combination of perforated absorbing and smooth reflecting sandwich panels, which are also tilted or skewed to facilitate sound reflection. The edges of the architectural structure are emphasized by brighter projections. The contrast is enhanced by various degrees of illumination integrating the audio signals with a minimalist color flow.

CONSTRUCTION FACTS
Structure: new building, temporary.
Construction type: light-weight construction. **Material:** combination of perforated absorbing and smooth reflecting sandwich panels. **Special functions:** light installation: sound is turned into light.

Address: Munich, Germany. **Client:** The Free State of Bavaria represented by The Bavarian State Opera.
Completion: 2010. **Building type:** lightweight construction concert hall which must allow to be dis- and re-assembled quickly. **Other creatives:** ARUP, London (acoustics).

↑ | Detail of "spikes"
↓ | Frequence sections of music are translated into "spike constructions"
↓↓ | Section

↑ | Illumination at night
↓ | Diagram acoustical properties

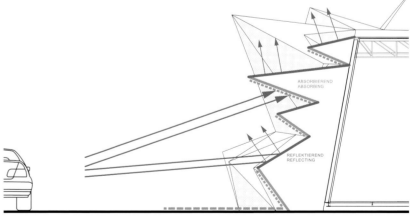

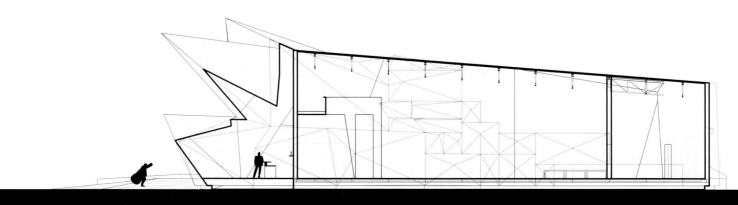

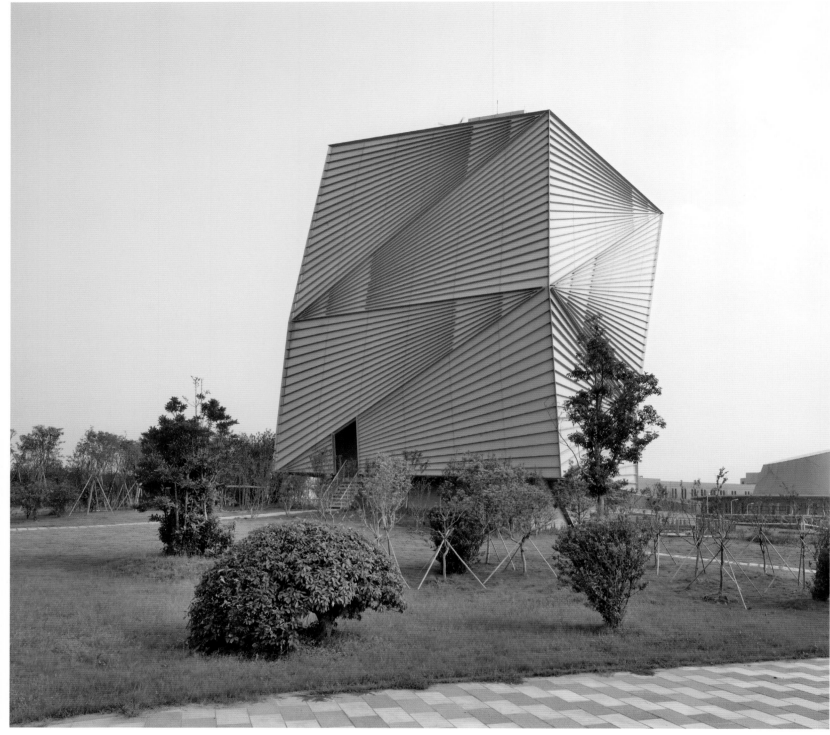

↑ | **View from campus**
→ | **Dynamic façade**

Center for Sustainable Energy Technologies

Ningbo

Situated on the Nottingham University campus in Ningbo, the Center for Sustainable Energy Technologies (CSET) accommodates a visitor's center, laboratories and classrooms. Its design is inspired by Chinese lanterns and traditional wooden screens. The façade folds dramatically to create a dynamic shape. The building is entirely clad with a double skin – an inner envelope of concrete and an outer envelope of glass. Lighting between the two skins changes the appearance of the building from day to night. The design employs various environmental strategies. A large rooftop opening brings natural light to all floors of the building and allows down-draught cooling and efficient natural ventilation. Geothermal energy is used to cool and heat the floor slabs.

CONSTRUCTION FACTS

Structure: new building on campus. **Construction type:** double-skin façade. **Material:** glass. **Fixing:** punctuated fixing. **Insulation:** thermal insulation. **Special functions:** gaining of solar energy.

PROJECT FACTS

Address: Ningbo, China. **Client:** University of Nottingham. **Completion:** 2008. **Building type:** university. **Other creatives:** Luca Turrini, Bologna, Italy (structural engineering), TiFS Engineers Srl., Padova, Italy, Prof. Roberto Zecchin (lighting design).

↑ | **Detail view façade**
↓ | **Energy strategies summer**

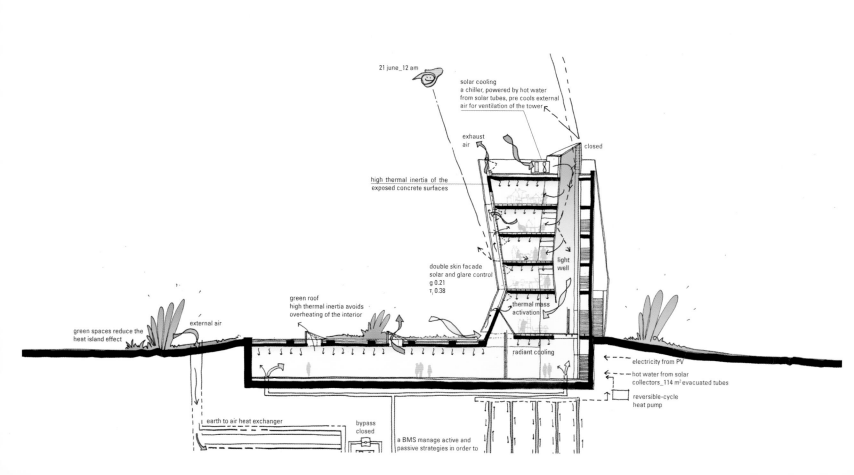

21 june_12 am

solar cooling
a chiller, powered by hot water
from solar tubes, pre cools external
air for ventilation of the tower

exhaust
air

closed

high thermal inertia of the
exposed concrete surfaces

double skin facade
solar and glare control
g 0.21
τ₁ 0.38

light
well

thermal mass
activation

green roof
high thermal inertia avoids
overheating of the interior

green spaces reduce the
heat island effect

external air

radiant cooling

electricity from PV

hot water from solar
collectors_114 m² evacuated tubes

reversible-cycle
heat pump

earth to air heat exchanger

bypass
closed

a BMS manage active and
passive strategies in order to

↖ | Façade with photovoltaic panels
↑ | Entrance area
↙ | View at night
↓ | Energy strategies winter

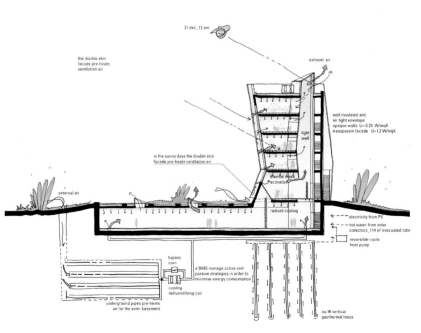

↑ | Rear view

Adaptonic Transfer Center

Darmstadt

The compact cuboid building supports the intensive communication among changing work groups at the Fraunhofer Institut. It contains a show room, offices, and laboratories as well as communication and seminar areas. The suspended façade consists of golden-bronze shimmering brass sheets, so-called TECU Brass plates, whose surfaces were pre-treated and that are disrupted by an irregular grid of quadratic openings. The perforation is intended to provide a filigree texture and spatial depth. The brass layer of the sandwich elements results in a changing color effect that gives different impressions depending on the change of light, the time of day and of yea. This reduces the complex scientific concept of smart materials symbolically to its basic premises: action and reaction.

CONSTRUCTION FACTS

Structure: new building, solitaire. **Construction type:** curtain wall. **Material:** perforated brass façade. **Fixing:** punctuated fixing with rivets. **Insulation:** glare shield on interior, sun screen on exterior.

Address: Bartningstraße 47, 64289 Darmstadt, Germany. **Client:** Fraunhofer-Gesellschaft e.V., Munich.
Completion: 2010. **Building type:** office.

↑↑ | **View from the street**
↑ | **View at night**
← | **Section of the façade**
↓ | **Detail façade**

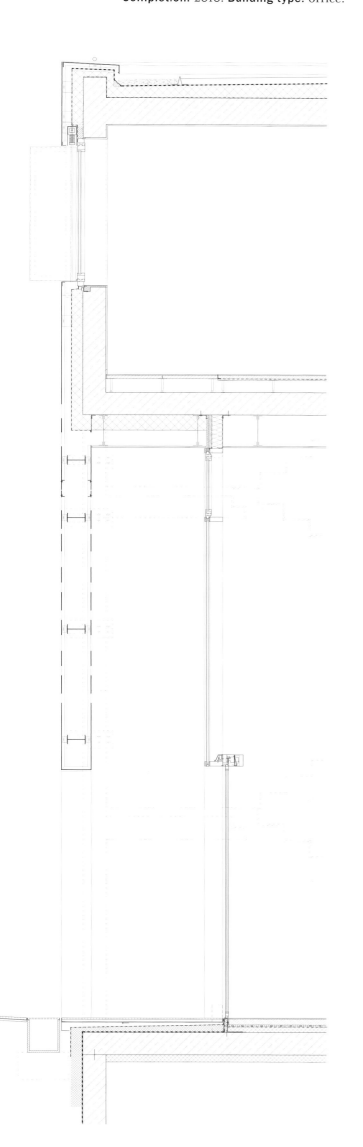

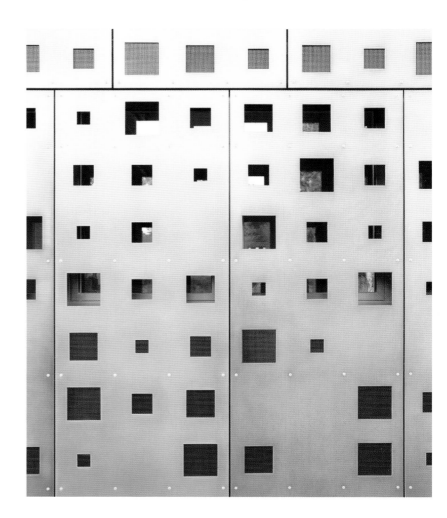

Schmucker und Partner
Planungsgesellschaft

↑ | Rear view

Käthe Kollwitz School

Mannheim

The design won an architectural competition for a "modular" school construction system. As a first step, a pilot project of sorts, the design was implemented at a total of five schools – the Käthe Kollwitz Schools with integrated children's center. The layout concept of the building consists of a central access zone to which two "room tracts" are connected. The western part contains the class and group rooms. The eastern part houses all the organizational functions (multifunctional rooms, administration, sanitary areas, warehouse, etc.). The closed staircases are situated at the building corners and equipped with a strikingly designed façade. Despite the modular construction method, the façade print designs, which are developed individually for every school, make each building unique.

CONSTRUCTION FACTS
Structure: new building, prototype. **Construction type:** rear ventilated curtain wall. **Material:** printed high pressure laminate. **Fixing:** punctuated fixing, not visible. **Insulation:** R-value: 0.28 W/(m²K).

Address: Zum Herrenried 1, 68169 Mannheim, Germany. **Client:** City of Mannheim. **Completion:** 2008.
Building type: school. **Other creatives:** Philip Gaedke, Hamburg (design printed motif).

↑ | **Front view**
→ | **Section façade**
↘ | **Elevations**
↓ | **East façade**

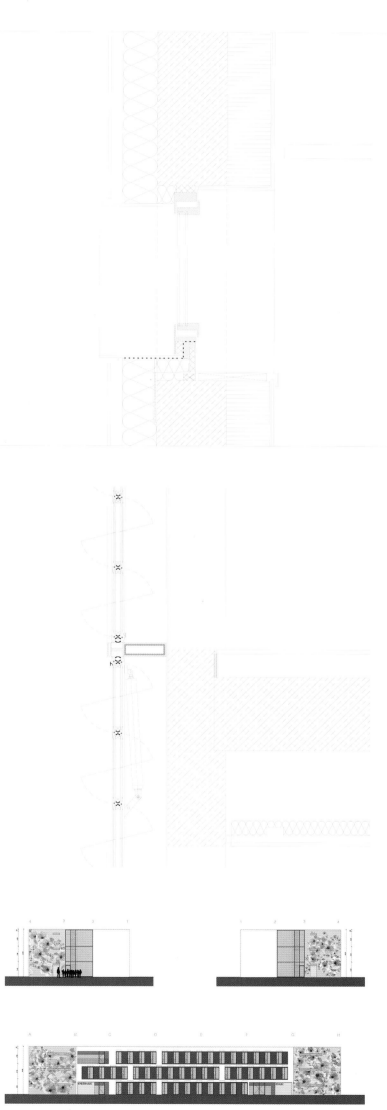

↑ | View from the street

Villaverde Health Care Center

Madrid

The Villaverde Health Care Center belongs to a series of three similarly designed health care centers. The building consists of a single floor. The units are ordered in an orthogonal grid with thirteen patios separating public from private spaces through three "non-corridors". The corridors ceased to exist as a linear structure because of the alternative arrangement of empty spaces and waiting rooms. The light flowing in from the patios forms a stark contrast to the façade, which is conceived as a blind mass of modulated glass. This façade does not allow an interior-exterior relationship and instead forces a vertical view.

CONSTRUCTION FACTS
Structure: new building, solitaire. Construction type: rear ventilated curtain wall. Material: laminated safety glass. Fixing: suspension.

Address: Avda. de la Felicidad 17, Madrid 28041, Spain. **Client:** Madrid+Salud, Ayuntamiento de Madrid. **Completion:** 2010. **Building type:** health care. **Other creatives:** Geasyt (mechanical engineering), Maria Jose Camporro (structural engineering).

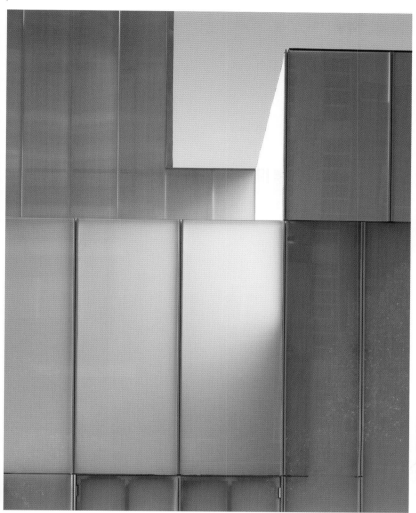

↑ | Detail façade
↓ | Construction scheme

↑↑ | View at night
↑ | View by day
↓ | Tectonic system

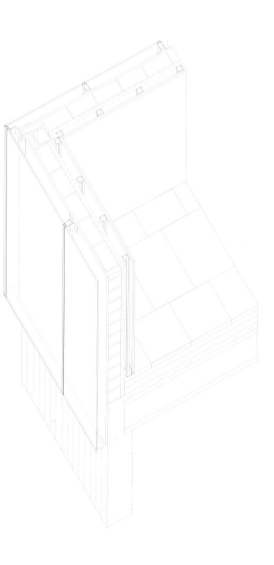

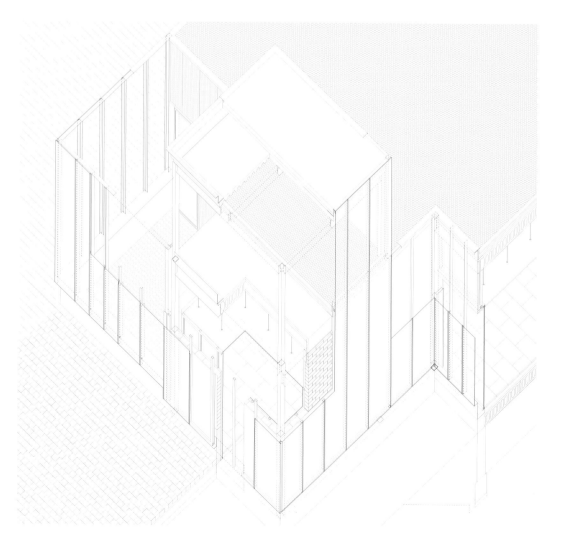

↑ | View with colorful slats

Kekec Kindergarten

Ljubljana

The main design concept of Kekec kindergarten was based on the existing kindergarten's lack of play equipment. The new façade eliminates this weakness by offering play elements along all three exterior walls. The revolving vertical toy slats are the color of natural wood on one side but painted into nine different bright colors on the other, giving the building an understated or a playful appearance depending on the children's play. As the children manipulate the colorful timber, they get to know different colors, experience wood as a natural material and change the appearance of their kindergarten, while the colorful revolving slats also function as shading elements for the windows behind.

CONSTRUCTION FACTS
Structure: new building, solitaire. **Construction type:** rear ventilated curtain wall. **Material:** colored pine timber slats. **Fixing:** metal bearing fixes the slats and enables their rotation. **Insulation:** sun shield. **Special functions:** interactive façade: kids can play and change the appearance.

Address: Hermana Potočnika 13, 1000 Ljubljana, Slovenia. **Client:** Mestna Občina Ljubljana. **Completion:** 2010. **Building type:** kindergarten. **Other creatives:** Jure Kotnik, Andrej Kotnik. **Construction engineer façade:** Riko Hiše d.o.o.

↑ | **View with closed slats in natural wood**   ↓ | **Detail slats**
↓ | **Detail drawing façade**

↑ | Main entrance

ASU Walter Cronkite School of Journalism & Mass Communication

Phoenix

Located in downtown Phoenix, the six-story, 20,900-square-meter building has become an integral part of the fabric of ASU's energizing downtown campus and a harbinger of Phoenix's redevelopment. Just as truth and honesty are guiding principles to journalism, they were also applied to the design of the building. The architecture is specifically expressive of function and materiality. The exterior is clad in glass, masonry and multi-colored metal panels whose patterns are inspired by the radio spectrum. The building's massing incorporates appropriate sun screens on each of the four façades; their specific architectural treatment reduces the heat loads and is one of many of the LEED Silver building's sustainable strategies.

CONSTRUCTION FACTS
Structure: new building. Construction type: curtain wall. Material: corrugated metal panels, aluminum curtain wall with clear glass and spandrel panels. Fixing: conventional. Insulation: thermal insulation.

Address: 555 N. Central Avenue, Phoenix, AZ 85004, USA. **Client:** Arizona State University. **Completion:** 2008. **Building type:** university building. **Other creatives:** Sundt (design builder), HDR Architecture, Inc. (executive architect). **Construction engineer façade:** CTS Structural Engineers, KT Fab Curtain Wall, Paul Deeb (public art component).

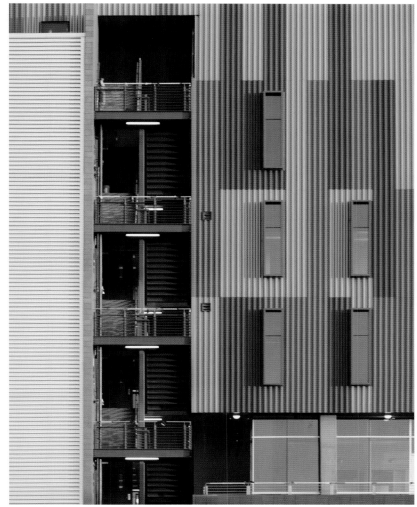

↑ | Detail metal panel façade

↑ | Detail façade

↓ | Elevation

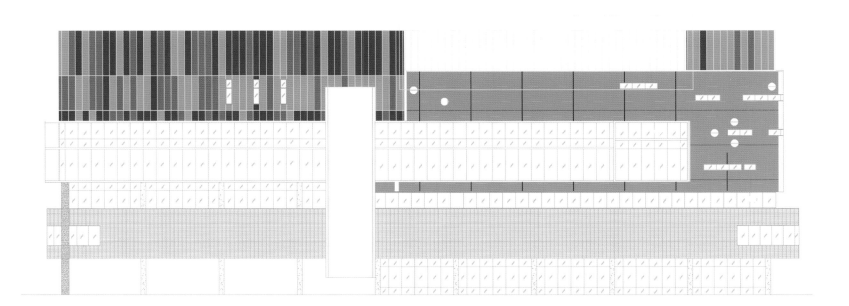

↑ | Exterior view

Martinet Primary School

Barcelona

All of the school's support facilities are housed in a block on the ground floor next to the primary playground. The classroom block has been designed as a three-story volume with classrooms on all three floors. The first and second floors are accessed through a south-facing corridor. A screen provides protection from the sun here and functions at various levels. The main façade of the school is visible from the nearby highway, clearly announcing the location of the school. It blends in with the large containers of a nearby industrial area. On the inside, a double façade creates a playful interaction of light and shadow.

CONSTRUCTION FACTS
Structure: new building. Construction type: double cladding, perforated façade. Material: stoneware ceramic and laminated safety glass. Fixing: steel rings, bracings. Insulation: sun screen.

Address: Carrer Martinet Nº1, Cornellà de Llobregat, Baix Llobregat, Barcelona, Spain. **Client:** City Council of Cornellà de Llobregat. **Completion:** 2011. **Building type:** school. **Other creatives:** Toni Cumella (Wall manufacturer).

↑ | Detail double façade
↓ | Elevation and section façade

↑ | Detail double façade in greens
↓ | Detail stoneware on the exterior

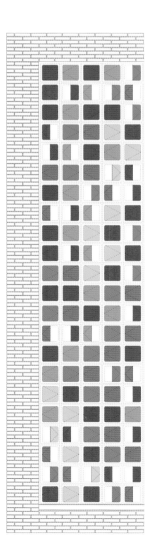

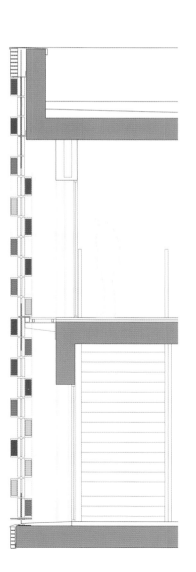

↖↖ I View with closed sun shades
↑↑ I Detail façade
↖ I Elevations
↑ I View of open sunshades

Kindergarten Ajda 2

Ravne na Koroškem

The signature design feature of Ajda kindergarten is its didactic façade, made from thick anthracite isolative and fire-resistant steel boards, which comply with high energy efficiency standards. They can be decorated with magnets in five colors. The lightweight magnets are foldable so that children can manipulate them with ease, for instance to create animals, vehicles, buildings and other shapes. The interactive façade helps improve the children's motor skills, eye-hand coordination and problem-solving techniques, as well as stimulate creativity. This first magnetic façade in the world can be a teaching tool, help the learning process and trigger the children's imagination by allowing for constant changes in the façade.

PROJECT FACTS
Address: Javornik 56, 2390 Ravne na Koroškem, Slovenia. **Client:** Občina Ravne na Koroškem. **Completion:** 2011. **Building type:** kindergarten. **Other creatives:** Jure Kotnik, Andrej Kotnik, Tjaša Mavrič, Tina Marn. **Construction engineer façade:** Trimo d.d.

CONSTRUCTION FACTS
Structure: new building, solitaire. **Construction type:** insulated steel sandwich elements. **Material:** steel panels with magnetic shapes in four different colors. **Fixing:** punctuated fixing on container construction. **Insulation:** glare shield. **Special functions:** interactive façade: magnets serve as toy for kids.

↑↑ | View towards entrance
↑↗ | View from inside
↑ | View towards classrooms at night
↗ | Section

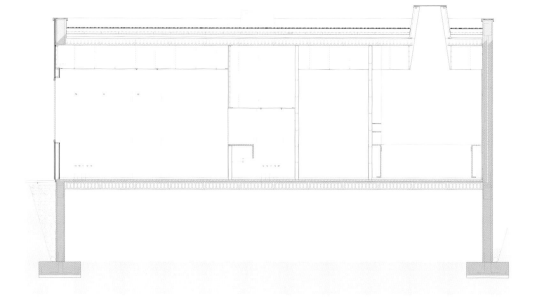

Nursery in the Park

Zaragoza

CONSTRUCTION FACTS

Structure: new building. **Construction type:** double cladding. **Material:** polycarbonate façades. **Fixing:** aluminum substructure. **Insulation:** thermal insulation, glare shield.

The building is located in a large green space where trees proffer an exclusive view that changes with the seasons. The floor is divided lengthwise into two parts – for services and classrooms respectively. The floor plan also provides for numerous courtyards to conserve the existing trees. The façade of the classrooms filters the incoming light through a double skin of green and opal polycarbonate, providing insulation as well as shielding from the light. The material effects subtle light changes in the classroom, thus aiding the development of the children's sensitivity to such changes.

PROJECT FACTS

Address: Echegaray y Caballero, 50003, Zaragoza, Spain. **Client:** Zaragoza Town Hall. **Completion:** 2010. **Building type:** nursery.

| Santiago Carroquino
architects

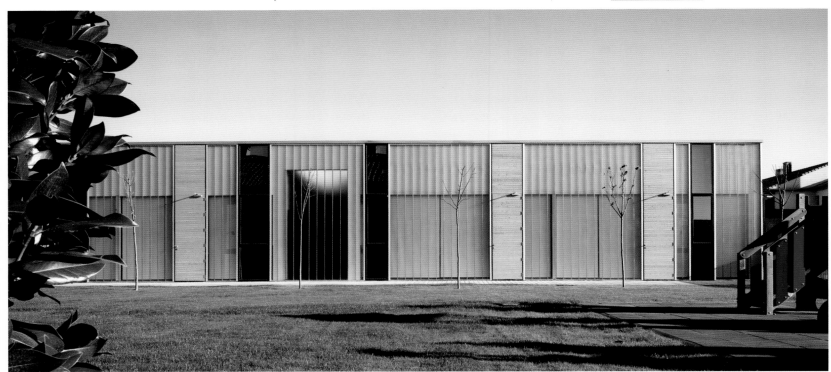

↑↑ | View towards classroms
↑ | View from playground

Santa Isabel Kindergarten

Zaragoza

This nursery school consists of two connected rectangular boxes containing, respectively, the educational and the service areas. The southern façade is dominated by glass while the northern façade is covered with timber wood. The boxes are closed off to the north to protect them from the inclemency of the weather and the street. In contrast, they open up to the south through a U-Glass pane fitted in a double braided comb structure, with timber and steel frames, to seek out sunlight and provide a view of the playground. The external sheet consists of timber shuttering with different squares patterns to highlight, through the texture, the vertical treatment of the enclosure as differing from the southern façade.

CONSTRUCTION FACTS
Structure: new building. **Construction type:** solid construction, double-cladding. **Material:** U-glass, timber. **Fixing:** self-supporting. **Insulation:** thermal insulation, glare shield.

Address: De la Iglesia Street, 50016, Santa Isabel, Zaragoza, Spain. **Client:** Zaragoza Town Hall.
Completion: 2007. **Building type:** kindergarten. **Other creatives:** Hans Finner.

↑ | **Detail view façade**
↓ | **Cross section**

↑ | **Combination of materials**

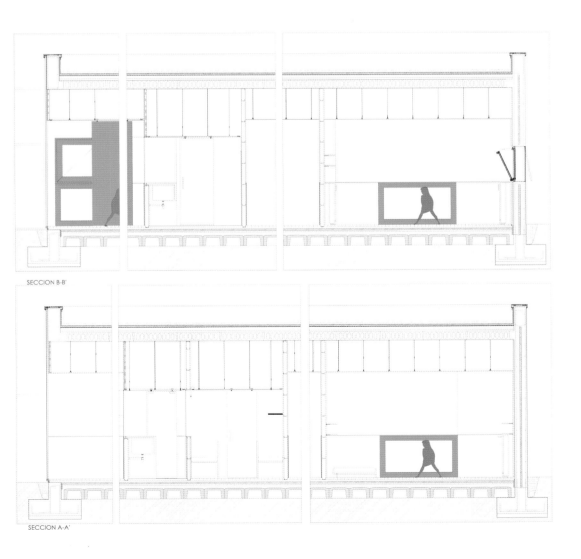

SECCION B-B'

SECCION A-A'

↑ | Entrance area at night

Center for Dialysis

Vienna

A clearly-structured friendly building, the center for dialysis Donaustadt in Vienna offers exceptional room qualities. The new addition is open towards the existing clinic complex. In addition to a large and clearly structured entrance hall, the ground floor contains a conference section with separate administration and service areas near it. The center contains 72 treatment spaces divided into four groups and equipped with all required main and peripheral rooms. All treatment areas face the green room towards the west. The outer façade is designed as a ribbon window strip. Ceiling-high suspended sun screen elements provide visual and glare protection and can be individually controlled as packages. They give the compact building a unique appearance.

CONSTRUCTION FACTS

Structure: new building, solitaire. **Construction type:** post-and-beam construction with rear ventilated curtain wall. **Material:** anodized aluminum. **Insulation:** R-value: 1.40 W/(m²K) (post-and-beam façade), 0.18 W/(m²K) (sheet-metal façade). **Special functions:** sun screen.

Address: Kapellenweg 37, 1220 Vienna, Austria. **Client:** Wiener Dialysezentrum GmbH. **Completion:** 2009. **Building type:** health care. **Other creatives:** ARGE Dialysezentrum Donaustadt Wien – Nickl & Partner Architekten AG (general planner); Rinderer & Partner ZT KEG (structural analysis); JMP (HVACR); Küttner, Wenger & Partner GmbH (medical technology).

↑ | **View from garden**
↓ | **Section façade**

↓ | **Detail opened and closed façade elements**

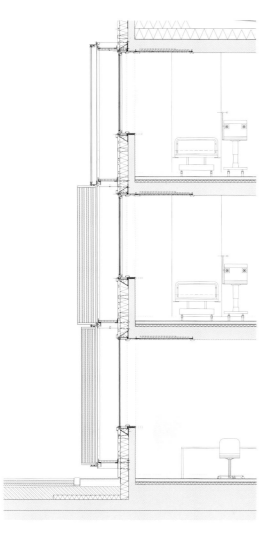

↑ | General view

Cib – Biomedical Research Center

Pamplona

The result of a competition, this building offers an image inherent to its intrinsic functionality, manifested by an enclosure that covers all formal functions. The outer skin 'fits' the internal structures. The project aims to link to the building's purpose of biomedical research, through the application of the biomimicry (adaptation of natural, models, systems, processes, and elements to human problems) in the generation of the architecture. The bio-types used to adopt similar systems were: the camel as a paradigm of functionality, the polar bear as an example of a multifunctional skin, and the leaf as the successful integration of structural resolution and flexibility.

CONSTRUCTION FACTS
Structure: new building. **Construction type:** rear ventilated curtain wall. **Material:** glazing, aluminum anodized lattice. **Fixing:** punctuated fixing, suspension. **Insulation:** thermal insulation, noise insulation, glare shield, UV-reduction.

Address: Navarre's Hospital Complex, Pamplona, Spain. **Client:** Navarre Health Service. **Completion:** 2011. **Building type:** research, health, office. **Other creatives:** Raúl Escrivá – Opera (structural engineering). **Construction engineer façade:** Marcial Lázaro – Altres, Jofebar.

↑ | Detail façade elements
↓ | Section, elevation, ground floor plan

↑ | Detail double façade
↓ | Detail view

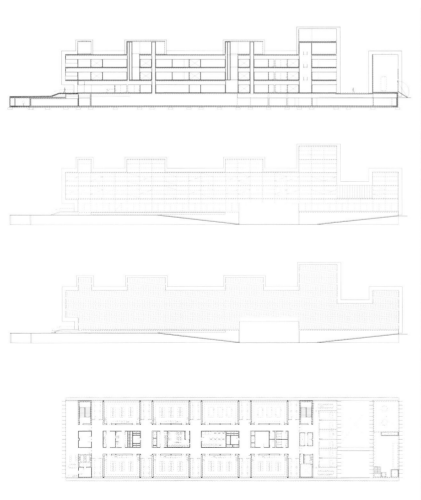

Architectenbureau Marlies
Rohmer

↑ | View up the façade

Smarties

Utrecht

The multi-story student dorm building at Utrecht University offers 380 housing units for students in a city with a chronic shortage of student accommodations. The façade consists of a grid of multicolored aluminum panels from which the windows were omitted. Seen from a distance, the colors blend into a grey, scaly skin. The closer you come, the more it appears as a colorful honeycomb for the bright young students – our 'smarties' – from all over the world. In front of the building is an open plaza under a 20-meter cantilever which serves as an urban meeting place. This building is part of a concept to give De Uithof more coherence and character.

CONSTRUCTION FACTS
Structure: new building. **Material:** semi-matt modular aluminum panels. **Insulation:** thermal insulation.

PROJECT FACTS

Address: De Uithof, Utrecht, The Netherlands. **Client:** SSH Utrecht, University of Utrecht. **Completion:** 2008. **Building type:** student living and public space design. **Other creatives:** Floris Hund (collaborating architect), ABT Adviesbureau voor Bouwtechniek (structural engineering).

↑ | Detail aluminum façade
↓ | Detail drawing façade

↑ | View from the street

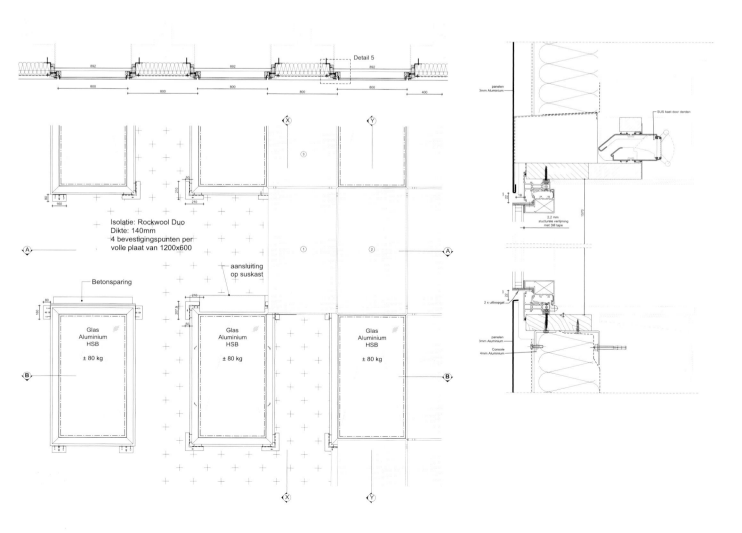

↑ | Detail west façade with terrace

Institute for Ornithology

Seewiesen

On the outside, the institute is covered by air-permeable larch wood sheating. The wood is untreated and roof protrusions are kept to a minimum to allow even weathering of the wood and aluminum façade. The windows are positioned in the insulation layer of the walls. The window surfaces were measured reduced to the necessary for energy-saving purposes, yet provide views of the lake and the forest. The windows on the west façade can do without sunshades as they are only next to a hallway and meeting point with a window height of only 51 centimeters. The eastern façade has windows in the doors and a row of windows on top. The door windows have push shutters and the top windows have window awning blinds.

CONSTRUCTION FACTS
Structure: new building, in context. Construction type: rear ventilated curtain wall. Material: untreated larch wood panels. Fixing: punctuated fixing. Insulation: R-value: 0.35 W/(m²K).

Address: Max-Planck-Institute for Ornithology, Eberhard-Gwinner-Straße, 82319 Seewiesen, Germany.
Client: Max-Planck-Gesellschaft. **Completion:** 2011. **Building type:** laboratory.

↑ | Detail east façade
↓ | Section façade

↑ | Interior with ribbon windows
↓ | Detailed drawings façade

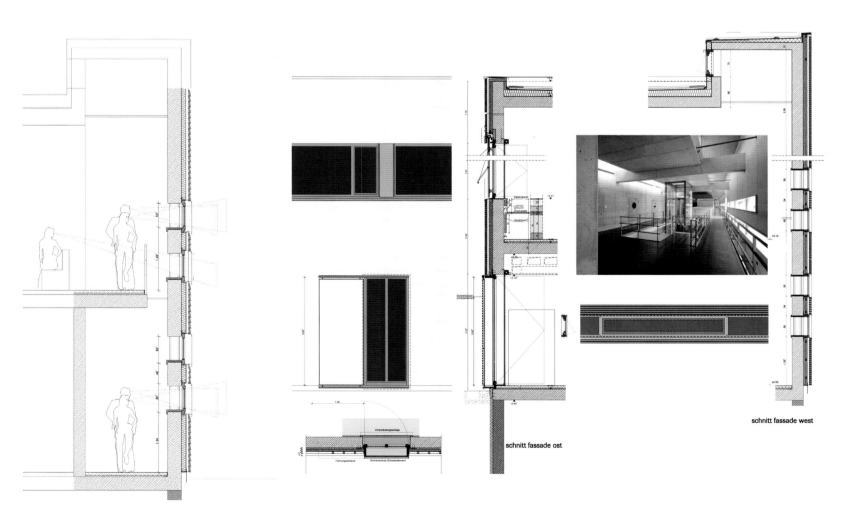

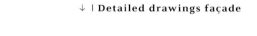

schnitt fassade ost

schnitt fassade west

↑ | View with opened lamellae
→ | Detail façade with reflection of inner courtyard

TU Chemie Graz

Graz

The new building consists of three distinguishable parts: the main glass building, the connecting metal element and the plastered building with a wooden roof terrace in the courtyard. The volume of the main building consists of different surfaces. The two longitudinal façades are large "smooth" glass membranes. The two recessed parts have a relief-style façade made of glass and aluminum. The glass surface is the showcase of the Technical University and its unique appearance creates a point of orientation in the "mental mapping" of visitors and residents. The look of the façade differs depending on the location of the observer, the weather, the time of day and the season. Sometimes the volume disappears by mirroring its surroundings, sometimes the pattern of the "molecules" appears in different colors.

CONSTRUCTION FACTS
Structure: new building. **Construction type:** glass curtain wall and post-and-beam construction. **Material:** fixed and moveable lamellae. **Fixing:** punctuated fixing. **Special functions:** sunscreen glass behind glass curtain wall, "colorstream" pigments on façade.

Address: Stremayrgasse 9, 8010 Graz, Austria. **Client:** Bundesimmobiliengesellschaft m.b.H. **Completion:** 2010. **Building type:** university. **Other creatives:** Robert Schaberl (artist, BIG-ART winner of competition: printed glass). **Construction engineer façade:** Fill Metallbau GmbH.

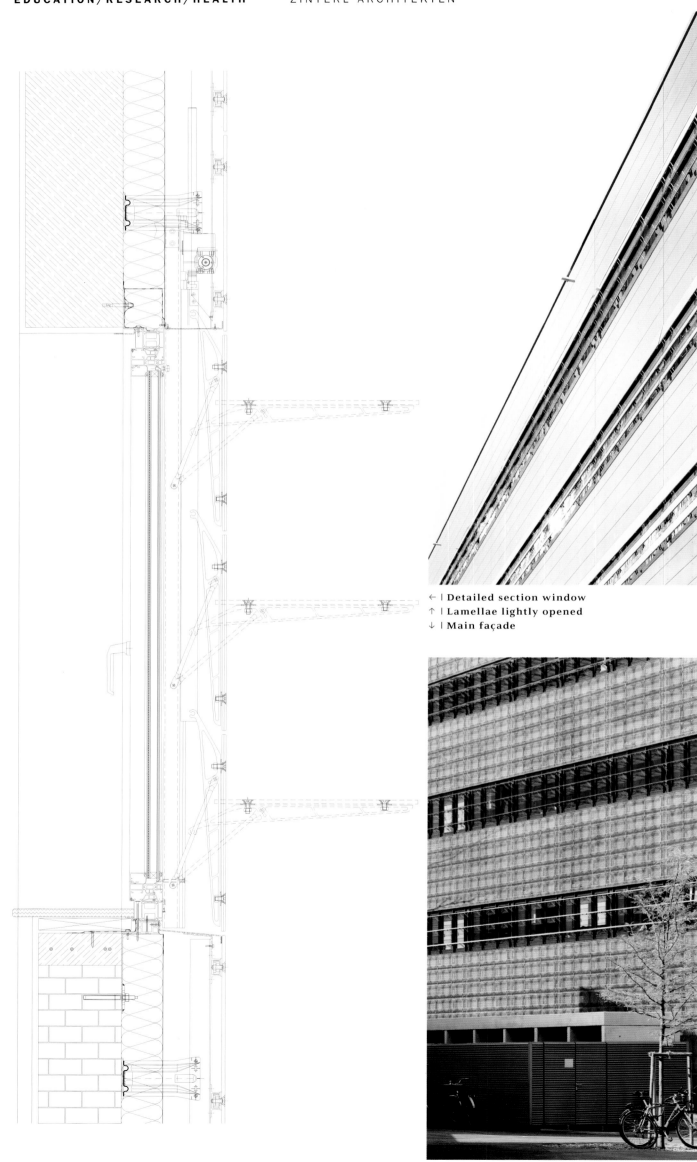

← | **Detailed section window**
↑ | **Lamellae lightly opened**
↓ | **Main façade**

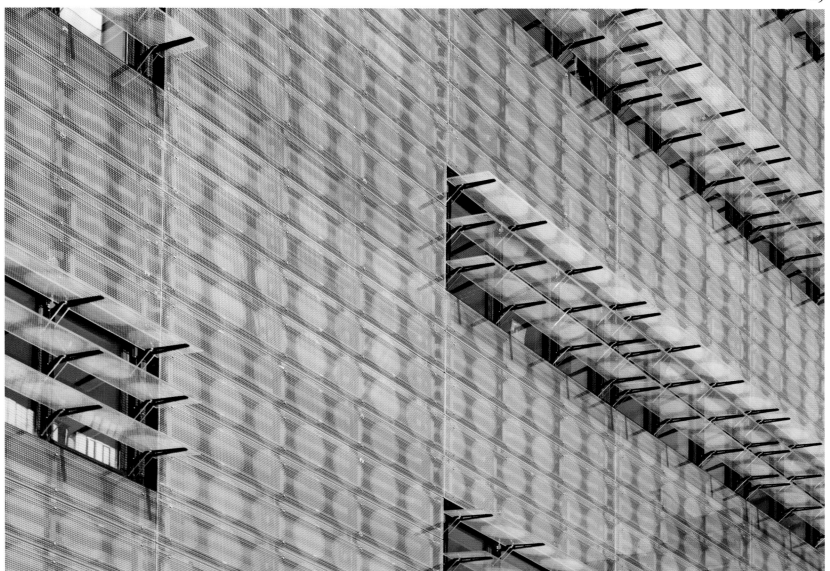

↑ I Detail view façade with different colors
↓ I Section

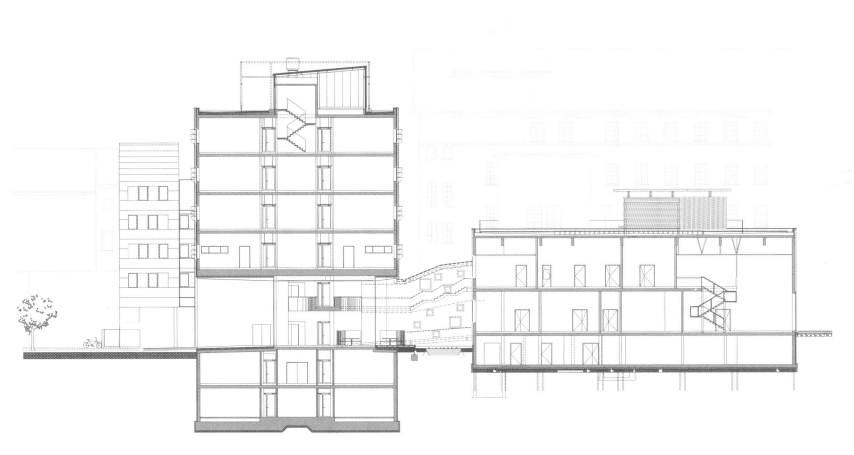

↑ | Façade with glass fields and colored elements

Secondary School

Bad Marienberg

The Evangelische Gymnasium (academic high school) Bad Marienberg is located at the edge of town in the immediate vicinity of other schools, the youth hostel and open fields. A metal façade with strips of glass and colored openings in different shades of green links the building to the surrounding nature and connects it to the neighborhood. The flexible ground plan offers the desired unrestricted development opportunities. Students enter the northern building section via the large entrance hall, from which all other sections can be reached quickly. The changing rooms for the sports hall and the refectory are located on the 1st level below ground level, the sports hall itself is dug one storey into the ground and is located on the 2nd level below ground level.

CONSTRUCTION FACTS

Structure: new building. **Construction type:** solid construction, post-and-beam construction, rear ventilated curtain wall. **Material:** lacquered aluminum, louvers as screens. **Fixing:** self-supporting. **Insulation:** R-value: 1.2 W/(m²K). **Special functions:** glare shield.

Address: Erlenweg 5, 56470 Bad Marienberg, Germany. **Client:** Evangelisches Gymnasium Bad Marienberg GmbH / Evangelische Kirche Hessen und Nassau. **Completion:** 2007. **Building type:** school.

↑ | **Generous glazing for views of the surrounding**
↓ | **Detail drawing glazing**
↓↓ | **Section**

↓ | **Detail façade**

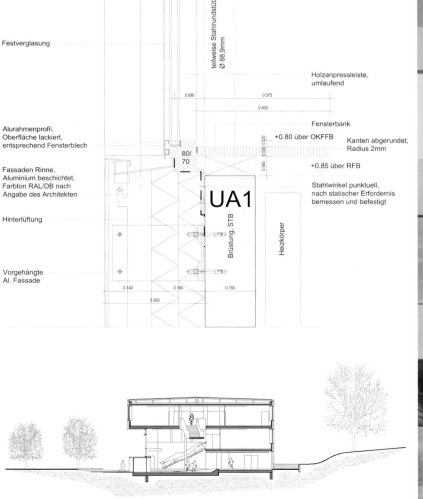

Festverglasung

teilweise Stahlrundstütze
Ø 88,9mm

Holzanpressleiste,
umlaufend

Fensterbank

+0.80 über OKFFB   Kanten abgerundet,
Radius 2mm

Alurahmenprofil,
Oberfläche lackiert,
entsprechend Fensterblech

Fassaden Rinne,
Aluminium beschichtet,
Farbton RAL/DB nach
Angabe des Architekten

+0.85 über RFB

Stahlwinkel punktuell,
nach statischer Erfordernis
bemessen und befestigt

Hinterlüftung

Vorgehängte
Al. Fassade

UA1

Brüstung, STB

Heizkörper

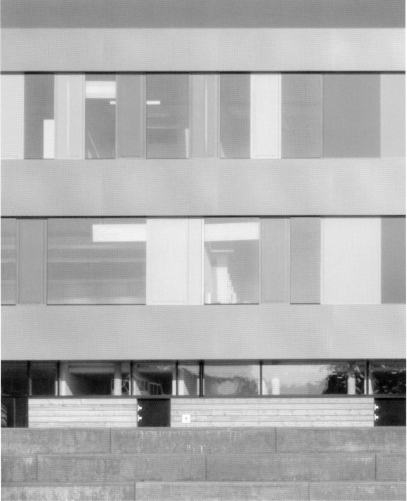

↑ | **Entrance in southwest façade**

Lecture Hall and Department of Real Estate Business

Regensburg

The new building is a distinctive entrance to the University of Regensburg and a central seminar and event building with an associated use by the department. Its exterior is dominated by the clearly distinguishable building structure into which few large openings and breaks were introduced. The department of real estate business has a slightly set back and connected structured façade, and the seminar rooms have a multi-story homogenous structure of matching openings, as well as "deep windows" for the illumination of the halls and foyers inside. All wall surfaces consist of jointless, two-tier exposed in-situ concrete with core insulation. The façades of the department are made of ceiling-high façade elements with external electrical wooden sliding shutters.

CONSTRUCTION FACTS

Structure: new building on campus. **Construction type:** double-skin solid construction. **Material:** exposed concrete, lamellae from larch wood. **Fixing:** on curtain-type anchor rod. **Insulation:** R-value: 1.2 W/(m^2K). **Special functions:** thermal insulation, natural ventilation.

Address: Universitätsstraße 31, 93053 Regensburg, Germany. **Client:** the Free State of Bavaria, National Building Authorities Regensburg. **Completion:** 2011. **Building type:** university.

↑ | **Interior view office**
→ | **Section façade with sliding panel**
↓ | **Space for maintenance between glazing and lamellae**

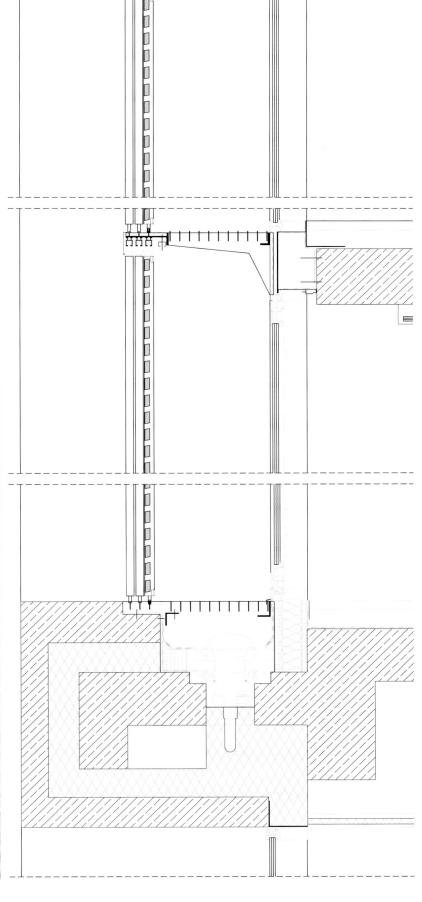

↑ | Exterior view

BioMedizinZentrum Bochum

Bochum

This building provides state-of-the-art laboratory, workshop, and office space for medical and biomedical research and health care. The compact structure inserts itself into the homogenous orthogonal fabric of its urban setting, but with its multicolored outer skin stands in deliberate contrast to the large stretches of exposed concrete characteristic of the surrounding university buildings. The articulation of the façade acts as visible expression of the equality of all rental units within. Its uniform cellular structure envelops the volume in a skin that unifies the various levels. Windows that open outward like ventilation flaps lend the façade a differentiated and individual look.

CONSTRUCTION FACTS

Structure: new building on campus. **Construction type:** rear ventilated curtain wall. **Material:** aluminum, double glazing. **Fixing:** aluminum post-and-beam construction with 6mm compression profiles. **Insulation:** R-value: 1.1 W/(m²K).

Address: Universitätsstraße 136, 44799 Bochum, Germany. **Client:** Entwicklungsgesellschaft Ruhr-Bochum mbH (EGR). **Completion:** 2008. **Building type:** laboratory and office.

↑ | Detail projected windows
↓ | Section façade

↑ | Detail façade
↓ | Detail drawing attic

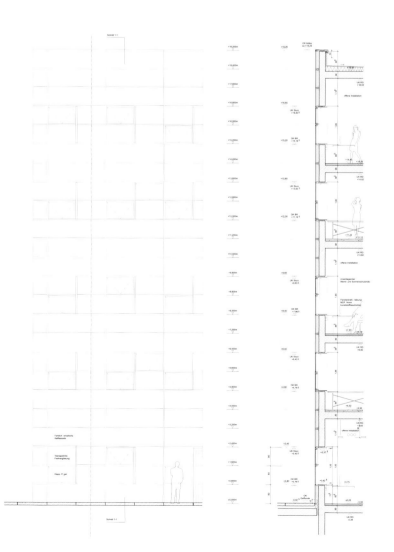

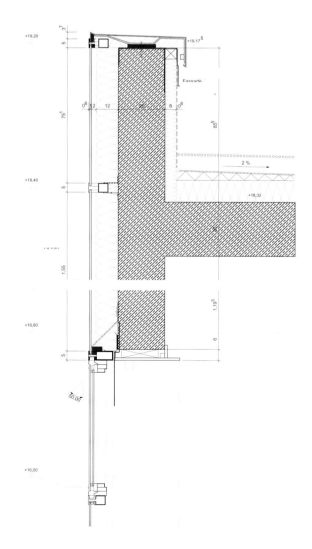

↑ | South-west view
→ | South façade

ZET – Sustainability Lab

Dresden

There are most various research activities in the sector of energy engineering. A building that houses such requirements will have to differ from traditional institute buildings in its exterior design. Technical "vertical blinds" embrace the sophisticated form and impart the beholder with various impressions of the building's cubature depending on the point of view. Once the complete shape becomes visible, the view through the blades allows for perceiving the building's interior, its technical contents, and its construction. Like a dazzlingly white weld seam, the staircase unites the old buildings' various levels with the differently high workrooms of the new building. The facilities presented inside the building contribute to its physical appearance: the wind tunnel's intake port dominates the façade; solar cells are used as sheeting. The power generated is fed into the university's power network, and is thus used in a rational way.

CONSTRUCTION FACTS

Structure: new building. **Construction type:** rear ventilated curtain wall. **Material:** aluminum lamellae. **Fixing:** punctuated fixing. **Insulation:** thermal insulation. **Special functions:** generation of energy (photovoltaics).

Address: George-Bähr-Straße 3b, 01069 Dresden, Germany. **Client:** Sächsisches Immobilien und Bau-management Niederlassung Dresden II. **Completion:** 2010. **Building type:** research.

↑ | **Detail view façade**
↓ | **Section**

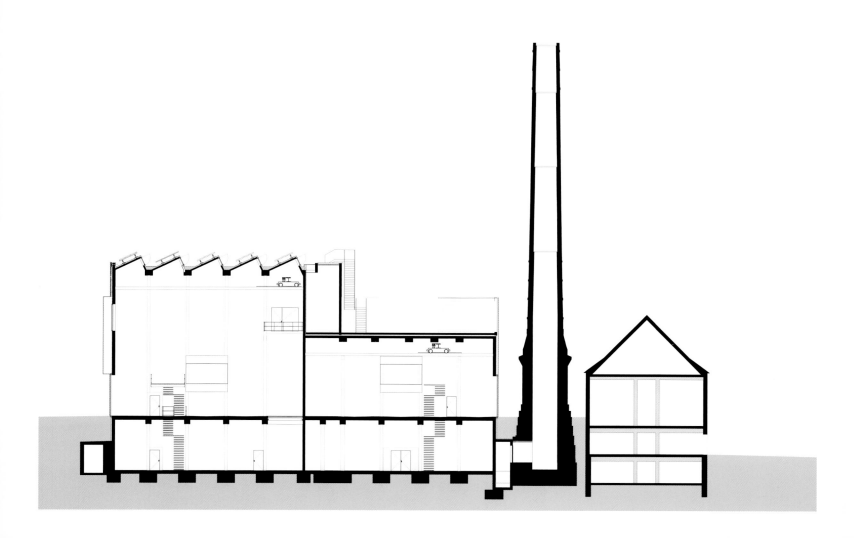

↑ | Façade closed
↓ | Façade opened

↑ | School with sports hall

Public Secondary School

Memmingen

The formerly intensively commercially used slaughterhouse premises are being reconstructed to become the home of a large educational and sports institution. The reconstruction aimed to create an independent and identity-shaping site that is in line with and suitable for the new educational use. In addition to the open and multi-purpose building design, the anthracite façade provides the premises with a new distinguished and clearly identifiable focal point. High-quality materials, such as acidulated glistening exposed concrete elements and anodized aluminum windows, create a very sustainable façade design. The façade's particular high-quality and long-service life reflect the spirit of the public school use.

CONSTRUCTION FACTS

Structure: new building, solitaire. **Construction Type:** rear ventilated, punctuated façade. **Material:** prefabricated elements from anthracite concrete. **Fixing:** self-supporting. **Insulation:** R-value: 0.16 W/(m²K). **Special functions:** sun screen and diverting of light.

Address: Schlachthofstraße 34, 87700 Memmingen, Germany. **Client:** City of Memmingen. **Completion:** 2010. **Building type:** school. **Other creatives:** Fraunhofer Institute for Building Physics IBP, Stuttgart.

↑ | **Anodized aluminum windows in block construction**
↓ | **Entrance area**

↑ | **Exposed concrete**
↘ | **Section façade**

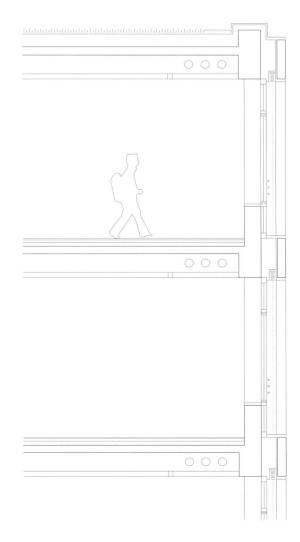

Jarmund/Vigsnæs AS
Architects

↑ | Façade covered with fiber cement boards
in 10 different colors

Oslo International School

Oslo

Oslo International School is a private school with about 500 children from more than 50 different nations. The building is divided into kindergarten, reception, primary, and secondary school. The primary goal of the building project was to upgrade the existing areas. Organically shaped walls are clad with specially milled wooden paneling in convex and concave shapes and treated with clear tar. In other places, the façade is covered with fiber cement boards in ten different colors. The exterior materials are also used inside. Daylight fills the rooms from narrow slits extending from floor to ceiling combined with circular roof lights. Inside, the wooden walls are whitewashed.

CONSTRUCTION FACTS
Structure: new building. Construction type: wooden stud frame with integrated steel columns for roof support. Material: milled wooden paneling, fiber cement boards. Insulation: R-value: 0.22 W/(m²K).

Address: Gamle Ringeriksvei 53, 1357 Bekkestua, Norway. **Client:** Oslo International School. **Completion:** 2009. **Building type:** school. **Other creatives:** AS Frederiksen (structural engineering).

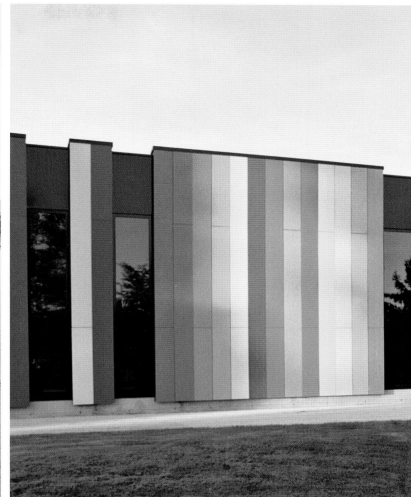

↑ | **Milled wooden paneling**
↓ | **Detailed section**

↑ | **Detail fiber cement boards**

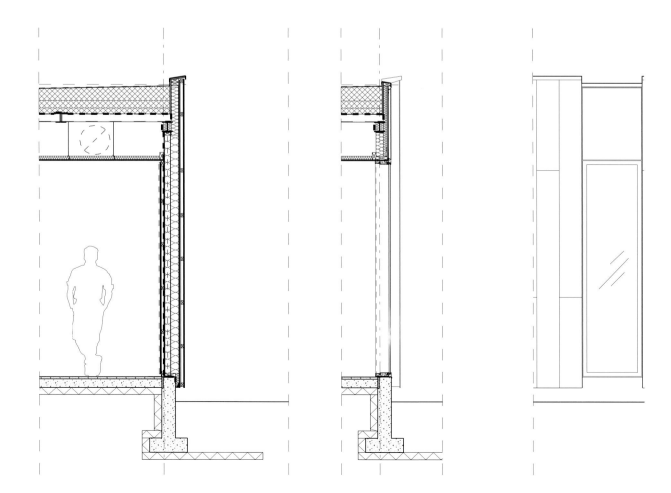

↑ | Colorful façade at night
→ | Detail façade

Center for Pediatric Medicine
Angelika-Lautenschläger-Klinik

Heidelberg

The new building of the pediatric clinic is based on the colorful Rubik's Cube. Similarly, the clinic consists of four major elements – a cube, functional building, entrance hall and parents' accommodations. The cube is used for patient care while the service building houses the diagnosis areas. The entrance hall located in between is the communication center. The façade of the upper floors consists of a comprehensive mullion and transom design with external metal sun screens. Colored glass elements are suspended in front, creating different sections and an interplay of colors. The lower-levels façade is made of quarry stone with external metal blinds and playfully arranged creeper cables for sun screen. The façade of the plinth is greened.

CONSTRUCTION FACTS
Structure: new building, solitaire. **Construction type:** post-and-beam façade, rear ventilated stone façade with ribbon windows. **Material:** aluminum, glazing, stone. **Fixing:** part of the construction. **Insulation:** 1.50 W/(m^2K) (post-and-beam façade), 0.29 W/(m^2K) (stone façade). **Special functions:** screens.

PROJECT FACTS

Address: Universitätsklinikum Heidelberg, Im Neuenheimer Feld 430, 69120 Heidelberg, Germany.
Client: The Federal State of Baden-Württemberg, represented by the building authorities of the
University of Heidelberg. **Completion:** 2008. **Building type:** hospital. **Other creatives:** Heiner Blum,
Gisela Kleinlein (artists).

↑ | **Entrance area**
→ | **Section façade**
↓ | **Interior view foyer**

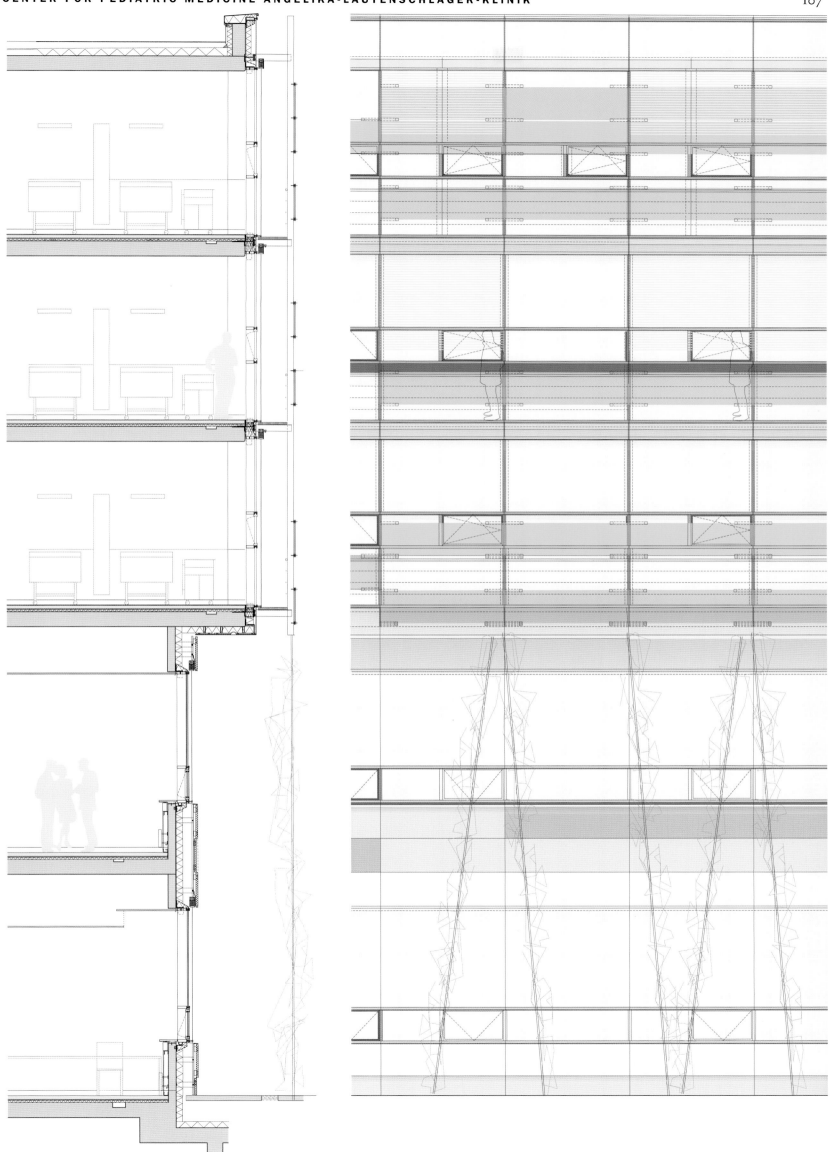

Dirk Melzer landscape
architecture + v-architekten

↑ | View from the street

Floodwater Pumping Station

Cologne

Where the city meets the countryside, the engineering building's side facing the Rhine is enclosed by a curved wall ending in a drive-on ramp. The great variation of heights and structures of the basalt stone wall result in a "flow around the engineering building." This image is continued on the metal façade in an abstraction of alluvial driftwood. The continuing pattern was manually created via CAD, adjusted several times for optimal static requirements, and finally cut out of the 10-millimeter steel plates by a plasma cutter. The substructure made of steel sections provides a clearance for stairs leading to functional areas and maintenance openings. The coating with two-component paint gives the surface a high-quality appearance with high weather and light resistance.

CONSTRUCTION FACTS
Structure: landscape architecture with new building. **Construction type:** curtain wall. **Material:** coated steel sheets. **Fixing:** punctuated fixing with steel hooks.

Address: Uferstraße, 50996 Cologne, Germany. **Client:** Stadtentwässerungsbetriebe Köln.
Completion: 2010. **Building type:** pumping station.

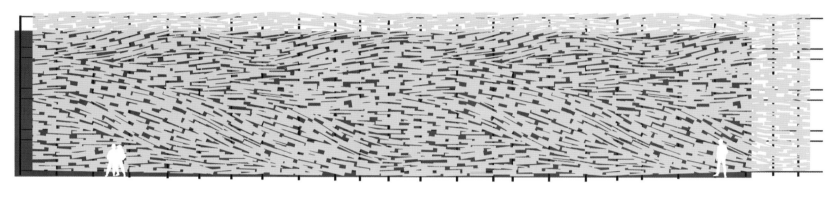

↑↑ | **View from the riverbank**
↓ | **Section**

↑ | **Elevation**
↓ | **Detail structure steel façade**

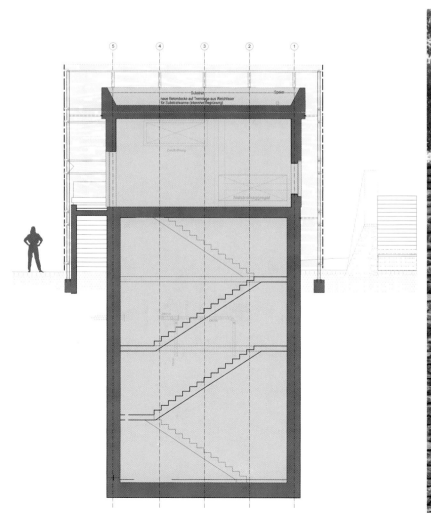

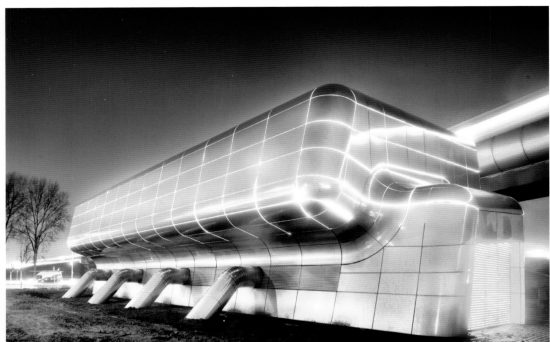

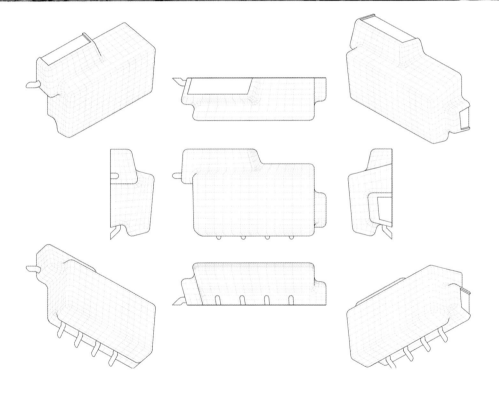

↖↖ | Exterior view at night
↑↑ | Detail of the façade, with pipes
↖ | Diagram façade, folded out
↑ | Detail façade panels

Booster Station South

Amsterdam

The Booster Station South is a sewage pumping station. The constant stream of passengers by car, metro, train, or bicycle perceives the Booster Station as a futuristic sculpture. The stainless steel skin consists of three types of panels: flat, single-curved, and double-curved. The single-curved sheets were rolled into shape. The double-curved spheroid corners were rubber press-molded and the double-curved saddle panels were fashioned using explosion techniques. With its cladding of stainless steel panels it reflects the movements, shapes, and colors of the environment. At night, the building's tectonics come to the surface. The illuminated seams in the steel skin make the pumping-engine look like a mesh-model as mass turns into mesh.

PROJECT FACTS
Address: Spaklerweg, Amsterdam, The Netherlands. **Client:** Waternet, Amsterdam. **Completion:** 2006. **Building type:** pumping-engine for sluicing out sewage. **Construction engineer façade:** Sorba Projects, Winterswijk, The Netherlands.

CONSTRUCTION FACTS
Structure: new building, solitaire. **Construction type:** cassette façade, system façade elements. **Material:** stainless steel panels. **Fixing:** suspended panels, punctuated fixing. **Insulation:** noise insulation.

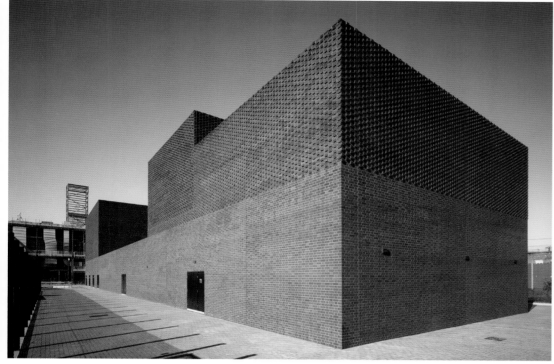

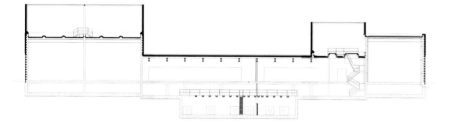

↑↑ | Exterior view
↑ | Sections
↗ | Detail brickwork

Primary Substation – 2012 Olympics

London

CONSTRUCTION FACTS
Structure: new building. **Construction type:** solid construction. **Material:** engineering brick. **Fixing:** self-supporting, brickwork tied to concrete structure. **Special functions:** brick bond modulated to perform different functions from blast protection to ventilation.

The building is not designed as an event in its own right but as part of a number of buildings that form the fabric of the Olympic site itself; having permanency, weight and dignity. Its architecture creates a sense of solidity appropriate to the building's role as a utilities building, whilst the use of brick reflects the traditional use of dark brick stock on the site. Appearing at first as an uninterrupted surface, the envelope is more of an open lattice than it appears. In lower sections, operating as a load-bearing structure, in others simply as a skin and in the upper sections and with subtle modulation it provides ventilation for the transformers that sit at either end of the building.

PROJECT FACTS
Address: Kings Yard, Carpenters Road, London 2012 Olympic Park, United Kingdom. **Client:** EDF Energy. **Completion:** 2010. **Building type:** substation. **Construction engineer façade:** Andrews Associates.

↑ | View from north

CUSWC – Central Urban Solid Waste Collection

Huarte

In this building, the local waste gets separated and compacted for either recycling or transportation to a waste disposal site. An underground pipe system connects it to the individual households of the neighborhood. The building's outer shell incorporates various layers of noise protection. The façade envelops the internal waste-compacting functions and machines such as turbines, decanters, compaction filters. It consists of large-format leaf-lacquered aluminum sheets made of recycled cans. They convey the image of swelling supported by the idea of an organic digestion occurring inside the building. At the same time, the iconography is intended to reflect the image of "patchwork."

CONSTRUCTION FACTS
Structure: new building, solitaire. **Construction type:** double-cladding. **Material:** recycled aluminum sheets. **Fixing:** punctuated fixing. **Insulation:** noise insulation.

PROJECT FACTS

Address: Calle Roma s/n, Ripagaina, Huarte, Spain. **Client:** Junta de Compensación AR1 of PSIS of Ripagaina. **Completion:** 2009. **Building type:** industrial. **Other creatives:** Tadeo Errea – Dasein Ingenieros (structural engineering). **Construction engineer façade:** Marcial Lázaro – Altres.

↑ | **Detail east façade**
↓ | **Elevations and roof plan**

↑ | **Detail aluminum sheets**

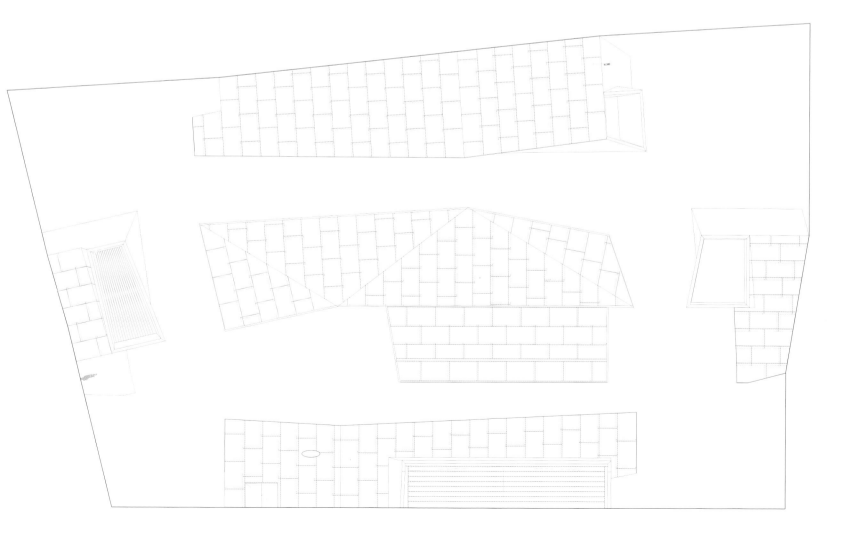

↑ | Detail of ornamental façade

Residential Complex Granatniy 6

Moscow

This residential complex's simple cubic forms and façades richly decorated with carved ornamentation are an architectural signature that has been considerably influenced by the development's surroundings – the old buildings on Granatny pereulok and the nearby Central House of Architects with its impressive portal created by Andrey Burov. The complex consists of three structures of different heights linked by glazed passages/vestibules and by a shared underground space. The way that the three blocks have been grouped around an internal courtyard results in a comfortable environment with a very human scale.

CONSTRUCTION FACTS
Structure: new building. **Construction type:** ventilated curtain wall. **Material:** natural stone plates. **Fixing:** suspension.

Address: 6, Granatniy lane, 123001, Moscow, Russian Federation. **Client:** Skanklin - invest. **Completion:** 2011. **Building type:** residential. **Other creatives:** Sergey Tchoban, Sergey Kuznetsov (architects).

↑ | **View from the street**
→ | **Detail drawing**
↓ | **Detail of the façade**

↑ | Entrance area
→ | Detail façade with glazing and stainless steel shingles

Aloft London Excel

London

The Aloft London ExCeL is a new high-quality hotel located on the ExCeL campus in London Docklands. The project was developed by ExCeL London's parent company, Abu Dhabi National Exhibitions Company, in partnership with Starwood Hotels & Resorts Worldwide. The plan of the building has a convex central spine containing bedrooms and the vertical circulation, flanked by two concave wings which house further bedrooms and corridors. These wings are clad in thousands of specially treated, highly reflective stainless steel shingles creating the extraordinary effect of constantly changing color with the passing of the day.

CONSTRUCTION FACTS
Structure: new building. **Construction type:** curtain wall. **Material:** toughened glass with screen printed ceramic frit, bead blasted and patterned stainless steel shingles. **Fixing:** adjustable steel brackets. **Insulation:** R-value: 0.15 W/(m²K), noise insulation.

PROJECT FACTS

Address: One Eastern Gateway, Royal Victoria Dock, London E16 1FR, United Kingdom. **Client:** Excel London (part of Abu Dhabi National Exhibitions Company). **Completion:** 2011. **Building type:** hotel. **Façade consultants:** Billings Design Associates.

↑ | **General view**
← | **Detail curved façade**

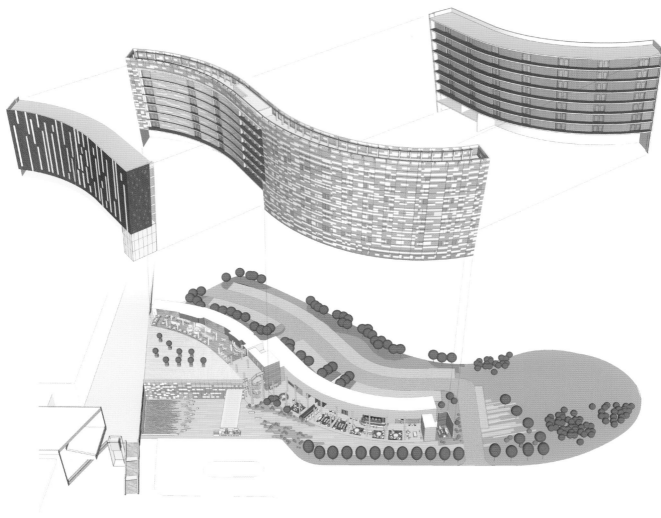

↑ | Exploded view drawing
← | Detail glass façade

| Toyo Ito & Associates, Architects (façade) | Carlos Basso, Toni Olaya (UDA Arquitectos) (building renovation) |

↑ | Detail steel structure

Suites Avenue Aparthotel

Barcelona

The boutique hotel is located on Passeig de Gràcia, across the street from Antonio Gaudi's "La Pedrera". The task was to turn an existing office building into a contemporary hotel. The new façade design implemented "waves" made of seamlessly connected 8-millimeter manufactured curved steel plates. The waves' convexity and concavity are shifted at different areas. The surface is coated in a light tint of pearl pink, allowing the color to slightly change according to the surrounding light conditions. Composite panels consisting of three types of glass with gently imprinted wave patterns were used to imitate the glimmering surface of a stream. Corresponding to the movement of people on stairs and elevators, the panels cause refractions, reflections, and an amplification of light to produce a serene, yet lively atmosphere.

CONSTRUCTION FACTS

Structure: façade renovation. **Construction type:** steel construction. **Material:** 8 mm curved steel plates coated in light pearl pink. **Fixing:** punctuated fixing.

Address: Paseo de Gràcia, 83, 08008 Barcelona, Spain. **Client:** Derby Hotels Collection. **Completion:** 2009. **Building type:** living. **Other creatives:** Manel Morilla (project manager).

↑ | View from the street
↓ | Diagram curving of the steel plates

↑ | Curved steel plates
↓ | View from inside

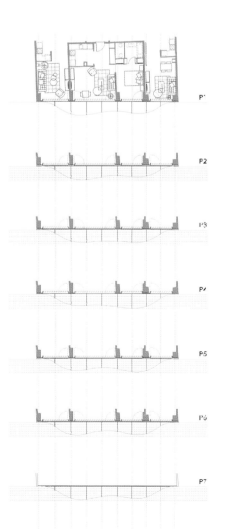

↑ | Exterior view

Residential Multi-family Home

Worb

The new building integrates into the historic center of Worb. It is cubic, simple, and clear, distinguished by a consistent energy-efficient and ecological design. The façade elements include ceiling-high glazing, paneling made of Duripanel particle bonded boards, and horizontal window strips. However, the distinguished volume and uniform contemporary look of the building is based on the incorporation of the balconies and staircase with green glazed fir timber cladding. At the same time, the structure, materials and texture of the building are closely related to the buildings at the town center.

CONSTRUCTION FACTS

Structure: new building. **Construction type:** composite construction. **Material:** rear ventilated wooden planking. **Fixing:** part of the construction. **Insulation:** R-value: 0.1 W/(m²K).

Address: Enggisteinstrasse 16, 3076 Worb, Switzerland. **Client:** Antoinette Hofmann Ganz. **Completion:** 2011. **Building type:** living. **Construction engineer façade:** Tschopp + Kohler Ingenieure GmbH, Bern; Daniel Hadron, Steffisburg.

↑ | **Detail of north view**
↓ | **Interior view**

↑ | **Detail façade**
↓ | **Elevation**

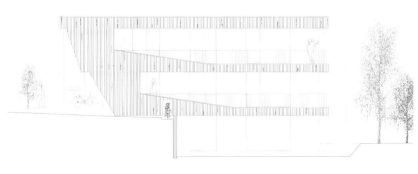

Chaix & Morel et Associés I
JSWD Architekten

↑ | **View from north**

Hotel Quai de Seine

Paris

A fire destroyed one of the twin buildings of the "Magasins Généraux", also disrupting the symmetry of the composition near the Bassin de la Villette. The faithful reproduction of the vanished building volume by a new building reintroduces this balance, while the new building differs from the old one in its lightness and transparency of its skin. The building is used as a hotel, youth hostel, and restaurant. Its oscillating silhouette creates clearances that direct the light and visitors to the central court of the block. The building's skin envelops the hotel and youth hostel, including the roof terraces. Behind the metal façade level, the building was covered in timber in reference to the former harbor function of the body of water and the building vis-à-vis.

CONSTRUCTION FACTS

Structure: new building. **Construction type:** double-cladding with translucent, metal curtain wall. **Material:** lamellae made of douglas fir. **Fixing:** part of the solid construction. **Insulation:** metal lamellae as glare shield.

Address: 68 Quai de Seine, 75019 Paris, France. Client: Cofitem - Cofimur. Completion: 2008. Building type: hotel. Construction engineer façade: AR & C, Bureau d'etudes Structure et Facades.

↑ | Detail façade
↓ | Section, vertical

↑ | Façade courtyard
↓ | Detail of lamellae

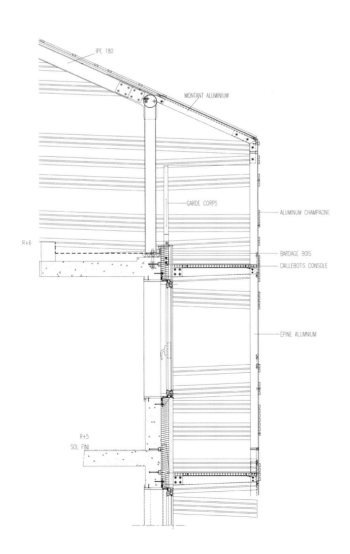

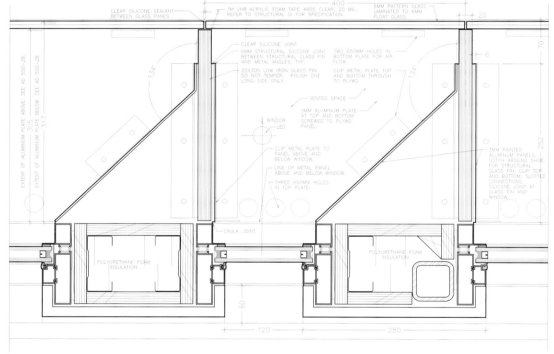

↖↑ | View of entrance and reflecting pool
↑↑ | Corner of living room/performance space
↖ | Detail of wall system at 500 level
↑ | Interior view staircase

The Integral House

Ontario

The Integral House serves as both a private residence and a performance space for musical events. It uses three distinct façade systems to articulate and weave together relationships between the surrounding landscape and the architectural program. The undulating perimeter of the living room/performance space is clad in a series of deep, wooden fins that modulate light, space, and sound. Lower floors are clad in a customized, curtain wall system, syncopated to accommodate changing radii while creating cinematic views of the forest beyond. The private spaces on the top floor are clad in etched glass to emphasize the feeling of floating above the tree tops.

PROJECT FACTS

Address: Toronto, ON, Canada. **Client:** Dr. James Stewart. **Completion:** 2009. **Building type:** residential/performance space. **Other creatives:** Blackwell Bowick Partnership (structural engineering), Julie Latraverse and Chris Oliver (interior design), Suzanne Powadiuk Design Inc. (lighting design), Swallow Consultants (acoustical consultant), Dr. Ted Kesik (envelope consultant).

CONSTRUCTION FACTS

Structure: new building. **Construction type:** double-glazed curtain wall (100-300 levels), punctuated façade (400 level), double-skin façade (500 level). **Material:** glazing, white oak fins, acid etched laminated glass. **Insulation:** thermal insulation. **Special functions:** wooden fins contribute to the acoustical performance of the concert hall inside.

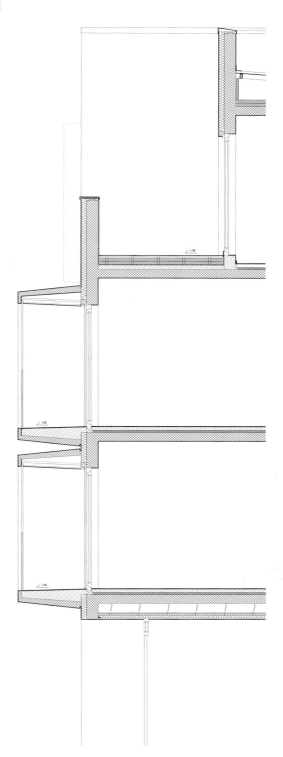

↑↑ | Street view
↑ | Detail prefabricated concrete frames
↗ | Prefabricated concrete frames
→ | Detail section façade

Jurčkova

Ljubljana

CONSTRUCTION FACTS
Structure: new building, solitaire in context.
Construction type: solid construction, seamless façade. **Material:** thermal insulation composite system. **Fixing:** bonding. **Insulation:** thermal insulation: R-value: 0.363 W/ (m²K).

The two buildings with fifty residential units are located directly on Jurčkova Street in Ljubljana. Their dominant design elements are the concrete window frames. The concrete is colored before fabricating the fitted elements. It is also made water resistant, thus requiring no additional protection. The conical shape of the loggias and window frames is due to the production technique, with heavy pre-fabricated elements pulled from the mould. The slightly rough effect of the concrete loggias matches the criteria of the street. Looking at the units from afar, the loggias seem playful and light. Yet they are strong enough to retain their uniformity despite any potential decorations by the residents.

PROJECT FACTS
Address: Jurčkova cesta 1, 1000 Ljubljana, Slovenia. **Client:** Regal GH. **Completion:** 2009.
Building type: housing.

Vaíllo & Irigaray + Eguinoa

↑ | Façade raised
→ | View of the terrace gallery

2C Houses

Corella

The strategy was to dig and contain the soil by means of a longitudinal wall, then construct glass boxes varying in size according to the clients' needs. The green latticework of the wall reminds the viewer of the rows of poplar trees growing at the river banks in this part of the country whose presence makes the river visible from afar. The house is designed so that it is sheltered from the north and exposed to the south, a circumstance that is abetted by the sloping of the ground in the southerly direction. The wall can be moved up and down. Between the green outer wall and the glass wall, which confines the living area, there is space to walk along the building.

CONSTRUCTION FACTS
Structure: new building. **Construction type:** double-cladding. **Material:** laminated safety glass, steel grating. **Fixing:** punctuated fixing, suspension. **Insulation:** thermal insulation, noise insulation, glare shield, UV-reduction. **Special functions:** façade can be raised and lowered mechanically.

Address: Calle de Cañete, CP: 31591, Corella, Spain. **Client:** Private. **Completion:** 2010. **Building type:** house. **Other creatives:** Tadeo Errea – Landabe (structual engineering). **Construction engineer façade:** Hermanos Chivite (motorized lattice), Altres (aluminum).

↑ | Façade lowered
↙ | South elevation and floor plans

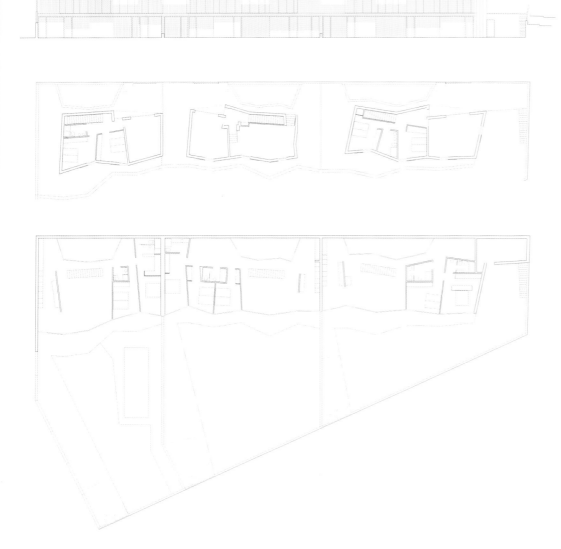

↑ | Façade in different positions
← | Gallery on ground floor

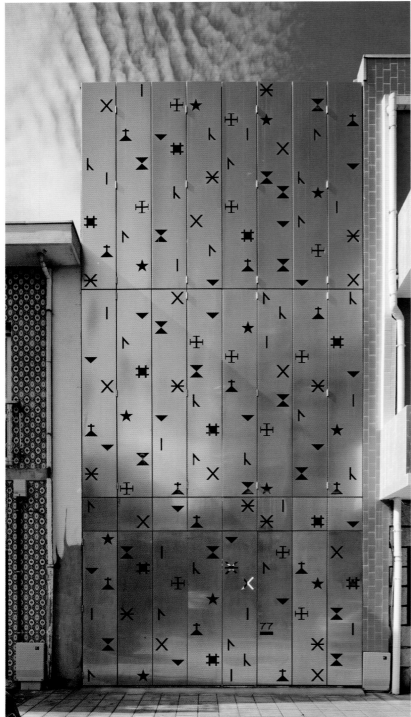

↖ | **East view of the façade, panels closed**
↑ | **Panels partially opened**

House 77

Póvoa de Varzim

House 77 is organized in a vertical and hierarchical way. The social areas are on the lower floors and the private areas on the upper levels. To achieve great visual amplitudes and dynamic interconnections between spaces, the interior was structured in half-floors. The street façade guarantees intimacy through stainless steel panels, perforated with the "siglas poveiras". These feature a proto-writing system once used as a way of communication and to mark personal and fishing belongings. They were not uniform but handed down from generation to generation. The opposite façade is covered in aluminum venetian blinds that not only shield the interior but also open up onto a small garden.

CONSTRUCTION FACTS
Structure: new building. **Construction type:** perforated façade. **Material:** stainless steel. **Fixing:** punctuated fixing, sliding sunshades. **Insulation:** thermal insulation, sun screen.

Address: Rua António Graça, nº 77, 4490 - 471, Póvoa de Varzim, Portugal. **Client:** Ana Paula da Silva Oliveira. **Completion:** 2010. **Building type:** living. **Construction engineer façade:** Abílio Rodrigues & Quantal.

↑ | View from inside
→ | Open views inside
↓ | Longitudinal section of the façade

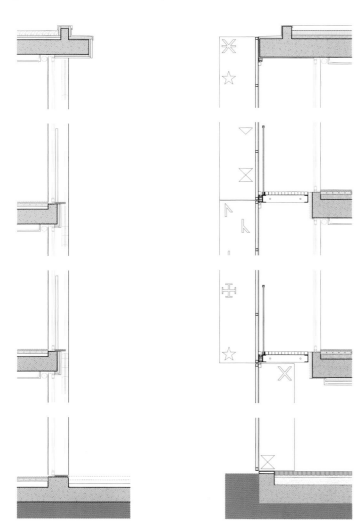

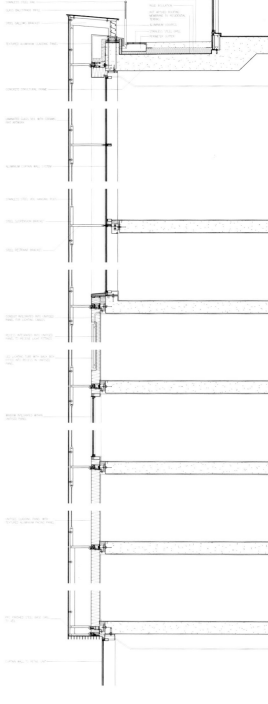

↖↖ | **Exterior view**
← | **Light installation at night**
↖ | **Detail double-skin façade**
↑ | **Section façade with lights**

W London Leicester Square

London

W London, Leicester Square is a landmark 192 bedroom, 5 Star hotel in the heart of London's West End, developed by McAleer and Rushe. In addition to the hotel, the new ten-floor building houses retail, leisure and residential accommodation spread over 18,500 square meters, including a spa, 11 penthouse apartments and two basement levels housing a new retail-leisure experience provided by a leading global brand. The façade is veiled in translucent glass suspended off the face of the building like a floating sheer curtain, evoking the cinematic heritage of this part of the West End. This veil functions like a huge pixel screen, the first of its kind in the UK. It allows the look of the building to change as day turns to night.

PROJECT FACTS
Address: 10 Wardour Street, London W1D 6QF, United Kingdom. **Client:** McAleer & Rushe. **Completion:** 2011. **Building type:** hotel. **Other creatives:** Concrete (interior design). **Construction engineer façade:** Billings Design Associates Ltd, Caldwell Consulting (engineering).

CONSTRUCTION FACTS
Structure: new building. **Construction type:** double-skin façade. **Material:** frameless glazing. **Fixing:** suspension. **Insulation:** thermal insulation. **Special functions:** light installations.

↑↑ | Façade at night
↑ | Lobby
↗↗ | Façade at daytime
↗ | Lit façade

Chrome Hotel

Kolkata

CONSTRUCTION FACTS
Structure: new building. **Construction type:** post-and-beam construction, perforated façade. **Material:** hume pipes, brick, plastered exterior finish with double-glazed windows, circular windows with LED lighting. **Fixing:** punctuated fixing. **Insulation:** thermal insulation, sun screen. **Special functions:** modulated lighting.

The façade of this hotel is punctuated by circular openings of 45 centimeters in diameter. These openings allow natural light to enter into the public spaces at daytime and are made of fritted glass preventing the exterior to be seen from the inside. This helps create an identity of its own for the entering visitor. Each opening is lit during the evening hours by LEDs that change color as the night progresses, promoting a dynamic image of the building as it glows in different hues like a large punctuated lantern. In addition to regular rooms, the hotel contains suites that cantilever out forming a wedge in the top half of the building.

PROJECT FACTS
Address: 226, A.J.C Bose Road, Kolkata 700020, India. **Client:** Chocolate Hotels Pvt. Ltd. **Completion:** 2009. **Building type:** hotel.

↑ | **Detail window panes**

Apartment House in Chelsea

New York

This extravagant apartment block in New York City stands out from the other buildings on the banks of the Hudson River. It features a façade of around 1,700 colorless windows which are tilted and skewed at various angles so that it appears like a glittering mosaic. The reflected images of the sky, the river, and the surrounding neighborhood present an uneven, twinkling appearance to passers-by, brightening the gray skyline of Chelsea with a sparkling look. Furthermore, although from the street the building appears slightly pivoted, there is no corner facing the viewer. Instead, the façade seems to wrap around the building because the surface is a continuous curve.

CONSTRUCTION FACTS
Structure: new building. **Construction type:** curtain wall (south façade), black brick (north, east façades). **Material:** tilted, colorless windowpanes. **Fixing:** steel frame. **Insulation:** thermal insulation.

Address: 100 11th Avenue, New York, NY, USA. **Client:** Alf Naman Real Estate Cape Advisors, Inc. **Completion:** 2010. **Building type:** living. **Other creatives:** Desimone Consulting Engineers, PLLC (structural engineering). **Construction engineer façade:** Front Inc.

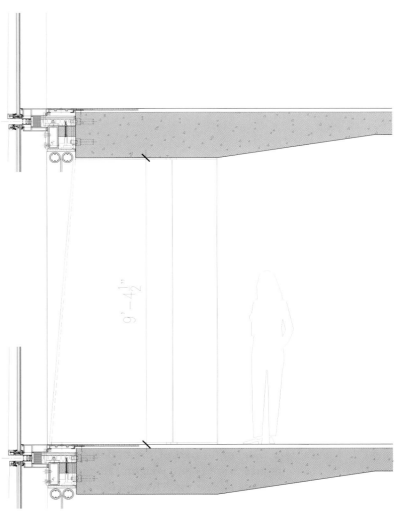

↑ | View from the river
↓ | Detail façade

↑ | View from 11th Avenue
↓ | Detail drawing façade

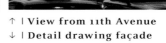

fischer berkhan architekten

↑ | **View from east**

House p

Zollernalbkreis

Clarity and austerity distinguish this classic modernity residence for two persons. The generous L-shaped rear living area extends into the garden and encloses the terrace. The façade is open towards the southwest. Glass sliding doors across the entire façade width allow the exterior and interior to interflow. Large roof overhangs highlight this effect. The exterior design clearly presents the different building bodies. The living area is designed in a combination of glass and aluminum. The upper part of the building, covered in variegated stone plaster, is impressive due to its massiveness and weight. Limited openings that can be totally closed by the sun screens accentuate its volume. The functional building has dark plastering. The colors and materials create a harmonious trio.

CONSTRUCTION FACTS
Structure: new building, solitaire. **Construction type:** solid construction. **Material:** mottled sandstone plaster. **Fixing:** bonding. **Insulation:** thermal insulation. **Special functions:** 8-meter wide lifting- and sliding elements from aluminum connect interior and exterior.

Address: Zollernalbkreis, Germany. **Client:** private. **Completion:** 2009. **Building type:** living. **Other creatives:** Interior design in cooperation with Michael Schad and Daniel Priester.

↑ | View from west
↘ | Cross section
↓ | View towards living room

↓ | Entrance area

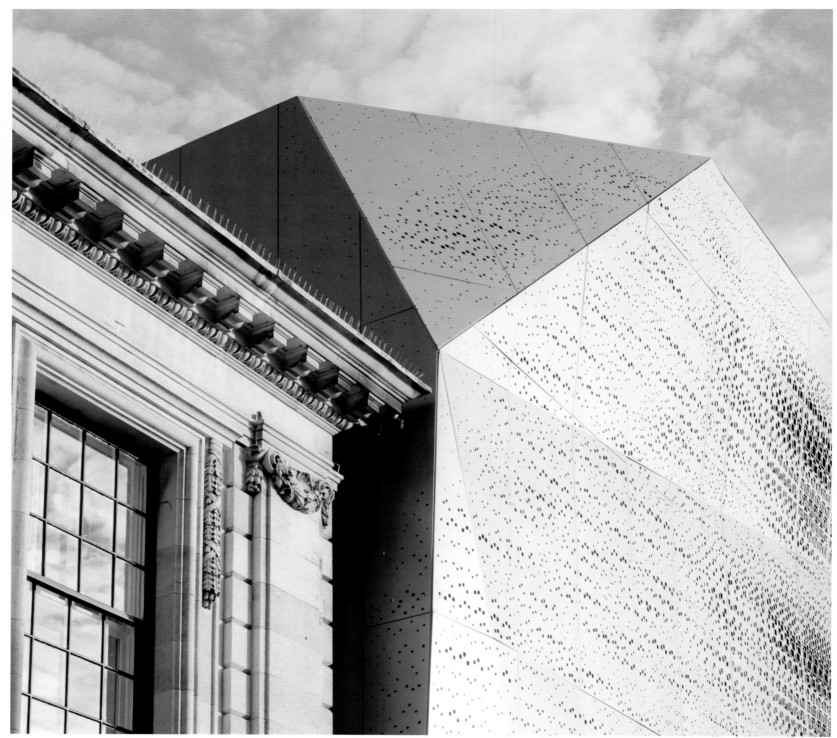

↑ | Detail old and new façade
→ | View through laser-cut skin from inside

Town Hall Hotel

London

In response to an architecturally eclectic structure, the Town Hall Hotel project design was affected by concerns over the access of light and views for the neighboring buildings. A pattern was deployed on the façade to regulate how much light enters the room behind it and to control the view available from the inside. Integral to the performance of the façade system, the laser-cut skin combines internal functions and context with a new visual grammar generated from an existing art-deco pattern. Associative digital modeling was used to create an abstract addition, which differentiates itself as a contemporary insertion whilst concurrently engaging its non-representational quality to act as an intentionally subtle backdrop to the classical façades.

CONSTRUCTION FACTS
Structure: redevelopment. **Construction type:** curtain wall, performative screen. **Material:** aluminum curtain. **Fixing:** self-supporting. **Insulation:** R-value: 1.8 W/(m²K).

PROJECT FACTS

Address: Patriot Square, London E2 9NF, United Kingdom. **Client:** Mastelle ltd. **Completion:** 2010.
Building type: hotel. **Construction engineer façade:** Arcora, Promet, OCSP.

↑ | Exterior view
↓ | Concept diagram perforated façade

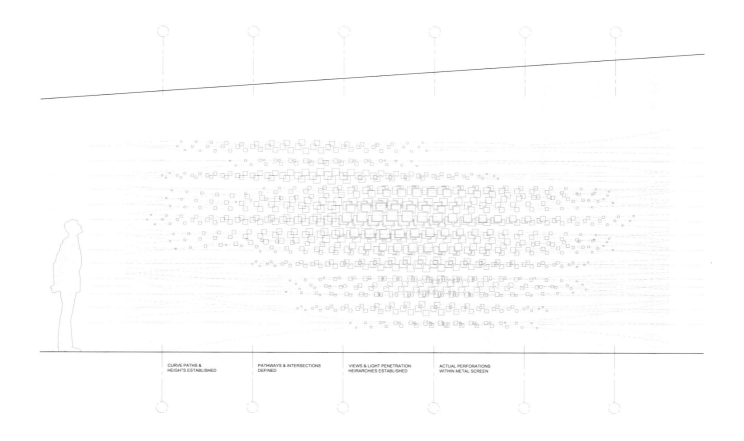

CURVE PATHS &
HEIGHT'S ESTABLISHED

PATHWAYS & INTERSECTIONS
DEFINED

VIEWS & LIGHT PENETRATION
HEIRARCHIES ESTABLISHED

ACTUAL PERFORATIONS
WITHIN METAL SCREEN

↑ | Roof extension
← | Detail cladding and balcony
↓ | Geometry new façade

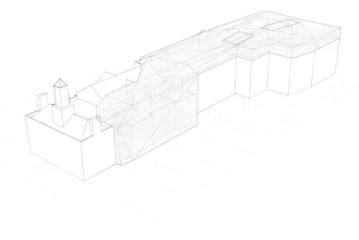

Jackson Clements Burrows
Architects

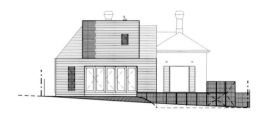

↖↖ | Detail canopy
↑↑ | Detail façade, in the evening
↖ | Façade completely covered with timber lattice
↑ | Elevations

Trojan House

Melbourne

This appendage to an Edwardian house in Melbourne, Australia, cantilevers above the garden. It provides additional rooms for a family with three children. The façade consists of a seamless timber skin covering roof, windows, and walls. Operable timber shutters are scattered across the façade where openings are required. The purpose was to keep as much green area at the back of the house as possible. The construction technique involves a cost-efficient waterproof fiber cement cladding system with timber battens and rain screen. The rain screen solution optimizes a passive thermal response by shading or insulating the house, depending on the weather.

CONSTRUCTION FACTS
Structure: addition. **Construction type:** curtain wall. **Material:** timber lattice. **Fixing:** punctuated fixing. **Insulation:** thermal insulation, sun screen.

PROJECT FACTS
Address: Illawarra Road, Hawthorn VIC, Australia. **Client:** Private. **Completion:** 2008. **Building type:** living. **Other creatives:** Adams Consulting Engineers (structural engineering).

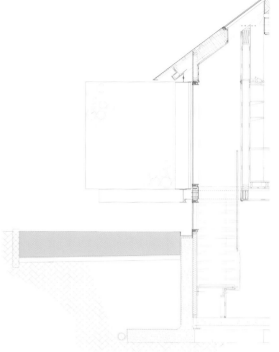

↑↑ | West façade
↑ | Detail cedar logs
↑↗ | Section façade
↗ | View from inside

House on Henry's Meadow

Quebec

CONSTRUCTION FACTS
Structure: new building. **Material:** stacked cedar logs in steel frame in front of pull-truded fibreglass windows with double-glazed, etched glass. **Insulation:** reducing solar heat gain.

The principal façade of this rural house forms direct relationships to both the adjacent log house and to the local tradition of stacked firewood walls. Situated at the edge of a woodland meadow, the stacked wood wall is contained in a large steel frame and floats above a reflecting pool to form a seemingly opaque exterior wall by day, and a glowing screen by night. Conversely, from behind the etched thermal glass units, the stacked logs create an abstract image of the wooden wall, which dramatically modulates the interior quality of light throughout the day and seasons.

PROJECT FACTS
Address: Quebec, Canada. **Client:** confidential. **Completion:** 2008. **Building type:** living.
Construction engineer façade: Blackwell Bowick Engineering (structural engineering).

↑ | View from the street

Hotel Courtyard by Marriott

Vienna

The hotel building near the Prater in Vienna responds to the concave-convex shape of the neighboring high-rise with a boomerang-shaped curving eight-story wing of rooms, which extends over a single-story plinth. Entrance lobby, restaurant, conference rooms, and the offices of the hotel management are located in the all-round glazed plinth level. A key design feature of the hotel room wing is the façade made of transparent and opaque elements. The design was based on a bar code with alternating slim light and dark strips of aluminum sheet panels and dark window sections. Horizontally displaced across each level, this interaction results in a simple, yet far from bland façade look, which is very attractive, especially when seen from a distance.

CONSTRUCTION FACTS

Structure: new building, solitaire. **Construction type:** post-and-beam construction (ground floor) and system façade elements (upper floors). **Material:** glass, enamelled glass, coated panel sheets. **Fixing:** mounted on solid construction. **Insulation:** R-value: 1.5 W/(m²K) (ground floor), 0.3 W/(m²K) (upper floors). **Special functions:** controlled venting holes.

PROJECT FACTS

Address: Trabrennstraße 4, 1020 Vienna, Austria. **Client:** IC Projektentwicklung GmbH. **Completion:** 2008. **Building type:** hotel. **Other creatives:** KS Ingenieure ZT GmbH, structural engineers. **Construction engineer façade:** IFFT Institut für Fassadentechnik.

↑ | **Play of dark glass fields with light aluminum panels**
→ | **Detail drawing façade**
↓ | **Entrance area**

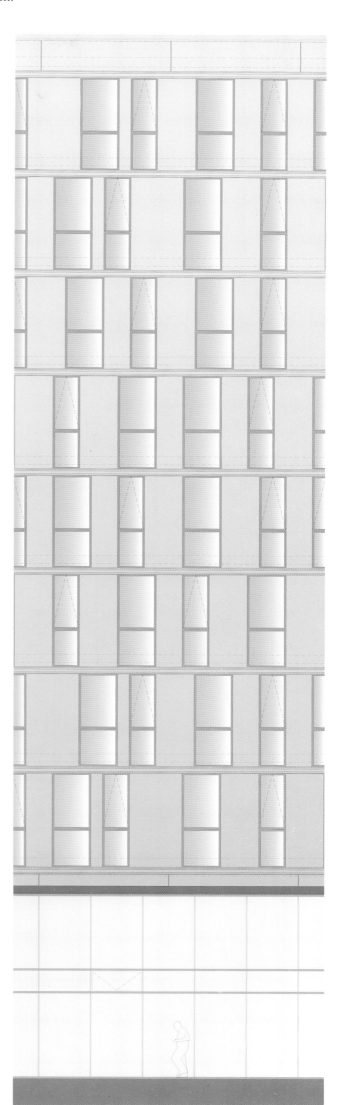

René van Zuuk Architekten

↑ | **View from bridge**

Block 16

Almere

Block 16 ("The Wave") is part of the master plan designed by Rem Koolhaas (OMA) for the prestigious town center of the young Dutch city of Almere. The seven-story residential block contains 49 apartments with an unobstructed view of a lake as well as a fitness center. The most unique feature of the new building is the southwestern façade that is expressively turned outwards. The organically curved and scale-like structured external skin consists of individual elements in a timber post-and-beam construction covered in aluminum sheets. The individual modules of the shimmering façade not only protrude and retreat step-like but are also tilted vertically and horizontally, giving them the appearance of organic scales.

CONSTRUCTION FACTS
Structure: new building. **Construction type:** wooden post-and-beam structure clad with aluminum panels. **Material:** anodized aluminum panels. **Fixing:** suspension. **Insulation:** thermal insulation.

Address: Koetsierbaan, Almere, The Netherlands. **Client:** Ontwikkelingscombinatie Almere Hart c.v.
Completion: 2004. **Building type:** living.

↑ | **Façade elements**
↓ | **Vertical section façade**

↑ | **Detail façade**
↓ | **Horizontal section façade**

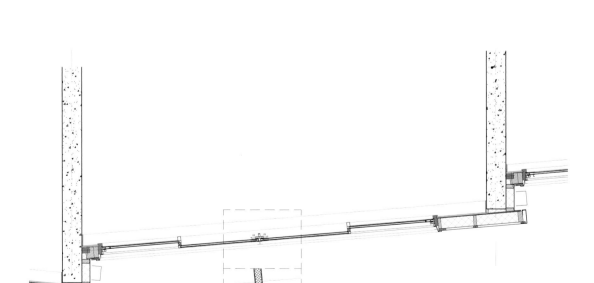

↑ | **Entrance area**

Sotelia

Podčetrtek

The Wellness Hotel Sotelia fills the gap between two existing hotels. In the design process the primary concern was to avoid an immense building mass that would have blocked the last remaining view of the forest behind. The originally planned single volume was therefore broken up into smaller units arranged in landscape-hugging tiers. The specific shape of the hotel is a direct result of seeking to link it with the landscape. From the front, the building appears almost as a two-dimensional set composed of parallel planes placed one behind the other. A clear division between the glass façades of the public section and the wooden paneling of the hotel rooms is unified by a raster of vertical elements made out of natural wood that visually interacts with tree trunks in the background.

CONSTRUCTION FACTS
Structure: new building, solitaire in context. **Construction type:** rear ventilated curtain wall. **Material:** partly pre-stressed printed glass, aluminum, wood-resin composite, dyed wood. **Fixing:** structural glazing, suspension. **Insulation:** R-value: 0.36 W/(m²K).

Address: Zdraviliška cesta 24, 3254 Podčetrtek, Slovenia. **Client:** Terme Olimia. **Completion:** 2006.
Building type: hotel.

↑ | Façade of atrium
↓ | Sections

↑ | Detail façade
↓ | Detail side view

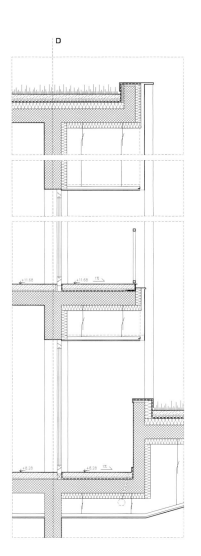

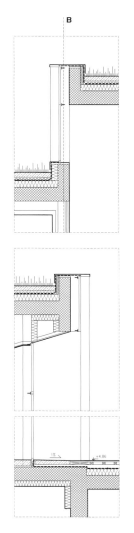

Jo. Franzke Architekten

↑ | View of both buildings from the street

Town Villas Siesmayerstraße

Frankfurt/Main

With the move of the American consulate the former parking lot became available for re-development. Four and five-story residential buildings were erected at the rear of the plot. With a strictly axial alignment, these houses featuring primarily roof-high windows, emulate in an abstract way the style of the neo-classicist residential homes that can still be found today in Frankfurt along the banks of the Main. Designed with one to four housing units on each floor, the layout accommodates expansion of the individual spaces by subsequently combining units. The concept of careful integration is also applied to the landscaping. It pays reference to the landscape forms of the neighboring Palmengarten (palm garden).

CONSTRUCTION FACTS
Structure: new buildings, solitaire. **Construction type:** rear ventilated curtain wall. **Material:** lime stone from Portugal, Porto de Mos. **Fixing:** ground anchor from mortar. **Special functions:** integrated air outlets.

Address: Siesmayerstraße 23-25, 60323 Frankfurt/Main, Germany. **Client:** Groß & Partner Grund-stücksentwicklungsgesellschaft mbH. **Completion:** 2008. **Building type:** living. **Construction engineer façade:** AMP Albrecht Memmert & Partner GbR.

 ↑ | Entrance area

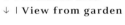 ↓ | View from garden

↑ | Detail window

↓ | Section

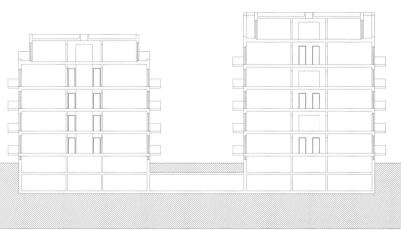

Gewers & Pudewill
architects designers engineers

↑ | Exterior view
→ | Detail façade with windows

Residential Suites Linienstrasse

Berlin

The residential building in the Spandau suburb of Berlin contains apartments and duplexes. Five floors are crowned by a penthouse that offers a magnificent view of the Mitte city district. Its bright white marble façade with in part round glass surfaces gives the building a noble elegance that strikingly distinguishes it from the existing buildings of the neighborhood. Large-scale windows, offset from one floor to another, create a lively sophisticated area into which the large terraces on the back fit in seamlessly. The façade thrives on the precision and refinement of its finishing and its creative detailed solutions.

CONSTRUCTION FACTS

Structure: new building, perimeter block development. **Construction type:** post-and-beam construction, rear ventilated curtain wall. **Material:** white marble. **Fixing:** stainless steel anchor. **Insulation:** thermal insulation.

PROJECT FACTS

Address: Linienstraße 218/219, 10119 Berlin, Germany. **Client:** Concept Bau-Premier. **Completion:** 2011.
Building type: living. **Other creatives:** soup, Berlin (furniture design).

↑ | Detail windows
↓ | Elevation Rückerstraße

↑ | View of corner
↓ | View at night

↓ | Vertical sections façade

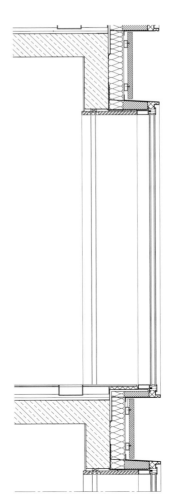

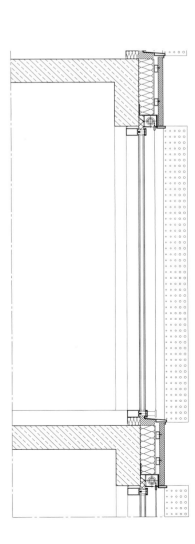

↑ | View from lake

Duplex House

Rüschlikon

The two-party house near lake Zurich has a lively silver-grey shiny surface. The two cubic interlinked residential units appear completely separated. From the separate entrances to the outdoor areas that are integrated on different sides, the neighbors never notice each other and only share the underground garage. The three-dimensional intertwining provides both units with a view of the lake, sun, and private outdoor areas on the very terraced plot. The façade is completely clad in hand-tinned copper sheets, each with its individual grain and its own shine. The building opens up towards the lake by large-scale aluminum-framed glazing.

CONSTRUCTION FACTS

Structure: new building. **Construction type:** solid construction with rear ventilated curtain wall. **Material:** tin-coated copper plates. **Fixing:** punctuated fixing. **Insulation:** Minergie-standard.

Address: 8803 Rüschlikon, Switzerland. **Client:** private. **Completion:** 2010. **Building type:** living. **Other creatives:** Scherrer Metec AG Zurich (façade systems).

↑ | **View towards lake**
↓ | **Detail drawing façade**

↑ | **Detail copper sheets**
↓ | **Detail west façade**

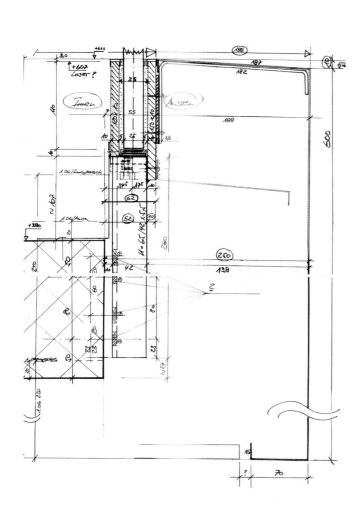

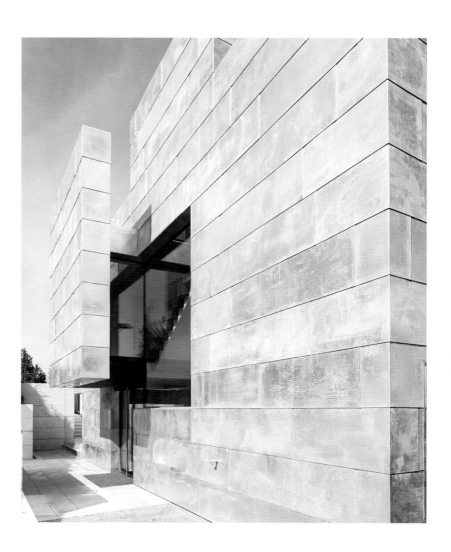

↑ | **View from south**

Kraton 230

Rotterdam

The building is home to the regional radio and television station RTV Rijnmond and other firms. The façade of the building is made of rusty brown cast-iron panels that are decorated with maritime and audio-visual motifs designed by Studio Job. The window openings in this cast-iron section extend across two levels. The ground-floor façade facing Lloydstraat is a transparent wall of glass below two cantilevered levels clad in steel panels. That gives this section of the building the character of a large awning that directs attention to the entrance and studios of RTV Rijnmond. The structure of the building and the square are clearly visible from the street through the glazed façade.

CONSTRUCTION FACTS
Structure: new building. **Construction type:** rear ventilated curtain wall. **Material:** cast-iron panels. **Fixing:** suspension. **Insulation:** R-value: 3.5 W/(m²K).

Address: Lloydstraat 23, 3024 EA, Rotterdam, The Netherlands. **Client:** Ontwikkelingsbedrijf Rotterdam. **Completion:** 2007. **Building type:** office. **Other creatives:** Robert Winkel, Robert Platje, Hennie Dankers, Erwin Verhoeve, Theun Frankema, Michel Zaan. **Construction engineer façade:** Pieters Bouwtechniek, Delft.

↑ | **Detail of the façade, corner panels**
↓ | **Cross section façade corner**

↑ | **Transparent curtain façade**
↘ | **Cross section façade**

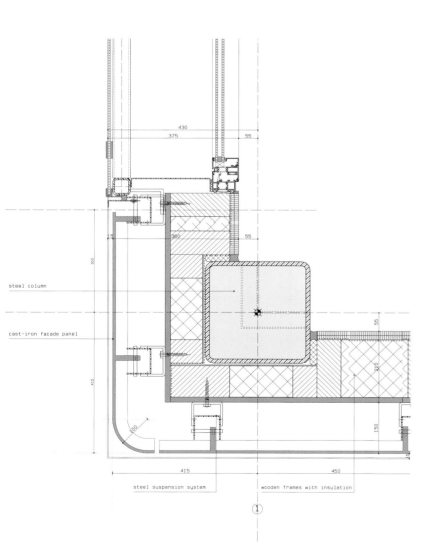

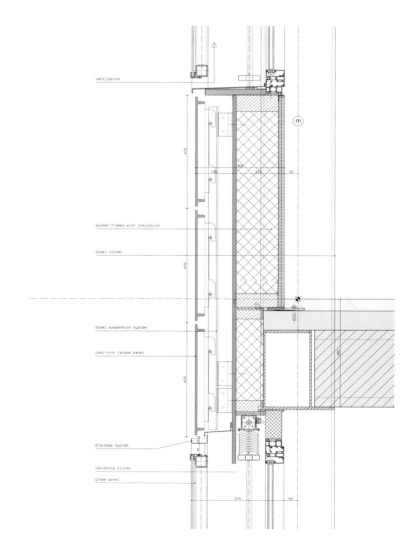

Patrick T I G H E Architecture

↑ | **View from the street**

Mixed-Use Affordable Housing

West Hollywood

This affordable housing project addresses a severe housing shortage for tenants living with disabilities. The 4,650-square-meter mixed-use program brings higher density into the urban core of the city. Situated on a 1,200-square-meter lot, the building contains 42 one-bedroom residential units organized around a central courtyard. Commercial / retail space is located along Santa Monica Boulevard. Parking is provided at the subterranean levels. Each apartment has its own private front porch that overlooks the outdoor courtyard garden. Arrays of photovoltaic panels are integrated into the façade and roof of the building and supply most of the peak load electricity demand whilst serving as a trellis for shading the roof top decks. A solar hydronic system is used and provides free hot water to the residents. The north and south façade is screened with custom laser cut panels of aluminum.

CONSTRUCTION FACTS
Structure: new building. **Construction type:** rear ventilated curtain wall. **Material:** custom laser-cut aluminum panels. **Fixing:** braced frame cladding. **Insulation:** thermal insulation.

Address: West Hollywood, CA, USA. **Client:** City of West Hollywood. **Completion:** 2010. **Building type:** living. **Structural Engineering:** Gilsanz.Murray.Steficek.Inc (GMS). **Other creatives:** AHBE Landscape Design (landscape design).

↑ | **Detail façade**
→ | **Diagram**
↓ | **Access balcony**

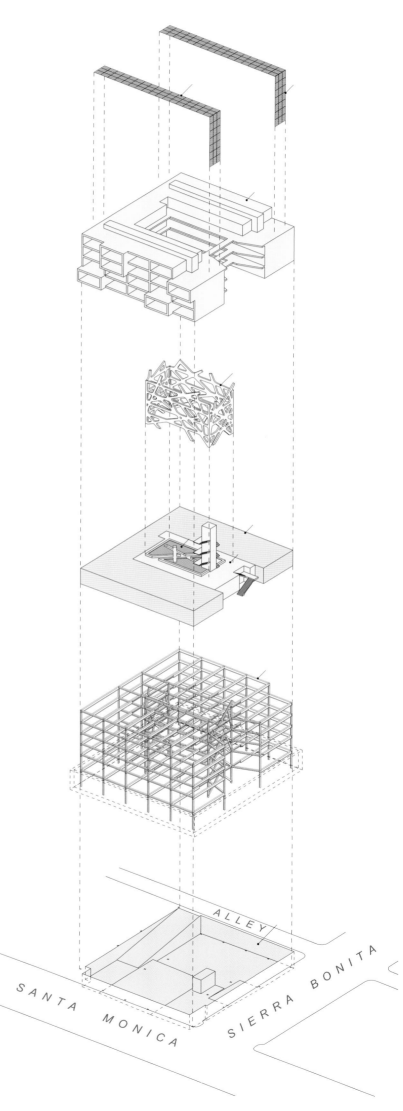

↖ | **View from south**
↑ | **View from east, entrance**

Hotel + Office Tower

Vitoria

The two buildings' design concept is closely connected to the essentially flat landscape, dominated by factories, warehouses, and barracks. The buildings differ in volume, geometry, and use. They combine similar materials for different utilization purposes and in different configurations: aluminum lattice surrounding glazed façades. They share the use of latticework. At the same time, it highlights the composition of each, depending on the angle of vision: from afar, the lattice disappears, and shades can be seen from inside the box and the glass; the perspective reveals a compact volume of "coarse grain", which outlines the pure geometry of each body.

CONSTRUCTION FACTS
Structure: new building. **Construction type:** rear ventilated curtain wall. **Material:** glazing, aluminum lattice. **Fixing:** punctuated fixing, suspension. **Insulation:** thermal insulation, noise insulation, glare shield, UV-reduction.

Address: Calle Zaramaga 3, CP: 01013, Vitoria, Spain. Client: Construcciones Andía S.A. + Construc-tora Principado + Avanco. Completion: 2011. Building type: office, hotel. Other creatives: Raúl Escrivá, Javier Errea – Landabe Ingenieros (structural engineering). Construction engineer façade: Marcial Lázaro – Altres.

↑ | Detail view of the two buildings
↘ | Detail drawings different types of façade

↑ | Detail aluminum structure

Neutelings Riedijk
Architecten

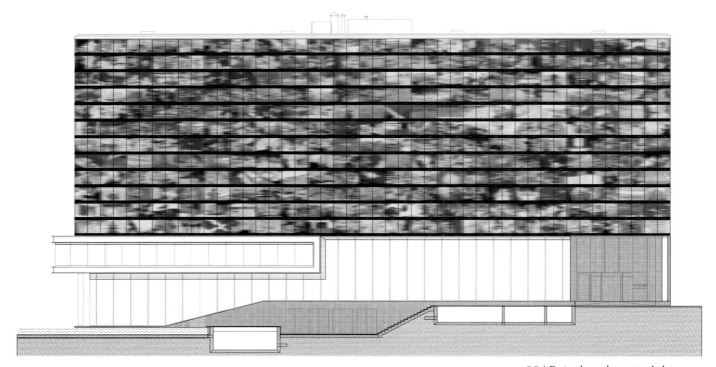

↖↖ | Exterior view at night
↑↑ | View towards façade from atrium
↖ | Elevation

Netherlands Institute for Sound and Vision

Hilversum

The new building for the Netherlands Institute for Sound and Vision consists of five underground levels and five levels above ground. Below ground, the national archives of Dutch radio and television recordings are stacked around a deep canyon. Above ground, a staged volume contains the media museum. The third element is the office building of the institute. The three volumes together enclose a large public atrium. The façade of the building is a screen of colored relief glass that depicts famous images of Dutch television, a composition created by graphic designer Jaap Drupsteen.

CONSTRUCTION FACTS

Structure: new building. **Construction type:** rear ventilated curtain wall. **Material:** colored relief glass. **Fixing:** custom-made horizontal aluminum profiles. **Insulation:** thermal insulation.

PROJECT FACTS

Address: Sumatralaan 45, Mediapark, 1217 GP Hilversum, The Netherlands. **Client:** Netherlands Institute for Sound and Vision. **Completion:** 2006. **Building type:** public.

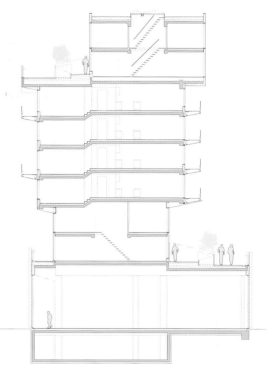

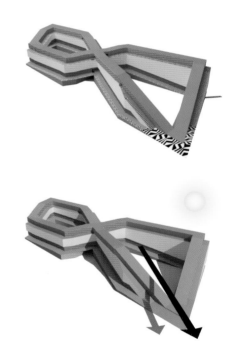

↑↑ | Interior courtyard
↑ | Detail façade towards inner courtyard
↗ | Sloping façade
↗↗ | Section
→ | Building diagrams

8 House

Copenhagen

CONSTRUCTION FACTS
Structure: new building, solitaire. **Construction type:** curtain wall. **Material:** concrete, aluminum, glass, steel. **Insulation:** thermal insulation.

The 8 House combines residential housing at the top with retail and office space at the base of the 61,000-square-meter building. Rather than a traditional block, the 8 House stacks all ingredients of a lively urban neighborhood into horizontal layers of typologies connected by a continuous promenade and cycling path up to the 10th floor. Two sloping green roofs totaling 1,700 square meters are strategically placed to reduce the urban-heat-island effect as well as providing the visual identity to the project and tying it back to the adjacent farmlands towards the south. The 8 House creates two intimate interior courtyards, separated at the center of the cross with communal facilities available to all residents.

PROJECT FACTS
Address: Copenhagen, Denmark. **Client:** St. Frederikslund Holding. **Completion:** 2010. **Building type:** living, retail, office. **Other creatives:** Hopfner Partners, Moe & Brodsgaard, Klar.

↑ | Detail façade

Rose am Lend

Graz

The eleven residential units of the "Rose am Lend" building offer high-quality living areas, while the salesroom on the ground floor reflects the era when the Lendplatz served as a market square. Instead of the customary demolition of the old forward-facing gabled houses in the area of the Lendplatz, this building was kept intact and renovated by adding another floor. The design also deliberately incorporates existing elements, transforming their context. Roses appears in different styles and sizes as a reference to the era of the original building's construction, when there was a "Schuhaus am Lend" (shoe store) in combination with a statue of Saint Rosalia on the Lendplatz. The wrought-iron blossoms on the balustrades complement the large roses of the façade.

CONSTRUCTION FACTS
Structure: redevelopment. **Construction type:** solid construction with thermal insulation composite system. **Material:** plaster, laminated panels. **Fixing:** bonded. **Insulation:** thermal insulation.

Address: Lendplatz 41, 8020 Graz, Austria. **Client:** GOLDEN NUGGET Bauträger GmbH. **Completion:** 2008. **Building type:** living.

↑ | **Building in surrounding**
↓ | **South elevation**

↑ | **Detail view façade**

GKS Architekten+Partner

↖ | View from the street at twilight
↑ | Detail façade clad with glass mosaics

Residential and Commercial Building

Wetzikon

The new residential and commercial building with five full floors and two attic floors is fitted into the urban development space as independent from all sides. The building stands alone, which is also expressed in its architectural and material language. The oriel increases the floor area of each story and adds to the individuality of the building. The glass mosaic mix, which was implemented as a façade design element surrounds the entire sculpted volume of the structure. Due to its high reflectivity and the depth effect of the glass mosaic, the impression of the building matches the atmosphere of the day. The base color of the glass mosaic mix was chosen in reference to the local Bollinger sand stone.

CONSTRUCTION FACTS
Structure: new building, solitaire in context. **Construction type:** rear ventilated curtain wall. **Material:** glass mosaics, 15x15 mm. **Fixing:** bonding. **Insulation:** thermal insulation.

Address: Bahnhofstrasse 117, 8620 Wetzikon, Switzerland. **Client:** Immoturicum AG.
Completion: 2009. **Building type:** shops, living.

↑ | Backlit mosaics in the entrance area
↓ | Longitudinal section façade

↑ | Glass mosaics
↓ | Underside view oriel

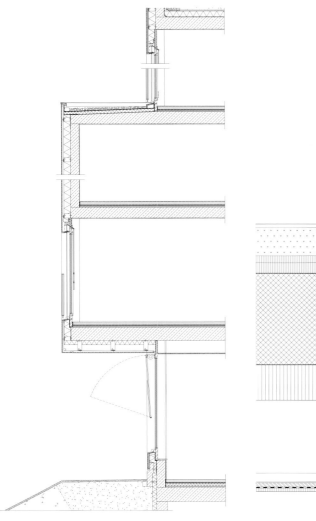

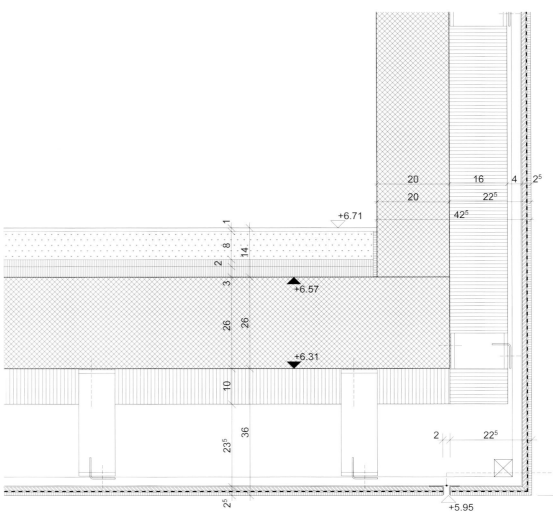

Hon.Prof. Johanne Nalbach,
Nalbach + Nalbach
Architekten

↑ | View of long façade

"The Wave"

Berlin

The horizontal alignment of the façade creates a link to the GDR architecture of its surroundings. The three types of uses of the building are differentiated by varying plasticity, height and surface material of the façade. The façade of the 4-star hotel reflects the quality rating of the hotel's category in the interaction between the spandrel building surfacing and window profiles – both anodized in black – with the gold metallic lower continuous apron. The slim linear element leads over to the higher iridescent silver continuous apron of the two-star hotel's metal façade with visible shear walls. The continuous apron tapers and rises gradually to the metal façade of the office block. The window profiles and the vertical night-cooling panel element are also anodized in black.

CONSTRUCTION FACTS

Structure: new building. **Construction type:** post-and-beam construction with curtain wall. **Material:** sheet steel with different alloys, anodized aluminum windows. **Fixing:** agraffe. **Insulation:** thermal insulation.

Address: Karl-Liebknecht-Straße 32, 10178 Berlin, Germany. **Client:** TLG Immobilien GmbH.
Completion: 2011. **Building type:** office and hotel.

↑ | Façade offices
↓ | Elevation

↑ | View from below

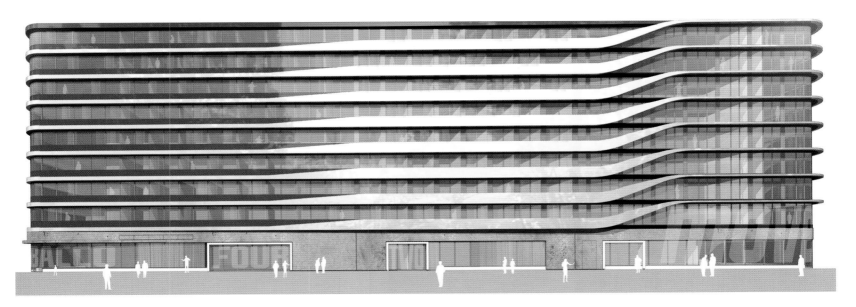

↑ | **South view**

Le Monolithe

Lyon

The urban superblock is a mixed-use development comprising social and rental housing, offices, and underground parking. The interiors of MVRDV's south-facing building are protected from the sun by aluminum shutters as a reference to traditional local architecture. With an environmentally responsive façade among many ecological characteristics of this building, "Le Monolithe" was developed as a highly efficient low-energy construction. When all shutters are closed they display the first article of the European Constitution, as a reminder of the values, ideals, and needs of the European Union.

CONSTRUCTION FACTS
Structure: new building. **Construction type:** environmentally responsive façade system. **Material:** aluminum shutters, double glazing. **Insulation:** highly-efficient low energy construction.

Address: Lyon, France. **Client:** ING Real Estate with Artemis. **Completion:** 2010. **Building type:** housing, office, commercial, parking. **Construction engineer façade:** Robert-Jan van Santen Ass..

↑ | Detail of west façade with perforated shutters

↓ | Detail window

↑ | View along the street

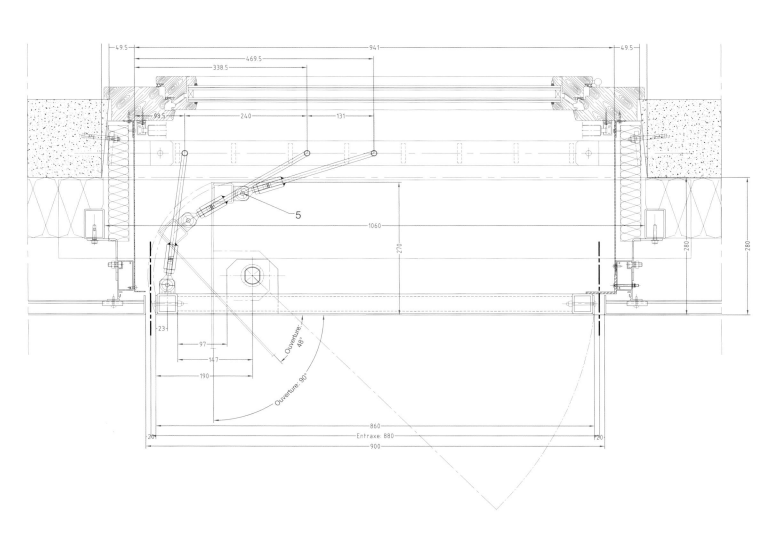

↑ | Detail façade with projecting roof
→ | View from south

Revitalization WestendGate

Frankfurt/Main

The building's architecture and energy efficiency were refurbished. Energy consumption, in part due to the introduction of solar façade modules, was reduced by more than 35 percent. The design concept of the old façade with dark elements and light colored pediment sides was maintained. The old static and flat façade was given a plastic effect through dynamic divisions that also created a sense of proportion which reveals itself to observers from nearby. The façade was made of three-dimensional elements. Each forms a sharp bend, which is offset from each panel to the next. The shadow and light reflections on the elements change, depending on the position of the sun.

CONSTRUCTION FACTS
Structure: redevelopment. **Construction type:** rear ventilated curtain wall. **Material:** laquered aluminum. **Fixing:** suspended panels, persistant pilaster strips. **Insulation:** R-value: 1.1 W/(m²K). **Special functions:** partially generation of solar energy.

PROJECT FACTS

Address: Hamburger Allee 2–4, 60486 Frankfurt/Main, Germany. **Client:** Aberdeen Immobilien Kapitalanlagegesellschaft mbH. **Completion:** 2011. **Building type:** office/hotel. **Other creatives:** a3lab, asterios agkathidis. **Construction engineer façade:** IFFT, Institut für Fassadentechnik, Frankfurt/Main.

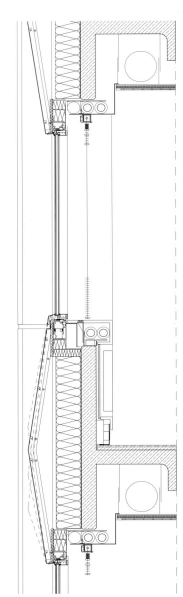

↖ | Detail façade
↑ | Section, detail drawing
↓ | Façade

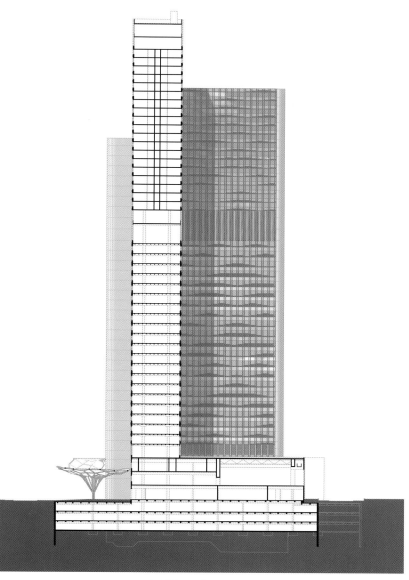

← | Elevation
↑ | Section
↓ | Detail canopy

Renzo Piano
Building Workshop

↑ | **Bird's-eye view**

Mixed-Use Development

London

The proposed concept for the site was to transform a single-use office building into a genuinely mixed-use development incorporating office, retail, restaurant, and residential use. Each facet is unique, differing in height, orientation, color, and relationship to natural light. Glass, steel, and ceramics are the primary elements of the skin. In each section the ceramic is used in different shades and colors that respond to the surrounding building, thus helping integrate the scheme in the immediate urban environment. At the core of the design is the courtyard with its cafes and restaurants. A six-meter full height glass façade provides maximum transparency, five passages through this courtyard create a permeable scheme and invite passersby to this piazza shaded by a 20-meter-high tree.

CONSTRUCTION FACTS
Structure: new building. **Material:** ceramic elements. **Fixing:** unitized façades are hung from the above concrete slab by brackets. **Insulation:** thermal insulation.

Address: London, United Kingdom. **Client:** Legal & General with Mitsubishi Estate Corporation Stanhope PLC. **Completion:** 2010. **Building type:** mixed-use development. **Other creatives:** Fletcher Priest Architects, Ove Arup & Partners (structural engineering). **Construction engineer façade:** Emmer Pfenninger & Partners.

↑ | Detail ceramic façade elements
↓ | Section façade

↑ | Ceramic elements with extrusions
↓ | Section façade ground floor

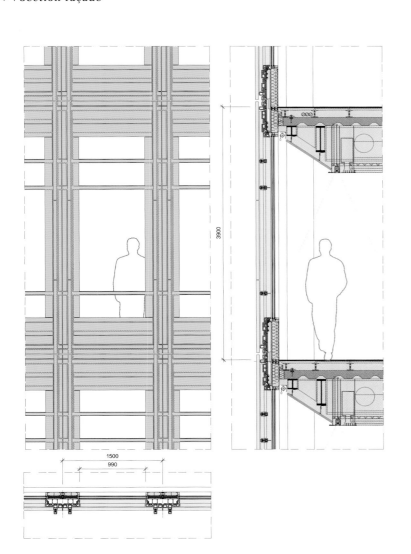

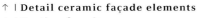

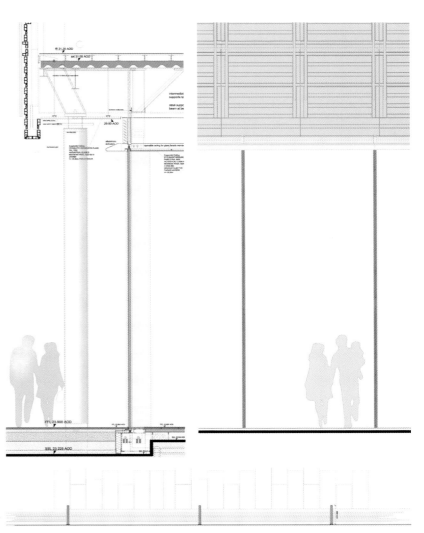

Faulders Studio
(façade design)
Studio M (building design)

↑ | **View from the street**

Airspace Tokyo

Tokyo

The project creates a 280-square-meter exterior building skin for a new four-story multi-family dwelling unit with professional photography studios in Tokyo, Japan. The original residence was uniquely wrapped by a layer of dense vegetation. Since then the entire site was razed to accommodate construction of the new development, with a design that invents an architectural system offering similar attributes as the demolished green strip and creating a new atmospheric space of protection. The artificial blends with the natural – sunlight is refracted along its metallic surfaces; rainwater is channeled away from exterior walkways via capillary action; and interior views are shielded behind its variegated and foliage-like cover.

CONSTRUCTION FACTS
Structure: new building. **Construction type:** perforated façade. **Material:** alpolic composite panels. **Fixing:** stainless steel rod supports, VHB tape for monolithic panel connecting.

Address: 1-23-1 Kitamagome Ota-ku, Tokyo, Japan 143-0021. **Client:** Masubuchi Photography. **Completion:** 2007. **Building type:** mixed use. **Other creatives:** Proces2 (computation design). **Construction engineer façade:** TONY Co., Ltd. (façade contractor).

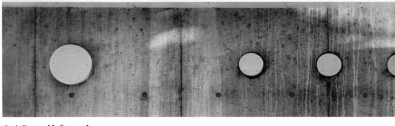

↑ | Façade glowing at night
↓ | Section façade

↑ | Detail façade
↓ | View from inside

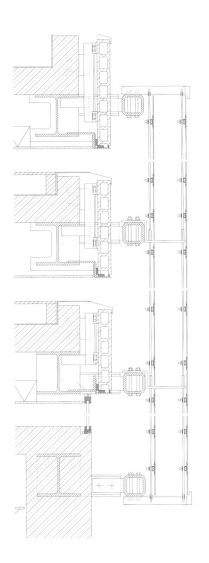

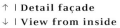

Jakob + MacFarlane
Architects

↑ | **Exterior view with hole**
→ | **Detail façade**

The Orange Cube

Lyon

The ambition of the urban planning project for the old harbor zone was to reinvest the docks of Lyon on the riverside and its industrial patrimony, bringing together architecture and a cultural and commercial program. The office building is designed as a simple orthogonal cube into which a giant hole is carved, responding to necessities of light, air movement, and views. This hole creates a void, piercing the building horizontally from the river side inwards and upwards through the roof terrace. A light façade with seemingly random openings is completed by another façade, pierced with pixilated patterns that accompany the movement of the river. The orange color refers to lead paint, an industrial color often used for harbor zones.

CONSTRUCTION FACTS
Structure: new building. **Construction type:** curtain wall. **Material:** perforated metal sheets. **Insulation:** R-value: <0.7 W/(m²K), sun screen. **Special functions:** daylight supply, improvement of natural ventilation.

PROJECT FACTS

Address: Quai Rambaud, Lyon, France. **Client:** Rhône Saône Développement. **Completion:** 2010.
Building type: offices and design showroom. **Construction engineer façade:** T.E.S.S.

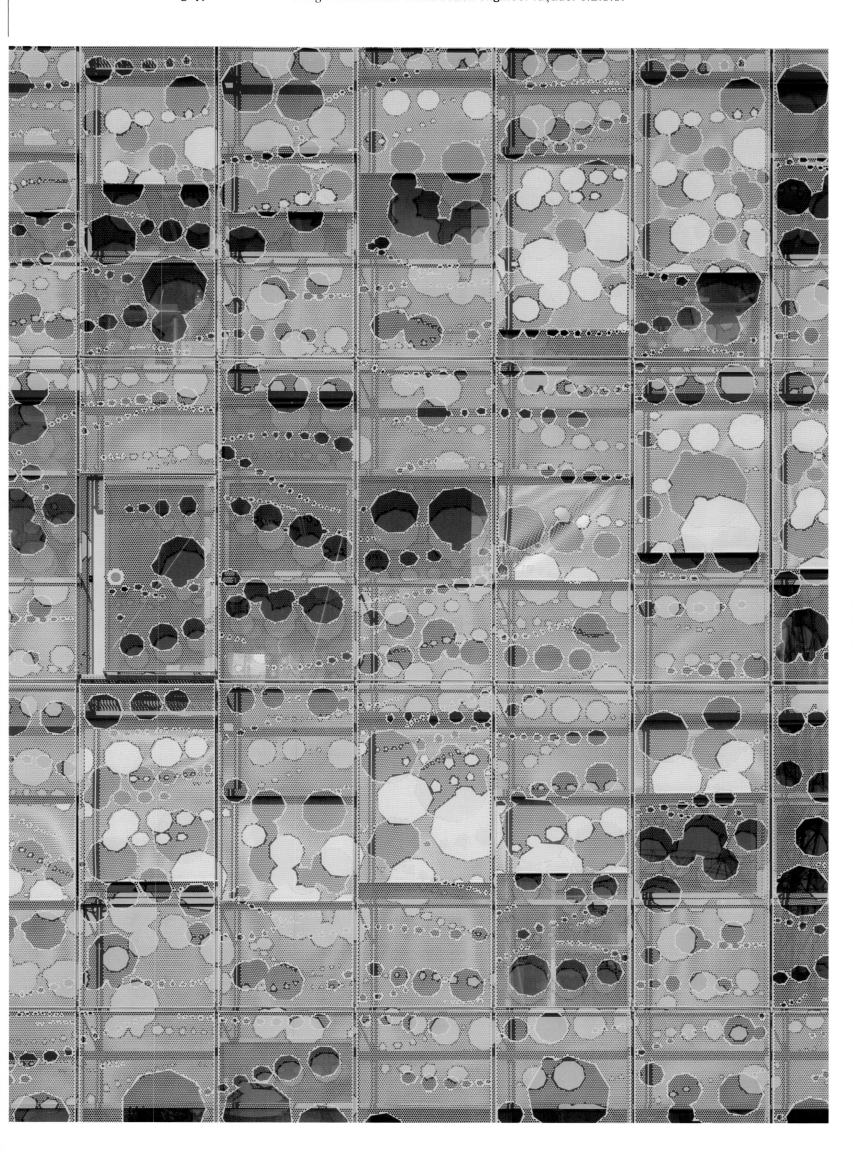

↑ | **Light façade**
↓ | **Section**

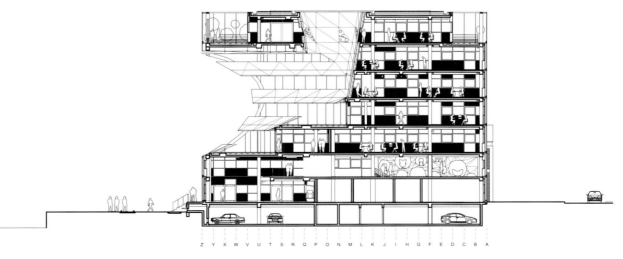

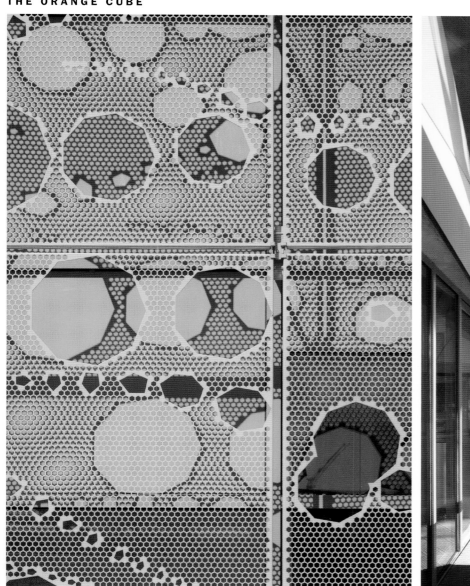

↖ | Detail window
↑ | Interior view hole
↓ | Diagram ventilation

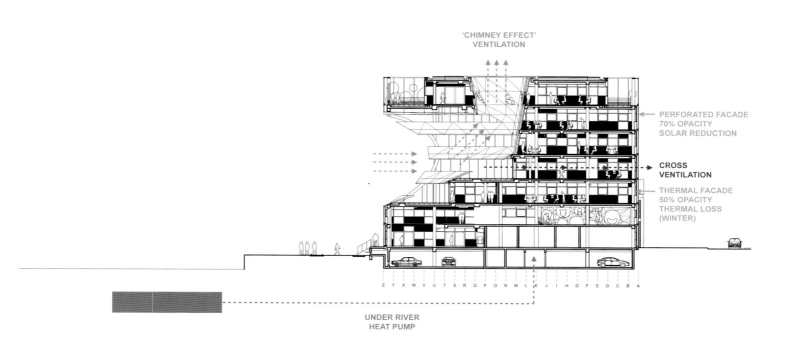

SPEECH
Tchoban & Kuznetsov

↑ | **Exterior view**

Office Building

Moscow

From the very start, this 12-story office building was intended as the head office of a big company, so the design incorporates the needs and desires of a specific client. The interior and landscape design are also by SPEECH Tchoban & Kuznetsov. This is a modern complex fitted with all the latest equipment as well as an energy-saving façade and three-level car park. The facade consists of 6-meter high glass and natural stone (limestone) using a 'dual façade' technology - there is an internal layer of glazing (double glazing units that open inwards) and on the outside continuous glazing with horizontal strips of stone every two floors (giving the building the appearance of a six-floor structure).

CONSTRUCTION FACTS
Structure: new building. **Construction type:** double ventilated curtain wall. **Material:** massive stone plates. **Fixing:** suspension, structural glazing. **Insulation:** thermal insulation.

Address: Leninskiy prospekt, 119415, Moscow, Russian Federation. **Client:** confidential. **Completion:** 2011. **Building type:** office. **Other creatives:** Sergey Tchoban, Sergey Kuznetsov (architects).

↑ | Detail of the façade
↓ | Section

↑ | Corner, with venetian blinds
↓ | Exterior view, from ground level

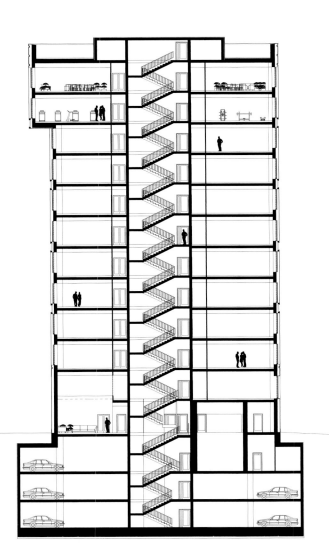

Thomas Pink
Petzinka Pink Architekten

↑ | View towards entrance area
→ | Entrance and vertical lamellae

Fin House

Constance

Holistic – integral – identity-shaping – in terms of its appearance and energy consumption, the "Lamellenhaus" (fin house) is the ideal location for a company representative office. The cube sets a clear urban development signal. The open nature of the façade links the landscape to the building. A significant and responsive fully-glated fin façade similar to a "sun dial" serves as sun and weather protection. Air conditioning technology and a comfortable climate create great user acceptance. Optimized primary energy use and trimmed building services sustainably minimize costs. The climate-friendly energy production leads to considerable CO_2 savings. Overall, it is an office building with high comfort, a house for the future.

CONSTRUCTION FACTS

Structure: new building, solitaire building in heterogeneous surrounding. **Construction type:** post-and-beam construction with cladding of vertical glass lamellae. **Material:** aluminum and glass lamellae. **Fixing:** punctuated fixing. **Insulation:** R-value: triple glazing: 0.7 W/ (m^2K), vacuum insulation panels: 0.2 W/ (m^2K). **Special functions:** sun shield.

Address: Byk-Gulden-Straße 2, 78467 Constance, Germany. **Client:** Nycomed GmbH. **Completion:** 2008.
Building type: office. **Other creatives:** DS-Plan, Stuttgart/Köln | WHP, Stuttgart | HPP, Bielefeld | ag
Licht, Bonn. **Construction engineer façade:** DS-Plan Ingenieurges. mbH.

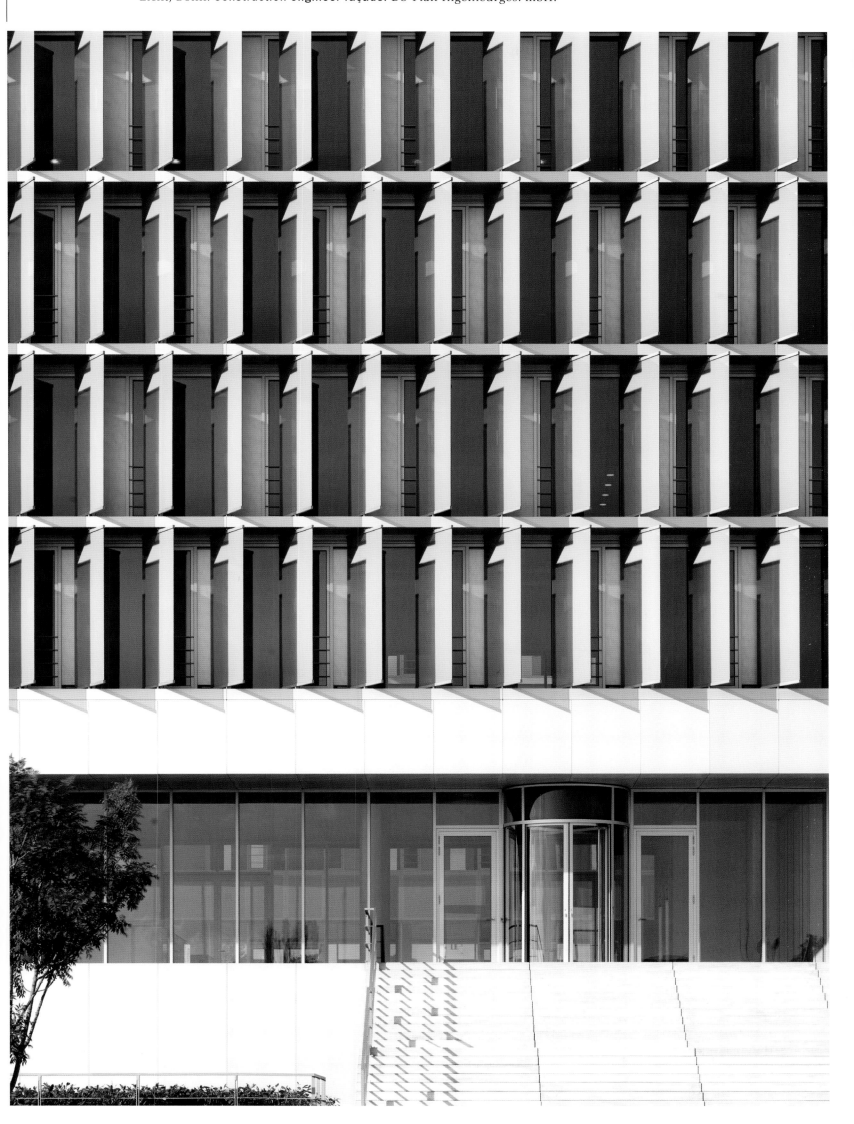

↑ | **Detail view vertical lamellae**
↓ | **Functioning lamellae**

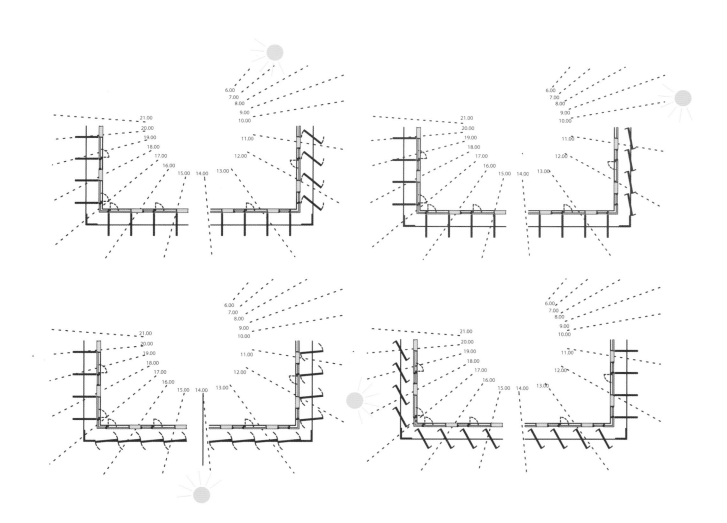

↑ | View outside from office
↓ | Detailed sections façade

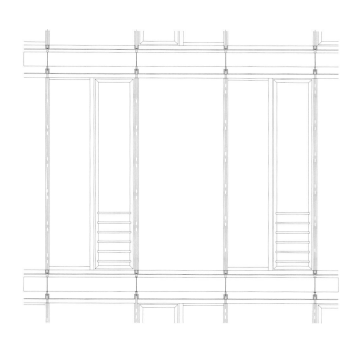
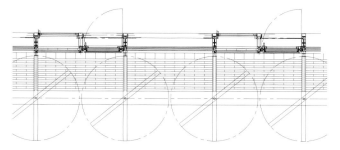

J. MAYER H. Architects

↑ | Exterior view Steckelhörn Street

S11 "Steckelhörn 11"

Hamburg

The project "Steckelhörn 11" is located in the harbor district of Hamburg. The floor plan is defined by the peculiarly shaped piece of land. The triangular-shaped lot stretches across the city block, resulting in a narrow façade of about 1.3 meters width facing the harbor and a main elevation of about 26.4 meters facing toward Steckelhörn Street. The vertical design was chosen due to the massive surrounding structures as well as local building-height regulations. Cantilevered elements in the main façade create a number of spatial features on the inside and outside. The ground level is conceived as a spacious lobby or café, the upper floors offer generous office space with balconies, loggias, and a roof terrace with a panoramic view of the city.

CONSTRUCTION FACTS
Structure: new building. **Construction type:** curtain wall (ceramics façade), self-supporting (aluminum-glass façade). **Material:** ceramic cladding, aluminum. **Insulation:** thermal insulation.

Address: Steckelhörn 11, Hamburg, Germany. **Client:** Cogiton Projekt Altstadt GmbH. **Completion:**
2009. **Building type:** office. **Other creatives:** WTM, Hamburg (structural engineering).

↑ | **Entrance area**
↓ | **Section**

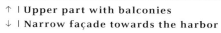

↑ | **Upper part with balconies**
↓ | **Narrow façade towards the harbor**

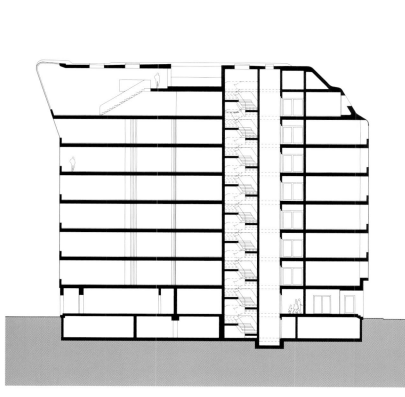

↑ | Gallery

Euro Space Center

Libin-Transinne

Situated at Libin-Transinne, the Euro Space Center boasts a façade clearly visible from the nearby motorway. It is prolonged by a 120-meter-long gallery that extends along the existing building. The reception hall and the gallery are evenly segmented into 4.8-meter side elements of slender steel tubes. Four horizontal layers of cables, 3.24 meters apart, connect the vertical tubes in both orthogonal directions to impede buckling. The stress induced by the cables and the wind is diffused by trellised girders. This is also the ideal support for large two- and three-dimensional banners that inform drivers about the activities of the center. The southern slopes of the roof and façade elements are equipped with photovoltaic panels covering a total of 5,060 square meters.

CONSTRUCTION FACTS
Structure: new building. **Material:** wood. **Insulation:** thermal insulation. **Special functions:** greenhouse (protects the wooden building).

Address: Rue devant les hêtres, 1 - 6890 Transinne (Libin), Belgium. **Client:** IDELUX. **Completion:** 2008. **Building type:** office. **Construction engineer façade:** Philippe Samyn and Partners sprl, architects & engineers.

↑ | **View across the motorway**
↓ | **Design sketch**

↑ | **The wooden building is protected**
↓ | **Elevation**

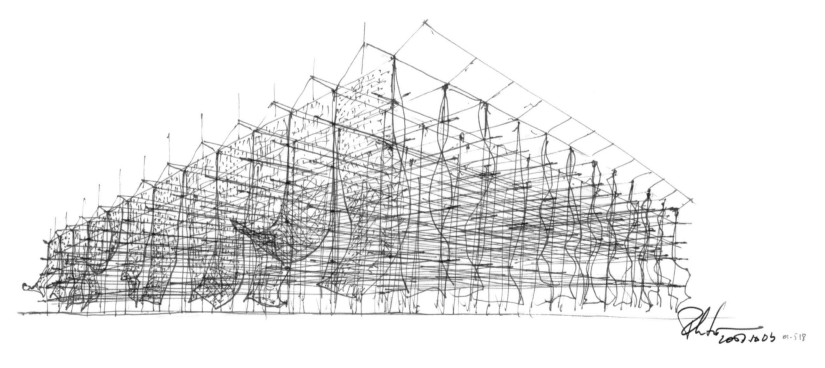

↑ | View chancellery from west
→ | Detail structured concrete on north side

German Embassy, Warsaw

Warsaw

The building's functions – chancellery, consulate, residence – are reflected in a multifaceted structure consisting of three buildings and three façades, which become cognizable when moving through the space. Soft and hard forms, solid structures and flowing spaces, light and dark, glossy and matte materials exemplify the polarity of natural and artificial elements. Large areas are covered in a suspended dyed concrete relief, which depicts the overgrowth of Virginia Creeper during the winter. The chancellery tract is covered in enameled structural glass, whose reflections resemble the surface of a lake in summer, while the plinth forms the base in mottled Nero Assoluto granite.

CONSTRUCTION FACTS

Structure: new building, solitaire. **Construction type:** rear ventilated curtain wall. **Material:** structured concrete with covering plants, enameled textured glass, natural stone. **Fixing:** agrafe (glass). **Insulation:** thermal insulation. **Special functions:** improving climate (with covering plants), reflection of light.

Address: 12 ul. Jazdòw, 00467 Warsaw, Poland. **Client:** Federal Republic of Germany, Federal Office for Building and Regional Planning (BBR). **Completion:** 2009. **Building type:** office and living. **Other creatives:** Topotek 1, Herbert Fink Ing., Brendel Ing., Akustik Büro Moll, building physics Axel C. Rahn.

↑ | **Virginia creeper on structured concrete**
↓ | **Section concrete façade**

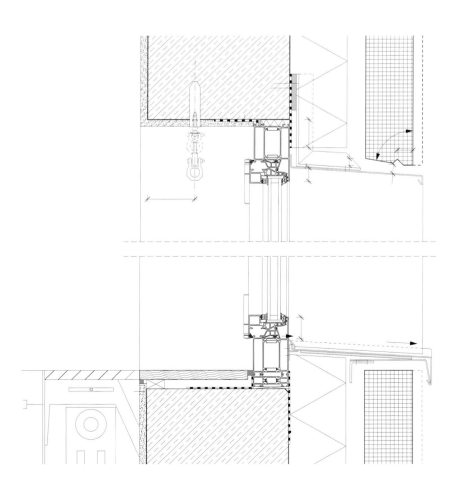

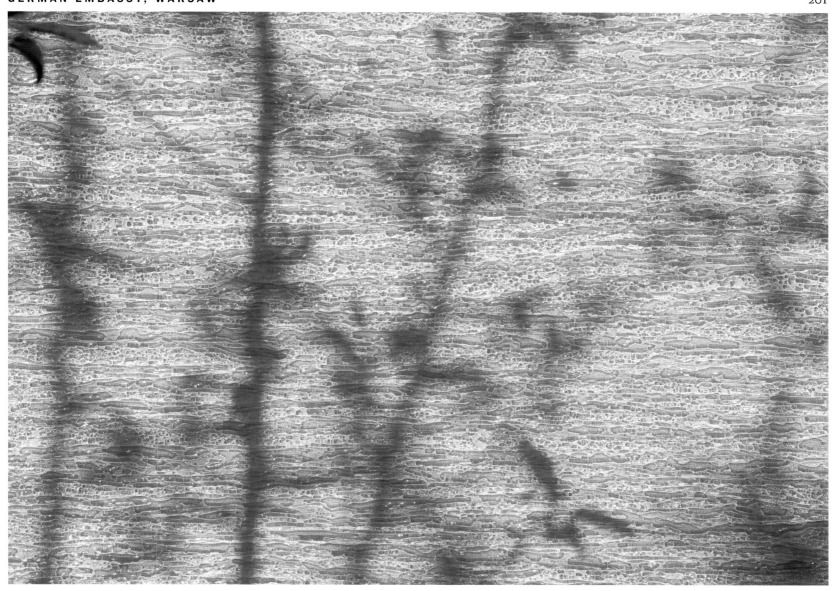

↑ | Textured glass façade
↓ | Section glass façade

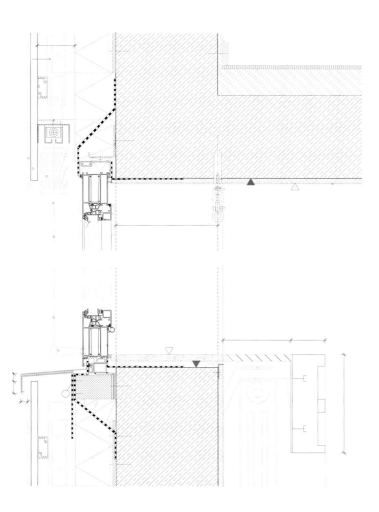

Thomas Pink
Petzinka Pink Architekten

↑ | **View from the sidewalk**
→ | **Detail façade**

Four Elements

Dusseldorf

Four Elements takes on the original concept of urban spatial disruption and repairs the public urban space based on the original urban planning and in harmony with its landmarked urban setting. The new building reacts with staggered façade projections and different story depths to the successive spatial expansions and reductions along Kaiserswerther Straße. The powerful ornamentation of the façade, reminiscent of the designs of Dutch Cubists, coupled with the snow-white surfaces of the cubic frames link 80 years of architectural history. This resulted in an office building with great visual power in the north of Dusseldorf. It received the "Best Architects 11" award in 2010.

CONSTRUCTION FACTS

Structure: new building. **Construction type:** rear ventilated curtain wall. **Material:** powder-coated aluminum. **Fixing:** punctuated fixing. **Insulation:** R-value: 1.1 W/(m²K).

Address: Georg-Glock-Straße 4 / Kaiserswerther Straße 22, Dusseldorf, Germany. **Client:** HOCHTIEF Projektentwicklung GmbH, Niederlassung Rhein-Ruhr. **Completion:** 2010. **Building type:** office. **Other creatives:** Lindner Group KG, Arnstorf. **Construction engineer façade:** IGF Zimmermann GbR, Mülheim.

↑ | View from the street
↓ | Horizontal section façade

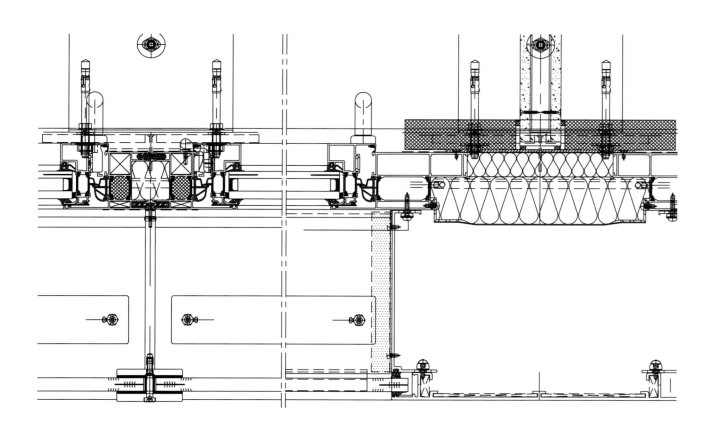

↑ | Inner courtyard
← | Detail entrance
↓ | Vertical section façade

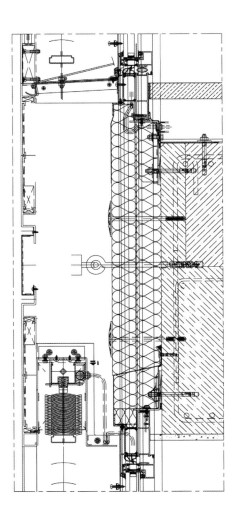

↑ | Screen-printed marble pattern

Origami Office Building

Paris

This office block near the Arc de Triomphe consists of a front and a rear building. The lobby of the front building plays on transparency between the street front and the main garden. On the avenue façade, the windows are furnished with an origami arrangement of marble panels to express elegance and modernity. The panels are comprised of a film of marble mounted on a twin layer of glass. This second skin is translucent and acts as a breast wall to ensure privacy as well as filter daylight, creating a soft interior atmosphere. Marble folds create a vibration along the 30-meter-long front. At both ends, in continuity with the façades of neighboring buildings, the origami becomes calmer and flattens out. But in the central part it forms a delicate bas-relief.

CONSTRUCTION FACTS
Structure: new building. **Construction type:** double-skin façade, curtain wall. **Material:** glass panels with screen-printed marble pattern. **Fixing:** punctuated fixing. **Insulation:** thermal insulation, noise insulation.

Address: 34–36 Friedland Avenue, Paris, France. **Client:** Gecina. **Completion:** 2011.
Building type: office.

↑ | Street view
↓ | Detail longitudinal section façade

↑ | View from inside
↓ | Detail façade

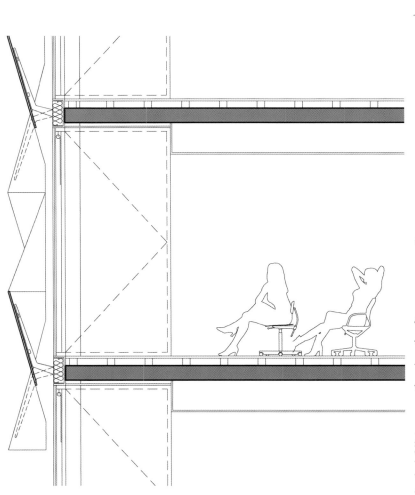

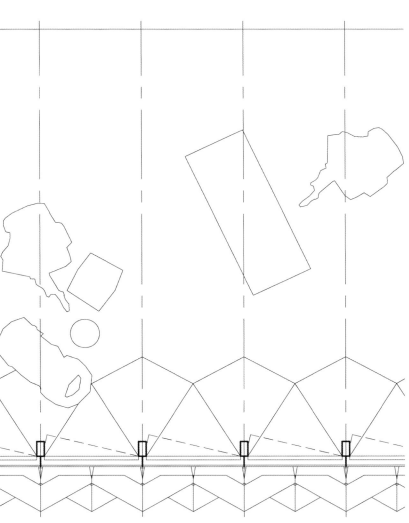

Philippe Samyn and Partners,
architects & engineers

↑ | Exterior view with bamboo sun screen

Office Block

Brussels

The original building from the 1960s was stripped bare and completely renovated. The new façade is made of wood with abundant glass surfaces and fitted with adjustable bamboo sunscreen Venetian blinds. A curtain of fixed-glass louver blades in a stainless steel frame provides protection from the rain. The top floor offers a complimentary glazed canopy. On the ground floor as well as at the corners, the façade is clad in stainless steel. The façade is fitted to the structure of the building in the form of a large wooden grid. Small balconies, protected by the glass louvers, are created by detaching the wooden window frames from the structure.

CONSTRUCTION FACTS

Structure: redevelopment. **Construction type:** double-skin façade. **Material:** wood, laminated glass, bamboo sun screen, glass louver blades, stainless steel. **Fixing:** punctuated fixing, self-supporting. **Insulation:** thermal insulation, noise insulation, UV-reduction.

Adress: n° 28 Avenue Marnix / Marnixlaan, Brussels, Belgium. **Client:** Immobiliere SEM s.a. **Completion:** 2009. **Building type:** office. **Construction engineer façade:** Philippe Samyn and Partners sprl, architects & engineers.

↑ | Ground floor and corners are clad with stainless steel
↓ | Detailed section

↑ | Detail fixed-glass louver blades
↓ | Section

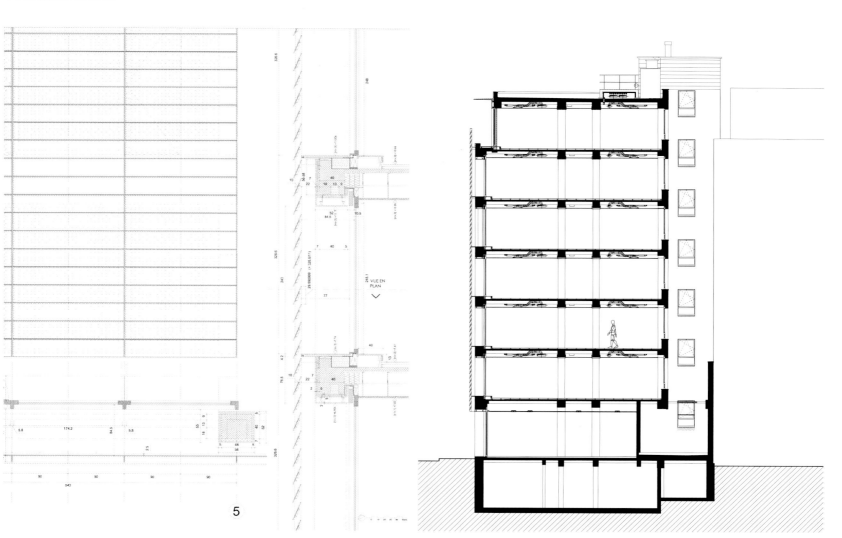

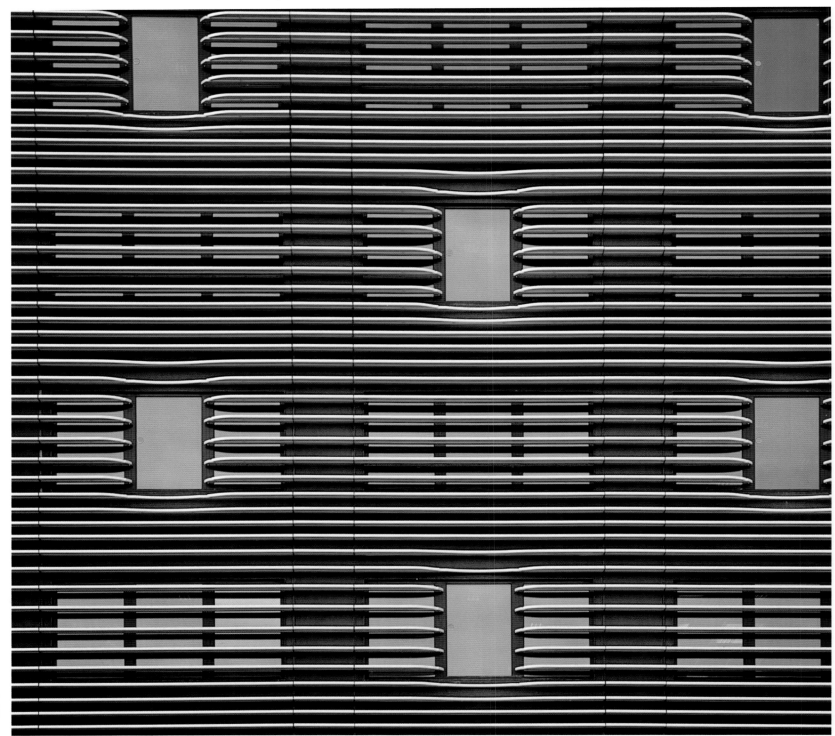

↑ | Detail façade with openings
→ | Swinging concrete veil

Galilée

Blagnac

Two distinct buildings are connected through a long white concrete veil. The coherence and balance of the whole is maintained by the homogenous treatment of the façades. The different shapes and similar materials make fraternal twins out of these two buildings, which works to maintain options for future users of the space. The differences between the buildings would allow multiple tenants to maintain an air of individuality while at the same time the continuous architectural themes provide an appropriate environment for a single occupant. The sunshade, a major element of the façade, brings the bright comfort crucial to the offices and open spaces of the building.

CONSTRUCTION FACTS
Structure: new building. **Construction type:** curtain wall. **Material:** aluminum, concrete. **Insulation:** thermal insulation, sun screen.

PROJECT FACTS

Address: Urban Development Zone Andromède, Blagnac, France. **Client:** Altarea Cogedim. **Completion:** 2010. **Building type:** office.

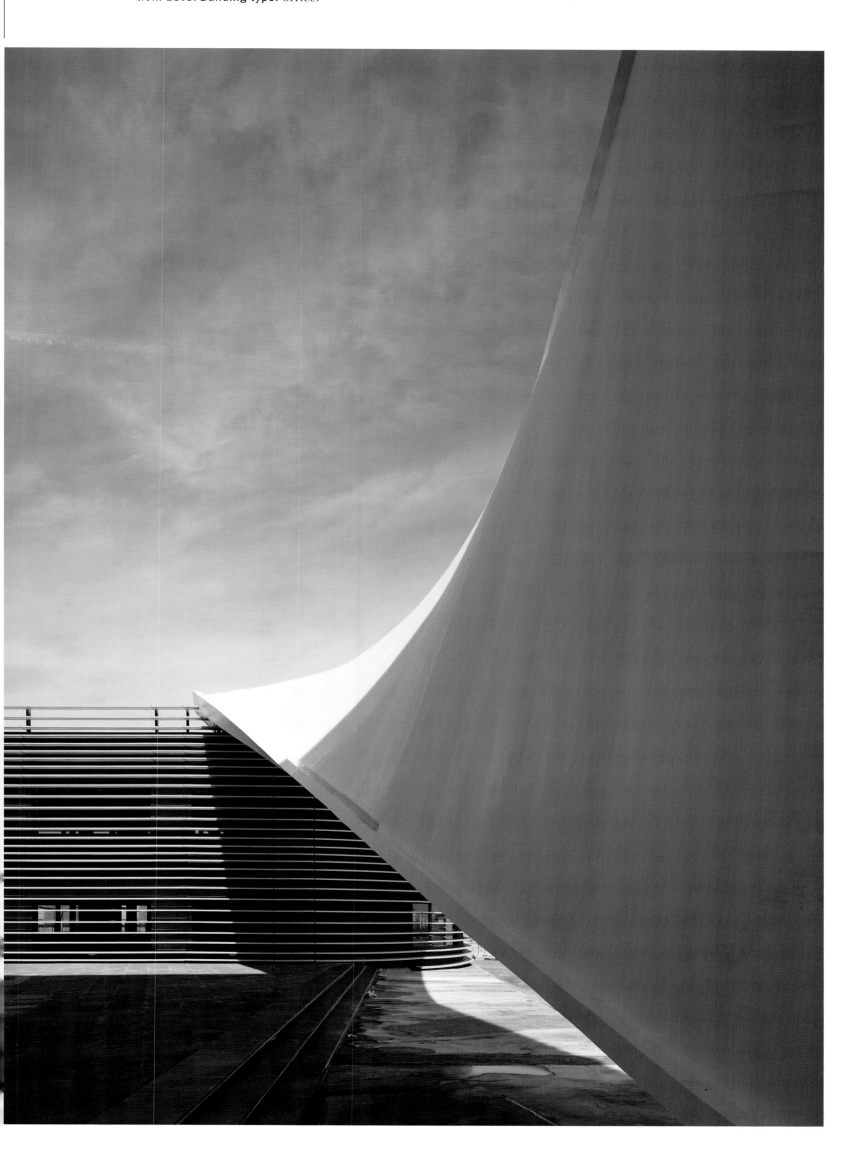

↑ | Detail façade and concrete canopy
↓ | Elevation main façade

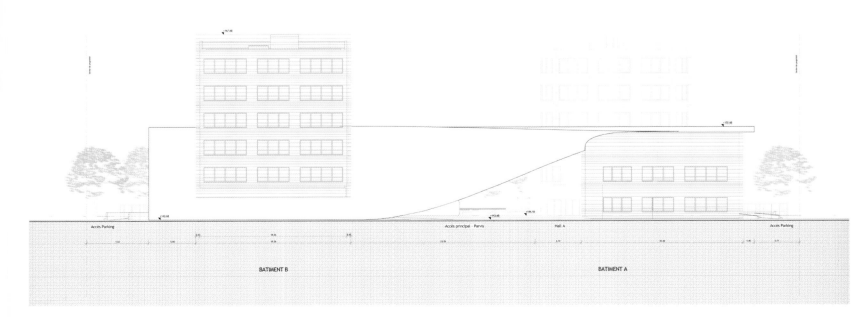

↑ | General view
← | Detail façade with sun screen

↑ I **View from banks**

IBA DOCK

Hamburg

The floating building in Hamburg rises and drops with the tide. Even in case of an extreme storm flood it rises along with the surface of the water. The entrance on the top deck is reached via a bridge. An exhibition space across three floors is complemented by an office section on the western part. The three-story building, a modular light-weight construction made of steel tubes, sits on a concrete pontoon, which also serves as a boat landing place. The modules were assembled on-site and can be varied and disassembled for maintenance. They are protected by a highly insulated curtain façade with colored cement fiber slabs. The system grooves and slab colors reflect the structure of the façade steel tubes. The choice of colors is based on the water – shiny blue-green was filtered out of black as the base color.

CONSTRUCTION FACTS
Structure: new building. **Construction type:** rear ventilated curtain wall. **Material:** colored fiber cement elements on metal substructure. **Fixing:** screw connect. **Insulation:** R-value: 0.19 $W/(m^2K)$. **Special functions:** insulation.

Address: Am Zollhafen 12, 20539 Hamburg, Germany. **Client:** Internationale Bauausstellung IBA Hamburg GmbH. **Completion:** 2010. **Building type:** office. **Construction engineer façade:** RISSE Ingenieurbüro für Fassadenplanung, Falkensee.

↑ | **Detail façade**
↓ | **Exploded view**

↓ | **Detail drawings window**

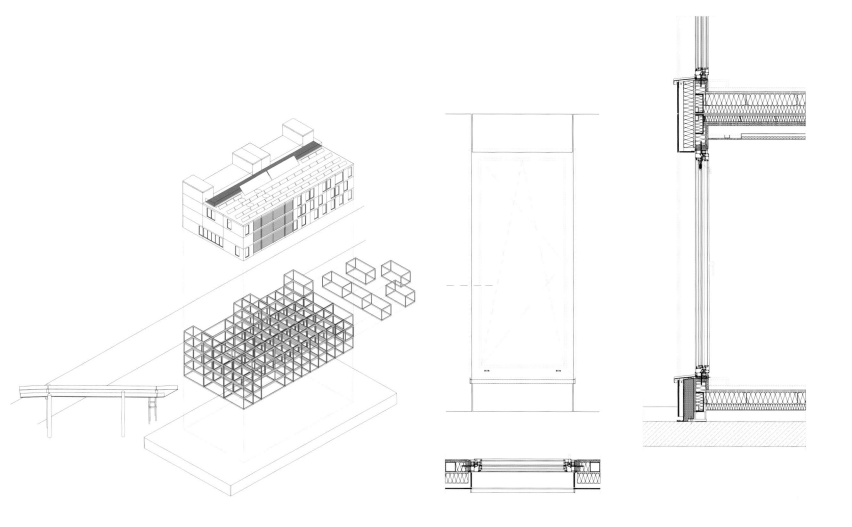

Thomas Pink
Petzinka Pink Architekten

↑ | **Detail façade during the day**

Lighthouse

Dusseldorf

With an area of approximately 11,300 square meters, the seven-story corner building demarcates the transition of a former industrial site into an attractive urban office and residential district. Its name is derived from all-round LED light strips that were fitted in shadowy grooves and covered with glass panels. A bus system controls the small LEDs that were fixed along a stretch of 1,400 meters. Reddish-brown dyed cut stone frames divide the skin of the building into diverse clusters. The impressive staircase made of the same colored concrete cut stones completes the sculptured effect of the building. In 2011, the building received the "silver" medal for sustainable construction by the DGNB e. V..

CONSTRUCTION FACTS
Structure: new building, solitaire in heterogeneous surrounding. **Construction type:** modular prefabricated elements. **Material:** dyed cut stone, illuminated grooves. **Fixing:** self-supporting. **Insulation:** noise insulation, sun screen. **Special functions:** integrated lighting in different colors.

Address: Derendorfer Allee 6, 40476 Dusseldorf, Germany. **Client:** Lighthouse Development GmbH. **Completion:** 2010. **Building type:** office. **Other creatives:** lighting planner façade: DS Ing. Büro Gebäudetechnik GbR Frank Stadermann. **Construction engineer façade:** Ingenieurbüro Franke.

↑ | **Lighthouse illuminated with green LEDs**
↓ | **Detail drawing section façade**

↓ | **Detail drawing attic**

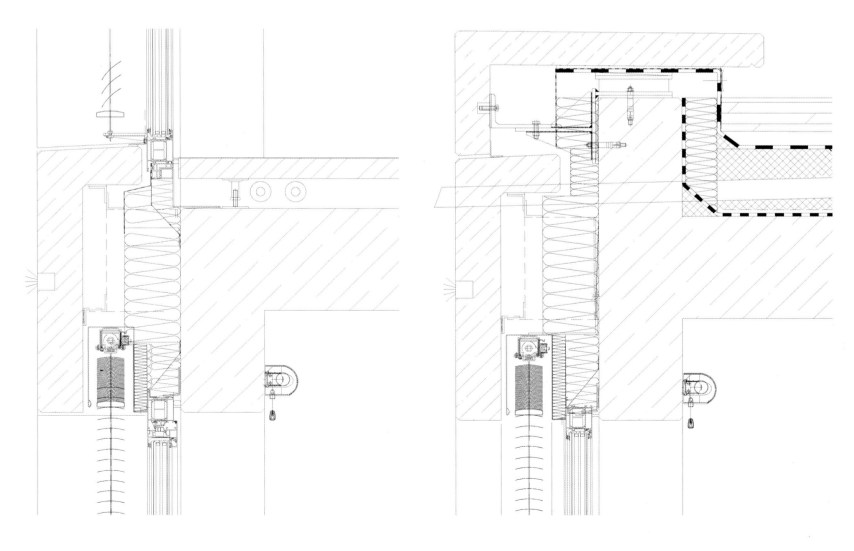

↑ | General view
→ | Detail façade

Kontor 19 in the Rheinauhafen

Cologne

The Kontor 19 building's visual effect is derived from the high contrast of the closed aluminum panels and the transparent glass sections of the IntegralFaçade. The aluminum panels are distinguished by a graphic structure etched in by a special cauterization and anodization process which provides a new look to the building ranging from dark gray to gold, depending on the time of day, weather and viewpoint of the observer. The office areas are ventilated naturally through shutters integrated into the façade. A well balanced energy concept, including thermo active building systems in the concrete ceilings, centrally controlled daylight controlling sun screen slats as well as night air cooling via the shutters provides air conditioning to the building.

CONSTRUCTION FACTS

Structure: new building, solitaire. **Construction type:** element façade, IntegralFaçade. **Material:** aluminum. **Fixing:** suspension. **Insulation:** R-value: 1.6 W/(m²K), noise insulation. **Special functions:** light-deflecting-blind.

PROJECT FACTS

Address: Anna-Schneider-Steig 8–10, 50678 Cologne, Germany. **Client:** moderne stadt, Gesellschaft zur Förderung des Städtebaues und der Gemeindeentwicklung mbH. **Completion:** 2006. **Building type:** office. **Other creatives:** Pete Bossley (artist ornamental structure). **Construction engineer façade:** Ingenieurbüro Rache-Willms GmbH.

↑ | Detail IntegralFaçade
↙ | Vertical and horizontal section façade
↓ | Open shutters

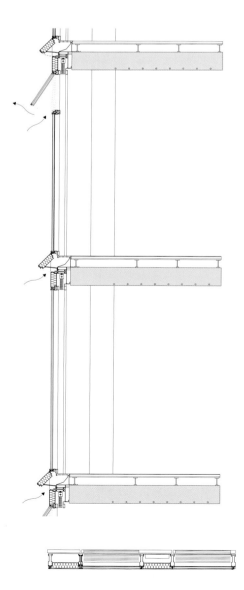

↑ | Detail aluminum element
← | New façade and old neighboring building

↑ | Façade folds like an accordion

Cinetic Office Building

Paris

The façades of this building vary according to the orientation and surrounding environment. The northwest façade on the avenue of the Porte de Lilacs is an original, irregular, folded construction. At a length of 112 meters, it has the shape of an accordion. Folds facing north consist of clear glass; those facing west are made of serigraphy glazing, depicting a work of the artist Elisabeth Ballet representing the close up image of a chestnut tree and its branches. The façade facing the Maquis-du-Vercors square and Doctor Gley Avenue draws its identity from a strongly defined pedestal and a progressive emptying of the superior levels and the attic. The piers consist of prefabricated concrete panels.

CONSTRUCTION FACTS
Structure: new building. **Construction type:** ventilated story-high glazing panels. **Material:** laminated tempered glass, printed on the PVB layer. **Fixing:** punctuated fixing, not visible. **Insulation:** thermal insulation.

Address: 12–16 avenue de la Porte des Lilacs, Paris, France. **Client:** COGEDIM/SOGEPROM/ADIM. **Completion:** 2009. **Building type:** office. **Other creatives:** Elisabeth Ballet (artist). **Construction engineer façade:** VP & Green.

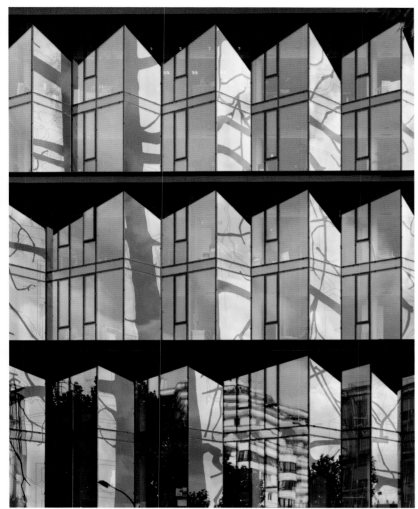

↑ | Detail folded façade with print
↓ | Concept printed motif
↓↓ | Elevation west façade
↓↓↓ | Elevation north façade

↑ | Façade with prefabricated concrete panels
↓ | View from inside through printed glass façade

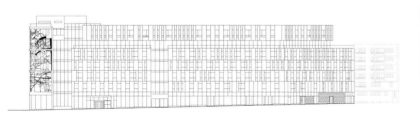

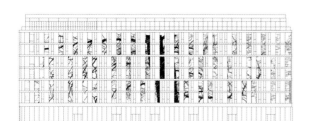

LAb[au], laboratory for
architecture and urbanism

↖↖ | Illuminated tower
↑↑ | Detail illumination
↗↗ | Illumination performance
↖ | Detail frequecy
↑ | Skyline with illuminated tower

spectr[a]um

Brussels

spectr|a|um presented a night with audio-luminous performances on the 145-meter-high Dexia
Tower in Brussels. A total of 4,200 windows were illuminated by laboratiorly renowned musi-
cians and artists who performed on Place Rogier's urban lounge and Dexia Tower. The title of the
design combines the idea of light and sound spectra with the German word "Raum" for space. The
frequencies of sound were related to the frequencies of light to describe the space. The event was
organized by LAb[au] with the aid of Dexia Bank and the City of Brussels.

CONSTRUCTION FACTS
Structure: new building. **Construction type:**
curtain wall. **Material:** glass, steel. **Insulation:** triple glazing: low-energy façade.
Special functions: media façade.

PROJECT FACTS
Address: Rogierplein, 1000 Brussels, Belgium. **Client:** RoDexia Banque Belgique. **Completion:**
2007. **Building type:** office. **Other creatives:** Philippe Samyn & Partners (architecture),
M & J.M. Jaspers – J. Eyers & Partners (architecture), Barbara Hediger (lighting engineer).
Construction engineer façade: Philippe Samyn & Partners.

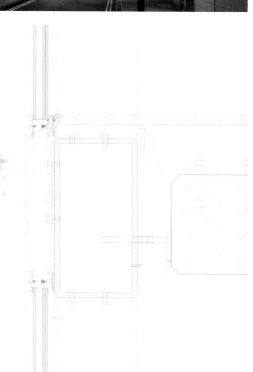

↑↑ | Exterior view at night
↑ | Longitudinal section façade
↗ | Detail façade

Reiss Headquarter

London

CONSTRUCTION FACTS

Structure: new building. **Construction type:** triple-skin facade, bright mild steel frame to acrylic rainscreen. **Material:** milled acrylic. **Fixing:** punctuated fixing. **Insulation:** thermal insulation. **Special functions:** lighting through integrated LEDs.

The façade consists of a double-glazed glass layer behind an acrylic rain screen. The acrylic layer has a complex machined profile – solid panels of acrylic are cut away by large vertical gauges of varying width and depth, within which even finer vertical striations are etched. When viewed obliquely, it takes on the shimmering quality of a sheet of silk. The effect changes at night when the acrylic is edge-lit, allowing it to vary the building's appearance. Horizontal slabs of up-lit fair-faced concrete balance the vertical emphasis of the façade, while the diagonal form of a staircase running from the second to the fourth floors offsets the orthogonal frame.

PROJECT FACTS

Address: 9–12 Barrett Street, London, W1U 1BA, United Kingdom. **Client:** Reiss Limited, London. **Completion:** 2008. **Building type:** office, concept retail, residential. **Other creatives:** Fluid Structures (structural engineering).

↑ | **View at night**
→ | **Detail of the façade**

The Crystal

Copenhagen

Freestanding on the site, the Crystal reads as a transparent, geometrical, glazed form which, resting only on a single point and a single line, floats as a visually light, crystalline structure above the plaza. It is an extension to the Nykredit premises and can accommodate an open plan office as well as single offices and meeting rooms. The building's multi-faceted glass façade reflects both daylight and the immediate surroundings, but the double glazing also features an integrated sun screen that allows the building to adapt to changing light conditions. In addition, the outer glazing system includes a subtle silk print design that both mitigates solar ingress and enlivens the ambience of the harbor area.

CONSTRUCTION FACTS
Structure: new building. **Construction type:** ventilated double-glazed façade. **Material:** safety glass, horizontal blinds, silk screen print design. **Fixing:** suspension. **Insulation:** thermal insulation. **Special functions:** integrated sun screen.

PROJECT FACTS

Address: Hambrosgade, 1562 Copenhagen V, Denmark. **Client:** Nykredit. **Completion:** 2011. **Building type:** office. **Other creatives:** SLA (landscape architect). **Construction engineer façade:** Grontmij A/S, Buro Happold.

↑ | **Side view**
← | **Section façade**
↙ | **Detail elevation**
→ | **Transparency effect of the façade**

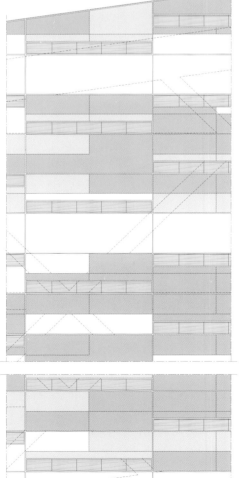

↑ I **Rear view**
→ I **Detail entrance**

Q1 in the ThyssenKrupp Quarter

Essen

In addition to two panorama windows with rear tensioning cables, the Q1 building of the ThyssenKrupp Quarter is distinguished by a new type of sunshade system. Resembling metal slats from a distance, the stainless steel sunscreen elements consist of approx. 3150 milled vertical double axes and approx. 400,000 horizontal slats bolted onto them, which are centrally controlled by engines depending on the situation of the sun. The rotating and foldable elements allow optimal light control with nearly unobstructed views. The division into trapezoid, triangular and rectangular individual elements creates a façade structure on which the reflected sunlight with its changing interplay of light creates an artistic interpretation of the architecture.

CONSTRUCTION FACTS

Structure: new building. **Construction type:** single-shell and double-shell façade (offices), insulated glazing. **Material:** glass, moveable louvers. **Fixing:** self-supporting (louvers), suspension (atrium). **Insulation:** R-value: 1.0 W/(m²K). **Special functions:** sun shield.

Address: ThyssenKrupp Allee 1, 45143 Essen, Germany. **Client:** ThyssenKrupp AG. **Completion:** 2010.
Building type: office. **Other creatives:** ECE Projektmanagement GmbH & Co. KG. **Construction engineer façade:** Werner Sobek, Stuttgart; Priedemann Fassadenberatung, Berlin.

↑ | **Detail façade**
↙ | **Scheme of sun shields**

↑ | Interior view office
↓ | Sections of office sun screen,
horizontal and vertical

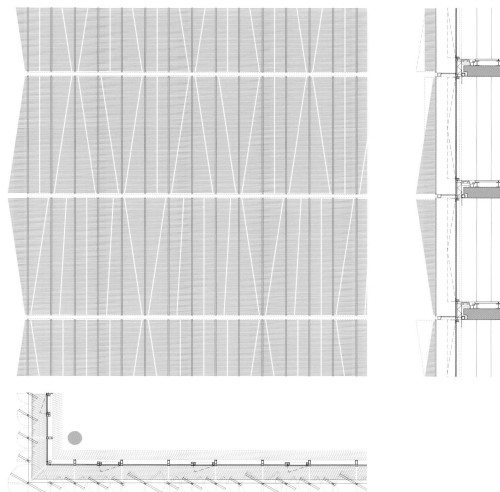
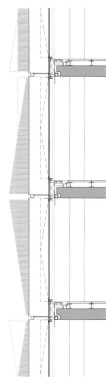

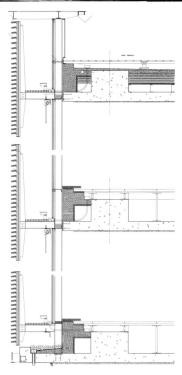

↖↑ | Night view
↑↑ | Detail wooden sun screen
↖ | South façade
↑ | Section

Transoceanica Headquarters

Santiago de Chile

The office building with underground car park is designed for optimal energy efficiency. It is composed of a main body with a great hall and two wings for open-plan offices, plus an independent body in the north as an auditorium and casino that is connected through an exterior marquise to become integrated into the building and the site. The building is designed in compliance with all passive energy saving requirements like orientation, use of natural light, renewable materials, insulation, etc. This involved, for instance, a façade in layers of DVH crystal, of low emissivity, plus a system of automated shades on the exterior, complemented by a wood skin, that protects from radiation, ensuring exterior views.

CONSTRUCTION FACTS

Structure: new building, solitaire. **Construction type:** curtain wall. **Material:** glass, wood, metal. **Fixing:** self-supporting. **Insulation:** R-value: 1.3 W/(m²K), noise insulation, glare shield, UV-reduction and protection.

PROJECT FACTS

Address: Av. Santa Maria 5888, Vitacura, Santiago, Chile. **Client:** Transoceanica. **Completion:** 2010. **Building type:** office. **Other creatives:** Hunter Douglas, Accura, Joma.

↑↑ | **Different colors stand for different temperatures**
↑ | **Illumination**
↗ | **Cold weather**
→ | **Visual weather forecast**

weather.tower

Brussels

The project took part in an illumination series entitled "Who's Afraid Of Red, Green and Blue" which LAb[au] conceived for Brussel's 145-meter-high Dexia Tower whose 4,200 windows can be individually color-enlightened by RGB-LED bars. The illumination series aimed for an artistic illumination of the tower every night during one year. The project displayed next day's temperature, cloudiness, precipitations, and wind by using colors and geometrical patterns to display these real-time data provided by the Royal Meteorological Institute of Belgium. The resulting geometric play of colors and shapes mirrors environmental data by means of light in order to reinforce the tower's role in the city as an urban landmark and a public light sign.

CONSTRUCTION FACTS

Structure: new building. **Construction type:** curtain wall. **Material:** glass, steel. **Fixing:** punctuated fixing. **Insulation:** triple glazing: low-energy façade. **Special functions:** media façade.

PROJECT FACTS

Address: Place Rogier, 1000 Brussels, Belgium. **Client:** Dexia Banque Belgique. **Completion:** 2007. **Building type:** office. **Other Creatives:** Philippe Samyn & Partners (architecture), M & J.M. Jaspers – J. Eyers & Partners (architecture), Barbara Hediger (lighting engineer). **Construction engineer façade:** Philippe Samyn & Partners.

GATERMANN + SCHOSSIG

↑ | View from street

Capricorn House

Dusseldorf

The large glass halls plus a second acoustic membrane constitute the frame for a modern office world that meets the requirement of a low-energy building. The specially developed façade modules, called "i-module façade" consist of two elements. The transparent section is designed as a rear ventilated box window with insulation glazing placed behind it. The interim space houses motor-powered sectional sun shades. The lower part of the module's closed field consists of highly insulated glass panels hiding technical equipment, the i-module. With an overall depth of only 200 millimeters, the i-module façade provides not only air conditioning, weather protection, natural ventilation, acoustic insulation, heating, cooling and aeration, but also heat recovery, sound absorption, and air purification.

CONSTRUCTION FACTS
Structure: new building, solitaire. **Construction type:** element façade. **Material:** aluminum, glass. **Fixing:** suspension. **Insulation:** R-value: 1.7 $W/(m^2K)$, noise insulation.

Address: Holzstraße 6, 40219 Dusseldorf, Germany. **Client:** Capricorn Development GmbH&Co.KG.
Completion: 2008. **Building type:** office. **Other creatives:** Trox Technik. **Construction engineer façade:**
Ingenieurbüro Rache-Willms GmbH.

↑ | Detail façade
↓ | Interior façade

↑ | Detail glazed atrium
↓ | Diagram ventilation

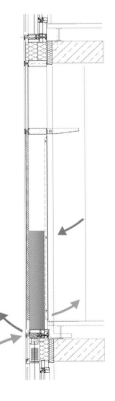

Architekten BKSP
Grabau Leiber Obermann
and Partners

↑ | **East façade**

Conference and Finance Center of the VW Bank

Braunschweig

The newly constructed multifunctional structure is not autistic but expresses the typical features of its neighbors such as volumes, construction style, and façade materials in a suitably emblematic architecture. Inside its compact volume it combines functional areas for training, conferences, restaurant, café, branch bank, as well as a central reception area. With a welcoming sweep, a bright canopy extends across the entrance to the new building, leading to the spatially transparent foyer containing the reception area, cafeteria and bank branch. Next to it is the restaurant, which, similarly to the café, extends into the water garden via a wooden deck. Containing flexible conference and training rooms, the upper level is connected to the foyer via a central elevator and the open staircase.

CONSTRUCTION FACTS
Structure: new building. **Construction type:** reinforced concrete with rear ventilated curtain wall. **Material:** sheets of polished stainless steel. **Fixing:** punctuated fixing. **Insulation:** thermal insulation.

Address: Schmalbachstraße 1, 38112 Braunschweig, Germany. **Client:** VOLIM Volkswagen Immobilien Vermögensgesellschaft mbH. **Completion:** 2003. **Building type:** corporate architecture. **Other creatives:** Prof.Nagel, Schonhoff + Partner, Hanover. **Construction engineer façade:** Kilimann Metallbau GmbH.

↑ | View from south with terrace and café
↓ | Northwest view of the façade

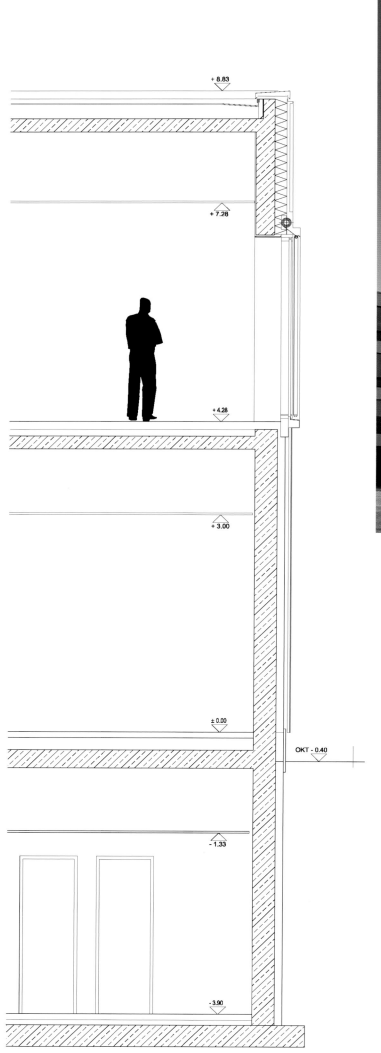

← | Cross section façade
↑ | View from east
↓ | Detail drawing stainless steel façade

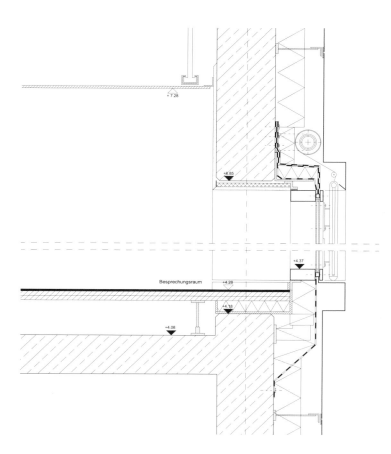

↑ | North-east view
↙ | Detail drawing
↓ | Interior view foyer

J. MAYER H. Architects

↑ | **Detail of the façade**

ADA 1 – Office Building "An der Alster 1"

Hamburg

The building site is situated directly on the shores of the Alster at the intersection between Hamburg's lively downtown area and urban cityscape. The horizontally striped façade with its floating "eyes" seems to mirror the water. This particular feature continues into the park next to the building with its eye-like platforms. The "eyes" of the façade also amplify the interior spaces which can be used either as an open plan office or subdivided further. The office building "An der Alster 1" links interior and exterior spaces to the public park in front of the building and to the city context of Hamburg, becoming a new anchor on the prestigious Außenalster waterfront.

CONSTRUCTION FACTS
Structure: new building. **Construction type:** double-skin curtain wall. **Material:** aerated concrete and glass. **Insulation:** thermal insulation.

Address: An der Alster 1, Hamburg, Germany. **Client:** Cogiton Projekt Alster GmbH. **Completion:** 2007.
Building type: office. **Other creatives:** Lydia Thiesemann, CBP (structural engineering).

↑ | View from the street
↓ | Section façade

↓ | Corner at night

1 - double skin facade
2 - "eye" loggia inside the double skin facade
3 - concrete core activation system
4 - convector heater

↑ | View building in context
→ | Detail façade with lamellae

Im Zollhafen 22, Rheinauhafen

Cologne

The sculptural volume of the building near the marina of the Rheinau Docks integrates all technical buildings and turns the roof into a fifth façade that is a suitable view from the "Kranhaus" buildings. The lively façade structuring is based on an organized rhythm, which creates the image of a cross-level verticality in a front and rear level. This results in an impression of depth, which is emphasized with light-colored anodizing in the front level and darker opaque infill elements in the rear level. In addition, the future-oriented ecological building and technology concept is distinguished by the optimal use of passive elements and the need-based and "simple" activation via a modern central building control system.

CONSTRUCTION FACTS

Structure: new building, solitaire. **Construction type:** element façade. **Material:** aluminum, glass. **Fixing:** suspension. **Insulation:** R-value: 1.3 W/(m²K). **Special functions:** light-deflecting-blinds.

PROJECT FACTS

Address: Im Zollhafen 22, 50678 Cologne, Germany. **Client:** moderne stadt, Gesellschaft zur Förderung des Städtebaues und der Gemeindeentwicklung mbH. **Completion:** 2011. **Building type:** office. **Project manager:** Holger Thor. **Construction engineer façade:** GATERMANN + SCHOSSIG with Rache Engineering GmbH.

↑ | **View from the marina**
↙ | **Detail drawing façade**

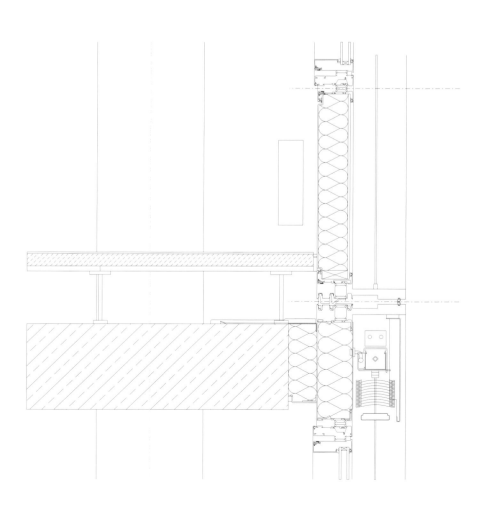

↑ | Detail façade with sun screen
← | Detail façade opened
↓ | Vertical section façade

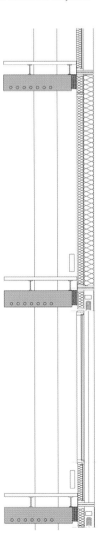

Renato & Reto Maurizio

↑ | **North-west view**

Commercial Center Punto Bregaglia

Vicosoprano

The floor plan offers different office and sales areas that can be adjusted within the systematic basic layout according to the current needs. To achieve the greatest possible flexibility, bearing walls were limited to the exterior walls and the inner dividing wall between the utilized areas and the access zone. To avoid static loads on cross walls and to enhance flexibility, the reinforcement of the building walls was designed as Saltire crosses outside the building skin. With its glazing and Saltire crosses, the center is in stark contrast to the other buildings. However, the use of larch wood as building material reflects the local architectural style.

CONSTRUCTION FACTS
Structure: new building. **Construction type:** wood stand construction with curtain wall. **Material:** larch wood. **Fixing:** glazing is fixed on the wood stand construction. **Insulation:** R-value: 0.5 W/(m²K). **Special functions:** crosses brace the building.

Address: Gewerbezentrum Punto Bregaglia, Val Torta 250, 7603 Vicosoprano, Switzerland. **Client:** Punto Bregaglia AG. **Completion:** 2008. **Building type:** industrial. **Construction engineer façade:** Ivo Diethelm, Blatten.

↑ | **Detail view of the bracing crosses**

↓ | **Detail elevation**

↓ | **Section of the façade**

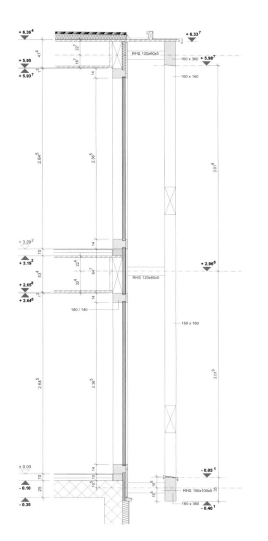

Renzo Piano
Building Workshop with
FXFowle Architects

↑ | View from inside
→ | Detail double-skin façade

The New York Times Building

New York

The 52-story glass and steel structure does not use the mirrored or tinted glass that renders towers mysterious and hermetic subjects. On the contrary, the building features a double-skin curtain wall with 186,000 ceramic rods that acts as a sun screen deflecting the heat and an inner wall of floor to ceiling water-white glass, which allow it to adapt to the colors of the atmosphere. Bluish after a shower, shimmering red after a sunset, the building speaks to the street. In addition to using 24 elevators (32 elevators in total including service), people move between its floors by using stairs located on the facades, which will foster communication between departments with their movement visible from the outside.

CONSTRUCTION FACTS
Structure: new building. **Construction type:** double-skin curtain wall. **Material:** ceramic rods, floor-to-ceiling water-white glass. **Insulation:** thermal insulation, sun screen.

PROJECT FACTS

Address: 620 Eighth Avenue, New York, NY, USA. **Client:** The New York Times / Forest City Ratner Companies. **Completion:** 2007. **Building type:** office. **Other creatives:** Ove Arup & Partners (structural engineering). **Construction engineer façade:** Heitman & Associates.

←←| View from west and south
↑ | Entrance area at night
← | Detail construction
↓ | Detailed section façade

↑ | Exterior view

Kuggen

Gothenburg

Kuggen at Lindholmen is a hub for formal as well as informal meetings between community and society. The building is constituted by repetitions of optimal office units. The façade is made of glazed terracotta tiles in various sizes and eight different colors. They are hung on prefabricated wall elements with stainless steel clips. Their length differs between 57 and 280 centimeters at a constant height of 57 centimeters. Most of the building lies in the shade of other buildings. The top two floors, however, feature a screen tracking the sun. The screen moves with the sunlight and blocks it during certain hours to prevent heat becoming an issue. The screen is made of a metal grid that replicates the colors of the façade, but on a smaller scale.

CONSTRUCTION FACTS
Structure: new building. **Construction type:** curtain wall. **Material:** glazed terracotta tiles in different sizes. **Fixing:** punctuated fixing. **Insulation:** thermal insulation. **Special functions:** moving sun screen on two top floors.

PROJECT FACTS

Address: Lindholmsplatsen, Gothenburg, Sweden. **Client:** Chalmersfastigheter AB. **Completion:** 2011.
Building type: office. **Construction engineer façade:** Staticus.

↑ | Windows maximize daylight, and the
energy-saving wall by the floor
↓ | Section

↑ | Motorized brise soleil
↓ | Horizontal section window
↓↓ | The building grows each upper floor

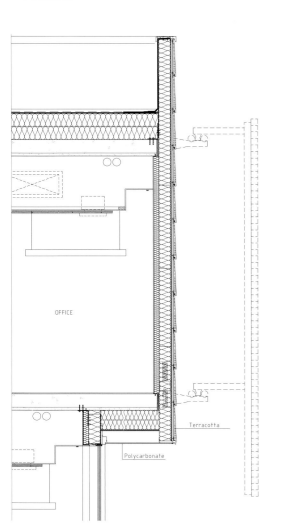

OFFICE

Terracotta

Polycarbonate

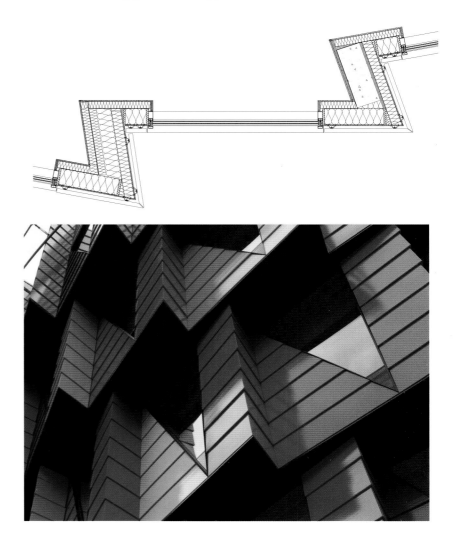

↑ | View from market place

New Façade of Galeria Kaufhof

Oldenburg

In the style of the famous honeycomb façade of Egon Eiermann, which had to be replaced due to damages, the architects designed a skin that is understated, yet distinctly modern, entering into a subtle dialog with the predominately Neoclassicist ancient quarters of Oldenburg. The new façade consists of large horizontally aligned translucent white glass elements and perforated aluminum sheets with a height of 275 centimeters each and varying widths of 30, 60, and 90 centimeters. The resulting shimmering skin is constantly changing – at times dissolving into the grey skies, at others turning into a shiny crystal or a mirror of the surrounding façades. At night, the full-surface backlighting turns the building into an illuminated body in the city.

CONSTRUCTION FACTS

Structure: façade reconstruction. **Construction type:** solid construction. **Material:** clear laminated safety glass. **Fixing:** elements clamped at top and bottom. **Special functions:** dimmable background lighting.

Address: Ritterstraße 17, 26122 Oldenburg, Germany. **Client:** METRO Group Asset Management GmbH & Co. **Completion:** 2011. **Building type:** shopping. **Construction engineer façade:** Arup GmbH, Berlin; BIS IKF GmbH, Oststeinbek; GIB – Büro Hellmann GmbH, Oldenburg.

↑ | **View by night**
↓ | **Detail drawing**

↑ | **View from street**
↓ | **Detail construction**

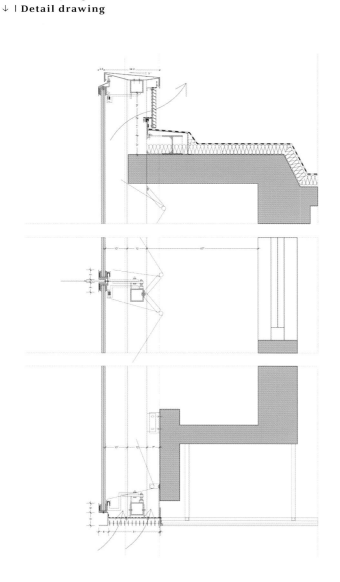

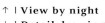

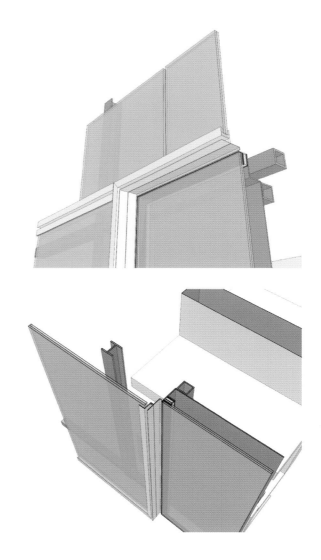

↑ | **Exterior department store**
→ | **Detail double shell façade with pattern**

John Lewis Department Store and Cineplex

Leicester

Department stores are conventionally designed as blank enclosures to allow retailers the flexibility to rearrange their interior layouts. However, the physical experience of shops is an increasingly important consideration to compliment the convenience of online shopping. The concept for the John Lewis store is a net curtain, providing privacy to the interior without blocking natural light. The store cladding is designed as a double-glazed façade with a pattern introduced. The use of pattern draws inspiration from Leicester's 200 years of textiles and weaving. The curtain concept is extended to the cinema, which is designed as an opaque stainless steel rain screen. It is treated in mirror finish and pleated at different scales to diffuse the large volume into a series of smaller reflective surfaces.

CONSTRUCTION FACTS
Structure: new building. **Construction type:** double shell façade. **Material:** glass with mirror frit (department store), stainless steel shingles (cineplex). **Insulation:** thermal insulation, noise insulation.

PROJECT FACTS

Address: Leicester, United Kingdom. **Client:** Hammerson. **Completion:** 2008. **Building type:** department store and cineplex. **Other creatives:** Adams Kara Taylor (structural engineering).

↑ | Exterior view cineplex
← | Sectional Axonometric department store
↗ | Detail façade cineplex
→ | Connection cineplex and department store
→→| Façade layering system department store

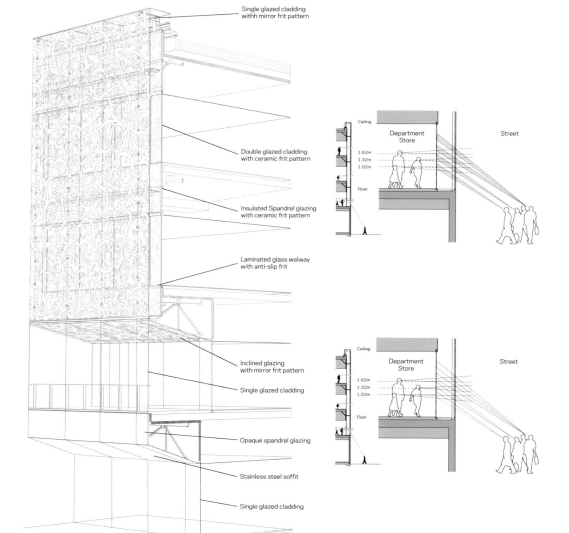

Single glazed cladding
withh mirror frit pattern

Double glazed cladding
with ceramic frit pattern

Insulated Spandrel glazing
with ceramic frit pattern

Laminated glass walway
with anti-slip frit

Inclined glazing
with mirror frit pattern

Single glazed cladding

Opaque spandrel glazing

Stainless steel soffit

Single glazed cladding

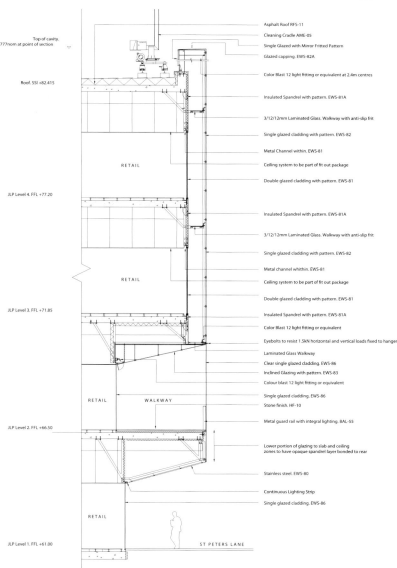

Top of cavity.
84.777?nom at point of section

Roof. SSI +82.415

Asphalt Roof RFS-11
Cleaning Cradle AME-05
Single Glazed with Mirror Fritted Pattern
Glazed capping. EWS-82A

Color Blast 12 light fitting or equivalent at 2.4m centres

Insulated Spandrel with pattern. EWS-81A

3/12/12mm Laminated Glass. Walkway with anti-slip frit

Single glazed cladding with pattern. EWS-82

Metal Channel within. EWS-81

Ceiling system to be part of fit out package

Double glazed cladding with pattern. EWS-81

JLP Level 4. FFL +77.20

Insulated Spandrel with pattern. EWS-81A

3/12/12mm Laminated Glass. Walkway with anti-slip frit

Single glazed cladding with pattern. EWS-82

Metal channel withihn. EWS-81

Ceiling system to be part of fit out package

Double glazed cladding with pattern. EWS-81

JLP Level 3. FFL +71.85

Insulated Spandrel with pattern. EWS-81A

Color Blast 12 light fitting or equivalent

Eyebolts to resist 1.5kN horizontal and vertical loads fixed to hanger

Laminated Glass Walkway

Clear single glazed cladding. EWS-86

Inclined Glazing with pattern. EWS-83

Colour blast 12 light fitting or equivalent

Single glazed cladding. EWS-86

Stone finish. HF-10

Metal guard rail with integral lighting. BAL-55

JLP Level 2. FFL +66.50

Lower portion of glazing to slab and ceiling zones to have opaque spandrel layer bonded to rear

Stainless steel. EWS-80

Continuous Lighting Strip

Single glazed cladding. EWS-86

JLP Level 1. FFL +61.00

ST PETERS LANE

↑ | Black and white façade as eye-catcher

Zeilgalerie – Façade Redesign

Frankfurt/Main

The look of the Zeilgalerie can be varied with the help of a complex light installation in its façade whose ambiguity provides room for individual interpretation and identification. In addition, several façade levels with different designs create attractive layer effects and optical depth. The softly pulsating light ornaments of the right-hand building's media façade produces a great variety of attractive images – clear geometric patterns turn into a flowing organic interplay of light and shadow, delicate linear accents alternate with impressive large-scale effects. While the characteristic tripartite structure of the building was maintained, the continuous matte black color of the façade and its repeated architectural elements create visual uniformity.

CONSTRUCTION FACTS
Structure: redevelopment. **Construction type:** rear ventilated curtain wall, post-and-beam construction (shop windows). **Material:** powder-coated aluminum panels. **Fixing:** punctuated fixing. **Insulation:** thermal insulation. **Special functions:** media façade: 42,000 individually controllable, white LEDs.

Address: Zeil 112–114, 60313 Frankfurt/Main, Germany. **Client:** IFM Immobilien AG. **Completion:** 2010. **Building type:** shopping mall. **Other creatives:** Meso Digital Interiors GmbH (programming). **Construction engineer façade:** KHP – König und Heunisch Planungsgesellschaft Frankfurt/Main.

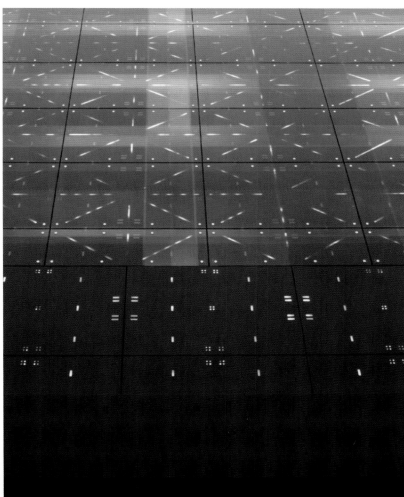

↑ | **View up the entrance area**
↓ | **Elevation**

↑ | **Detail view media façade**

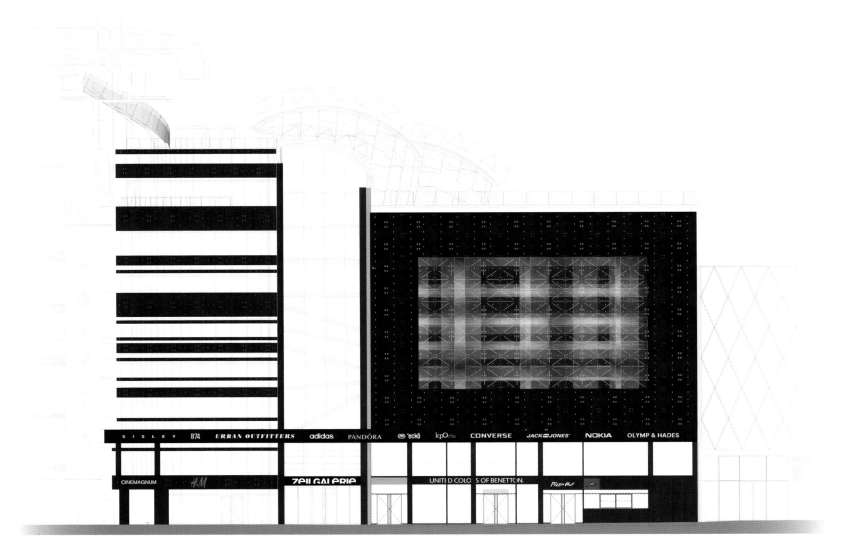

↑ | **Exterior view**

Placebo Pharmacy

Athens

The design process for this 600-square-meter regional pharmacy forced the designers to shift their viewpoint and come up with a virtual building – a placebo pharmacy. The octagonal shape of the existing structure was reshaped into a cylinder to create a spiral that seeks to converse with the rapid motion on Vouliagmenis Avenue, the urban artery on which the building stands. The panels of the façade are perforated using Braille, which alludes to the alphabet's use on pharmaceutical packaging and boosts visibility by allowing light to find its way into the interior. The new façade also protects the interior while attracting passers-by. Inside, the product display mirrors the circular front, while a ramp to the upper level extends the dynamism of the exterior spiral into the interior space.

CONSTRUCTION FACTS
Structure: redevelopment. **Construction type:** perforated façade. **Material:** steel, wood. **Fixing:** suspension. **Insulation:** sun protection.

Address: Vouliagnenis Avenue, Athens, Greece. **Client:** confidential. **Completion:** 2009. **Building type:** pharmacy. **Other creatives:** Xara Marantidou (artist), Enrique Ramirez (architecture).

↑ | **Detail perforated plates**
↓ | **Construction diagram**

↑ | **Interior view**
↓ | **Concept façade**

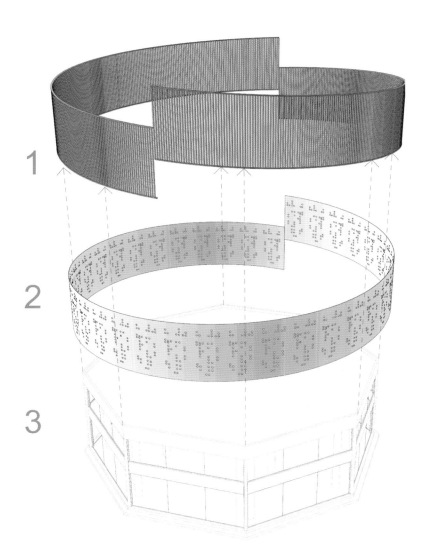

1

2

3

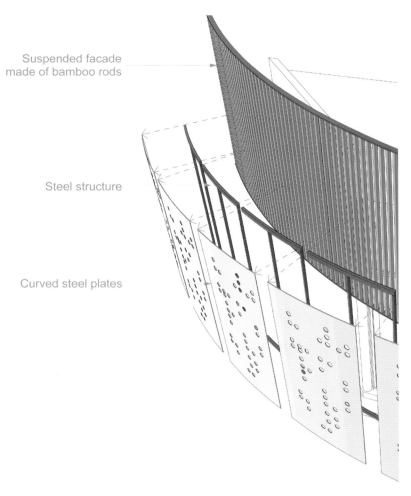

Suspended facade
made of bamboo rods

Steel structure

Curved steel plates

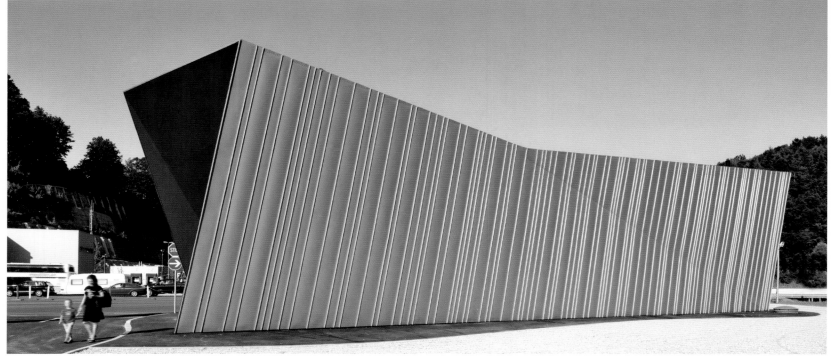

↑↑ | **View from the street**
↑ | **Side view**

Gruškovje

Podlehnik

Gruškovje Border Shop is situated on the border of Slovenia and Croatia. The simple two-story building has a longitudinal volume. The two smaller sides accommodate the main and the service entrance. Both entrances are funnel-shaped and slightly pushed into the interior so that the basic building volume also functions as a jutting roof. The two longer sides are solid and, like the roof, wrapped in metal sheets. In response to the dynamic environment, and with a simple design technique, the basic volume of the shop was distorted and twisted around the longitudinal axis. The unique appearance also facilitates easier spatial orientation of the passers-by owing to its greater visibility.

CONSTRUCTION FACTS
Structure: new building, solitaire in context. **Construction type:** rear ventilated curtain wall. **Material:** colored aluminum sheets. **Fixing:** punctuated fixing. **Insulation:** R-value: 0.33 W/(m²K).

Address: Zgornje Gruškovje BŠ, 2286 Podlehnik, Slovenia. **Client:** Regal GH. **Completion:** 2009.
Building type: shop.

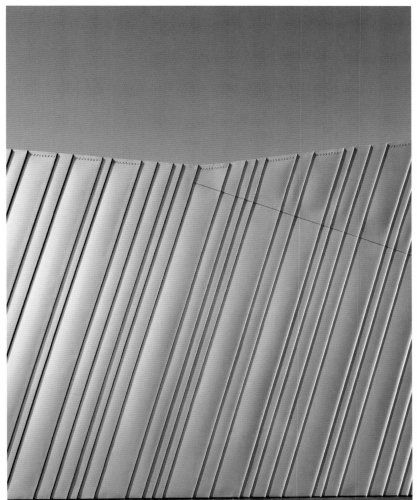

↑ | **Detail façade**
↓ | **Detailed sections façade**

↑ | **Façade along walkway**
↓ | **Entrance**

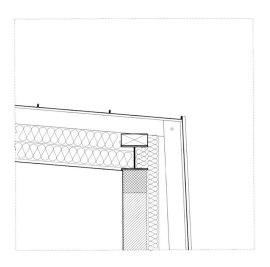

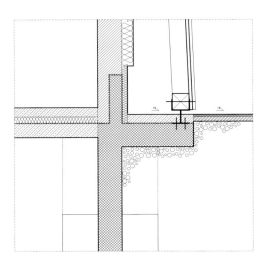

↑↑ | View from street
↑ | Parking place with entrance

"Nowy Swiat" Shopping Center

Rzeszow

Using the latest technology, Progress Eco S.A. offers innovative products that combine architectural steel structures such as nets, mesh, and sheet systems with LED lighting to deliver optimal solutions for architects and designers looking for new sources of inspiration and creativity. This is an interesting response to contemporary design, which continuously seeks new spatial and aesthetic effects. Thanks to high-quality materials and ease of cleaning, these innovative products are well suited for large surface areas in areas of extensive use, pollution, or humidity, like shopping malls, airports, railway stations, multi-level car parks, museums, universities, exhibition halls, and offices.

CONSTRUCTION FACTS
Structure: new building, solitaire. **Construction type:** curtain wall. **Material:** stainless steel mesh. **Fixing:** tensioned system with a compensating spring. **Special functions:** generation of light.

Address: Krakowska 20, Rzeszow, Poland. **Client:** Domena SP 20.2. **Completion:** 2009. **Building type:** shopping. **Other creatives:** Philips Lighting Poland S.A.

↑ | Detail façade
↓ | Detail section façade

↑ | Detail stainless steel mesh
↓ | Lit façade

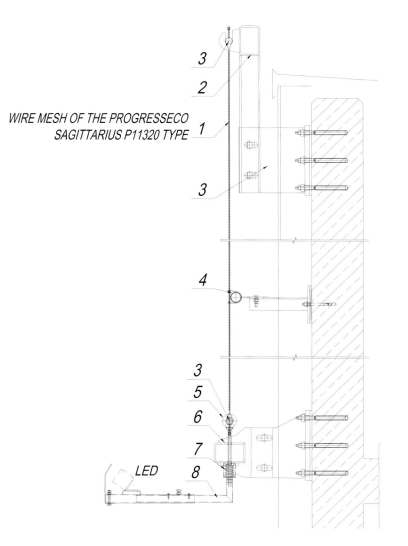

WIRE MESH OF THE PROGRESSECO
SAGITTARIUS P11320 TYPE

3
2
1
3

4

3
5
6
7
LED 8

↑ | Pilaster strips on the façade extend horizontally
→ | Detail glass façade

Leonardo Glass Cube

Bad Driburg

The graphically illustrated elements depicted on the glass façade were borrowed from the architecture and the surrounding landscape. A mix of photos and computer visualizations were printed on PVB sheets and laminated between the two glass panes. The print is transparent on both sides. To achieve an unobstructed view to the outside, the glass façade is free of columns across a width of 36 meters. Thin steel wires in the jointing equalize the distortion resulting from wind pressure. Vertical supporting profiles were also not needed in the building corners. Superimposed pilaster strips made of a white mineral material extend across the façade glass with a myriad of small lines, vertically extending the horizontal network of paths in front of the building without an optical interruption.

CONSTRUCTION FACTS

Structure: new building, solitaire. **Construction type:** double glazing without columns. **Material:** double glazing with printed foil between the two glasses. **Fixing:** clamped without frame. **Insulation:** thermal insulation.

Address: Industriestraße, 33014 Bad Driburg, Germany. **Client:** Leonardo / Glaskoch B. Koch Jr. GmbH & Co.KG. **Completion:** 2007. **Building type:** Corporate Architecture. **Other creatives:** Ingenieurbüro J. Steinkemper GmbH. **Construction engineer façade:** Schlaich, Bergermann und Partner GmbH.

↑ | **Pavilion at night**
↓ | **Detailed sections attic**

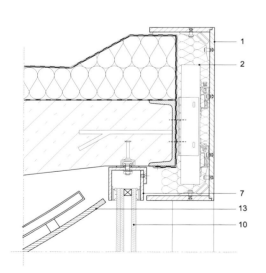

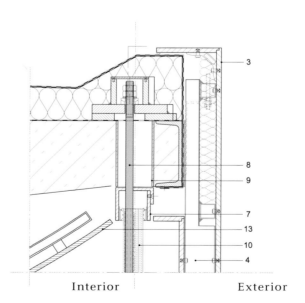

Interior   Exterior

1 cladding attic, 13 mm acrylic
2 curtain wall substructure
3 pilaster: 13 mm acrylic
4 substructure façade pilaster:
    2x aluminum U-profile 70/70 mm
7 above frame profile: aluminum
8 suspension rod: stainless steel
9 square profile stainless steel 25/25/2 mm
10 insulated glazing
13 suspended ceiling: curved gypsum cardboard

↑ | **Detail pilaster strips and glass façade**
↙ | **Detailed sections base**

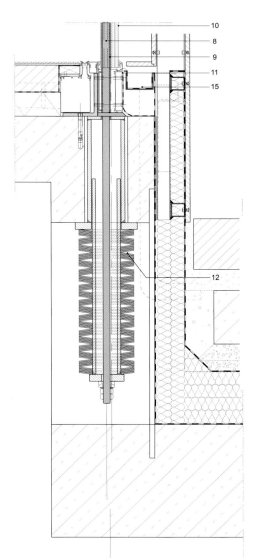

5 base, 13 mm acrylic
6 curtain wall substructure, base
8 suspension rod: stainless steel
9 square profile stainless steel 25/25/2 mm
10 insulated glazing
11 below frame profile: aluminum
12 spring
14 soil air outlet
15 draining channel

↑ | **Street view**

Hard Rock Cafe

Bangkok

The Hard Rock Café manages to reconnect visitors with music and design. By stripping back areas of the former cladding and structure, a two-meter-wide space between the existing building and the property line was created. The new construction occupies this two-meter wide space and the new façade consists of an undulating wall of hundreds of small black fiber cement panels, held in place by narrow horizontal and vertical trusses. The "sound wave" effect results in a curvature of the trusses that appears different depending on where the viewer stands. At times, the new façade reveals the concrete surface of the previously existing chophouse, allowing views of the surface underneath, while at others angles the overall elevation appears as a solid black wall.

CONSTRUCTION FACTS

Structure: refurbishment of existing building structure. **Construction type:** cantilevered steel structure off of existing concrete structure. **Material:** polyurethane-coated fiber cement panels. **Fixing:** steel hanger and frame.

Address: Siam Square Soi 11, Pathumwan, Bangkok, 10330 Thailand. **Client:** Hotel Properties Limited. **Completion:** 2011. **Building type:** restaurant & shop. **Other creatives:** Vichayuth Meenaphant, Pailin Paijitsattaya (façade), Prinda Puranananda (interior), Nopporn Sakulwigitsinthu (lighting), Anon Pairot Studio (product design), Alex Face (artist). **Construction engineer façade:** Montree Sayabovorn.

↑ | **Detail façade with surroundings**
↓ | **Detail drawing façade construction**

↑↑ | **Detail back wall**
↑ | **Detail wooden part**

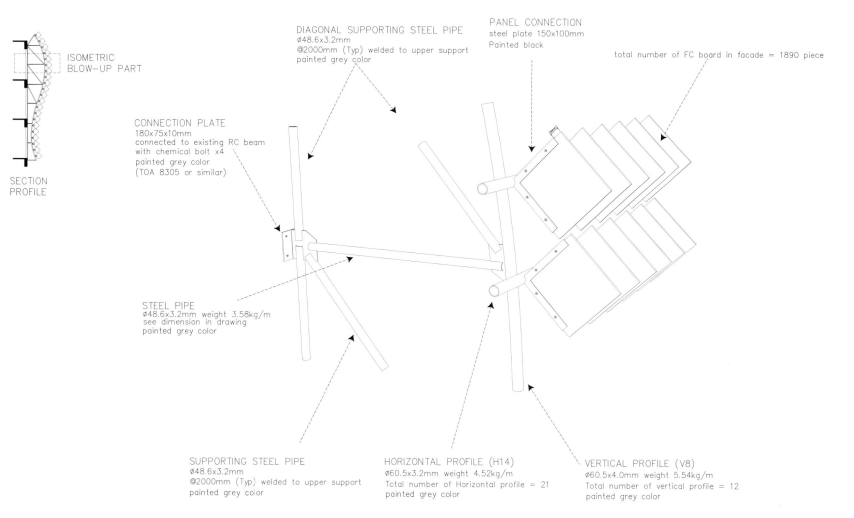

ISOMETRIC
BLOW-UP PART

SECTION
PROFILE

DIAGONAL SUPPORTING STEEL PIPE
ø48.6x3.2mm
@2000mm (Typ) welded to upper support
painted grey color

PANEL CONNECTION
steel plate 150x100mm
Painted black

total number of FC board in facade = 1890 piece

CONNECTION PLATE
180x75x10mm
connected to existing RC beam
with chemical bolt x4
painted grey color
(TOA 8305 or similar)

STEEL PIPE
ø48.6x3.2mm weight 3.58kg/m
see dimension in drawing
painted grey color

SUPPORTING STEEL PIPE
ø48.6x3.2mm
@2000mm (Typ) welded to upper support
painted grey color

HORIZONTAL PROFILE (H14)
ø60.5x3.2mm weight 4.52kg/m
Total number of Horizontal profile = 21
painted grey color

VERTICAL PROFILE (V8)
ø60.5x4.0mm weight 5.54kg/m
Total number of vertical profile = 12
painted grey color

↑ | View from street at night

Star Place

Kaohsiung City

Technically acting as a sun screen and weather barrier, the curved façade is fully glazed and combines the curtain wall glazing with horizontal lamellae and vertical glass fins. The position and size of each façade element are derived from a twisted frame system, which is related to the interior organization of the building. The concave front of the building displays different fluent forms when seen from varying distances and directs the visual field of the customers traveling on the spiraling escalators. Edge-lighting for the vertical glass fins spreads soft colors onto the façade by night. The lighting intensity and color effects are digitally controlled and choreographed.

CONSTRUCTION FACTS
Structure: redevelopment. **Construction type:** curtain wall. **Material:** steel, aluminum, laminated glass. **Fixing:** cast stainless steel clamps. **Insulation:** sun screen. **Special functions:** media façade: lighting effects can be choreographed.

PROJECT FACTS

Address: No.57, Wufu 3rd Road, Cianjin District, Kaohsiung City 801, Taiwan. **Client:** President Group, Kaohsiung, Taiwan. **Completion:** 2008. **Building type:** retail. **Other creatives:** HCF Architects, Planners & Associates (local executive architect), Dynasty Design Corp. **Construction engineer façade:** H&K Associates.

↑ | View towards entrance

↓ | Detail drawings façade

↑ | Interior view elevators and different levels

↓ | Longitudinal section façade

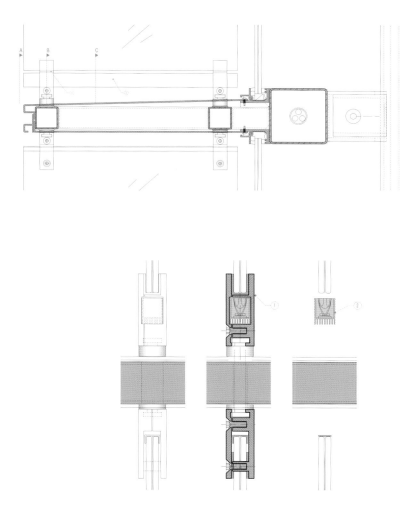

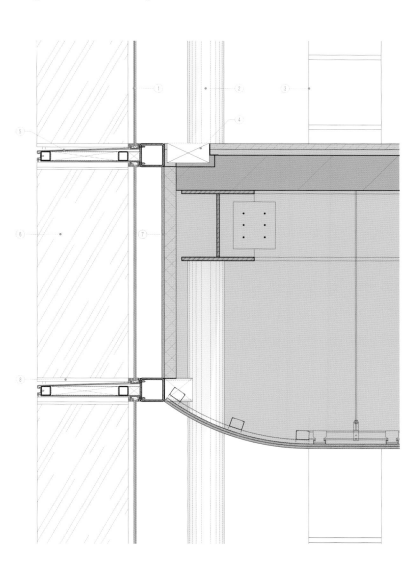

↑ | View from street

Sportalm Flagship Store

Vienna

The two-dimensional framework consists of alveolar stainless steel mesh with occasional reinforcements (closed hollow elements). This structure is statically effective and results in a very limited construction thickness with a façade height of five meters and free arrangement of the closed sections. The flat ceiling shell consists of milled mineral material plates, whose shape smoothly transforms from rounded to angular to achieve a three-dimensional look for the underlying triple glued laminated Corian sheets. this results in patterns of light and shadow that are found more in natural than in constructed contexts: This is the distinguishing façade element constituting a subtle hint of a snowy landscape in reference to the Sportalm Kitzbühel brand.

CONSTRUCTION FACTS

Structure: redevelopment. **Construction type:** curtain wall of glass. **Material:** tilted stainless steel sheets with glass filling and covered with corian. **Fixing:** self-supporting.

Address: Brandstätte 8–10, 1010 Vienna, Austria. **Client:** Sportalm Kitzbühel. **Completion:** 2009. **Building type:** shopping. **Other creatives:** DI Petr Vokal, DI Utko Mutlu, Bernhard Trummer. **Construction engineer façade:** Werkraum Wien.

↑ | **Detail façade**
↓ | **Structural diagram**

↓ | **Detail logo**

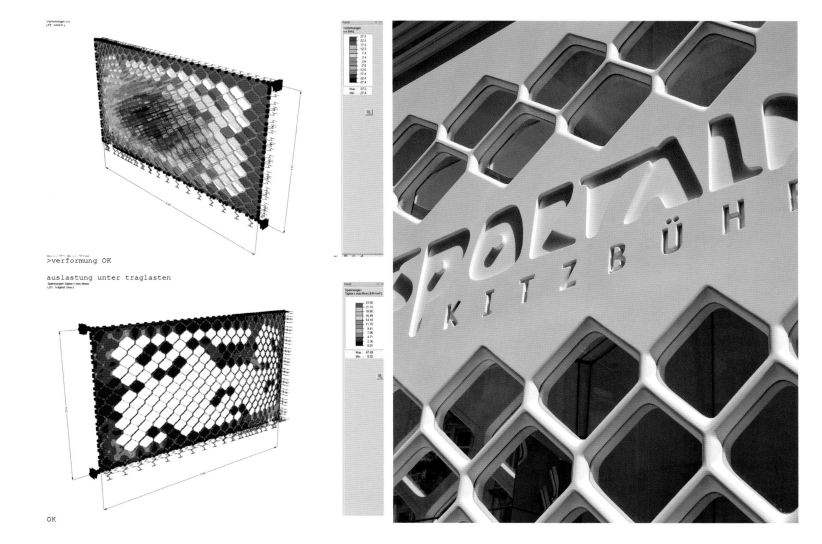

>verformung OK

auslastung unter traglasten

OK

Dietrich | Untertrifaller
Architekten

↑ | Entrance parking garage

Eurospar Vorkloster

Bregenz

A full-length signboard made of perforated copper trapezoidal sheet, large parts of which can be lowered mechanically, unmistakably signals to customers either "closed" or "open." The 100-meter-long structure consists of a single large unit that is distinguished from its neighbors by its clarity. Behind the fine shield which also serves the practical function of shading the glazed southern front, the space is shared by the sales floor and a ground-level covered parking area. Due to the height of the building and the light roof load, the supports of the building are slim and elegant. The Eurospar supermarket is distinguished by an architecturally appealing yet restrained construction style, a clearly laid out floor plan, carefully adjusted proportions and the perforated signboard.

CONSTRUCTION FACTS
Structure: new building. **Construction type:** curtain wall made of copper. **Material:** perforated copper sheets. **Fixing:** on top of metal structure. **Special functions:** permanent sun screen, façade can be mechanically raised and lowered.

Address: Rheinstraße 72, 6900 Bregenz, Austria. **Client:** Real Baubetreuungs- und Beteiligungs GmbH, Salzburg. **Completion:** 2006. **Building type:** shopping.

↑ | View of façade, lowered
↓ | Cross section of the façade

↑ | View of façade, raised
↓ | View of façade with shopping area

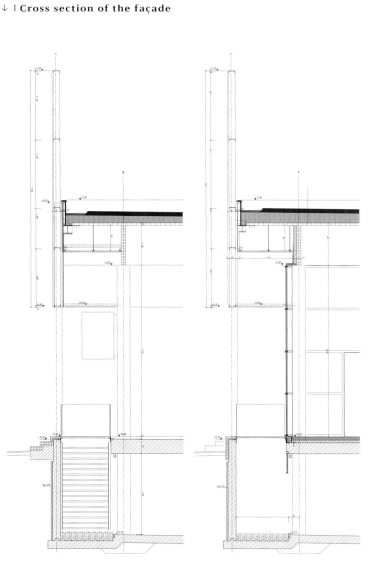

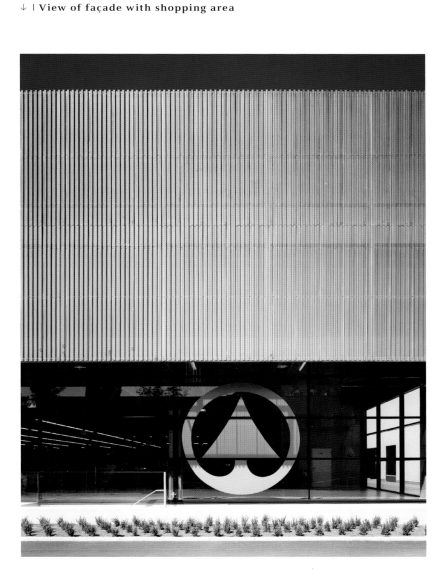

↑ | Illuminated façade

Breuninger Fabric Façade

Stuttgart

The 700-square-meter fabric façade was developed for the Breuninger flagship store to provide the building with a variable look. The timber façade is fitted with a suspended steel tube façade in front above the canopy at a height of about 5 meters. It is anchored to the existing façade structure. A rail system is fitted onto this light-weight construction to guarantee the guiding of the fabric material. The resulting corpus comfortably fits into the strongly recessed façade. The grooves between the fabric structure and the existing building sides underscore the three-dimensional nature of the design, while being in harmony with the building without becoming subordinate to it.

CONSTRUCTION FACTS

Structure: existing building. **Construction type:** curtain wall. **Material:** mesh, PVC. **Fixing:** clamped on substructure. **Special functions:** media façade, changeable, printable.

Address: Marktstraße 1–3, 70173 Stuttgart, Germany. **Client:** E. Breuninger GmbH & Co.. **Completion:** 2005. **Building type:** retail. **Construction engineer façade:** IWB Wörner.

↑ | **Motif bags**
↓ | **Elevation**

↑ | View of the façade with aluminum panels opened

Showroom Kiefer Technic

Bad Gleichenberg

When the façade is closed, light enters the showroom as if through a delicate fabric. This amount of natural light is quite sufficient for the presentation. The room climate is pleasant without consuming additional cooling energy. To open, the light metal panels are folded upwards in the lintel area and downwards in the parapet area, transforming into canopies. This keeps the panoramic view of the undeveloped landscape unobstructed. The 56 pairs of panels can be controlled individually, similar to the art of Origami. Light as paper and silent, within 30 seconds an almost infinite number of façade looks and views can be set. Of course, some particularly attractive positions are preprogrammed and can be initiated with independent movement sequences almost like a movie scene.

CONSTRUCTION FACTS
Structure: new building. **Construction type:** post-and-beam construction with folding elements. **Material:** perforated aluminum panels. **Fixing:** mounting brackets. **Insulation:** thermal insulation. **Special functions:** sun screen.

PROJECT FACTS

Address: Feldbacher Straße 77, 8344 Bad Gleichenberg, Austria. **Client:** Kiefer technic GmbH. **Completion:** 2007. **Building type:** office and showroom. **Construction engineer façade:** Kiefer technic GmbH.

↑ | Aluminum panels closed
↓ | Half closed and half opened panels

↑ | Façade partly opened
↓ | Play of opened and closed panels

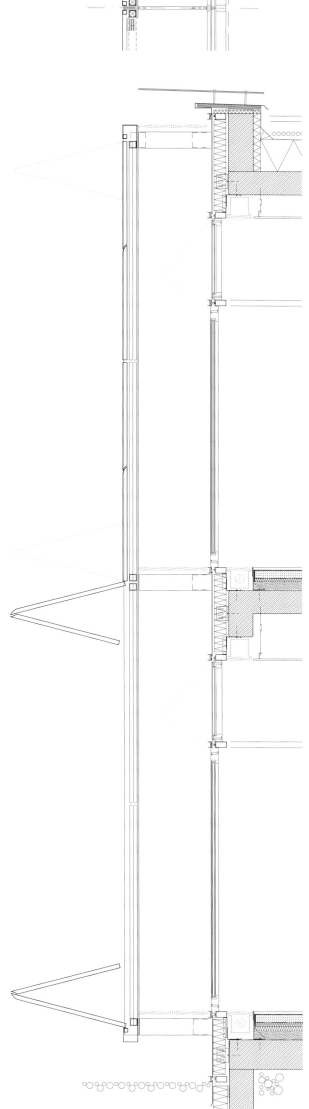

← | Section, façade detail drawing
↑ | Detail aluminum panels
↓ | Section
↓↓ | Ground floor plan

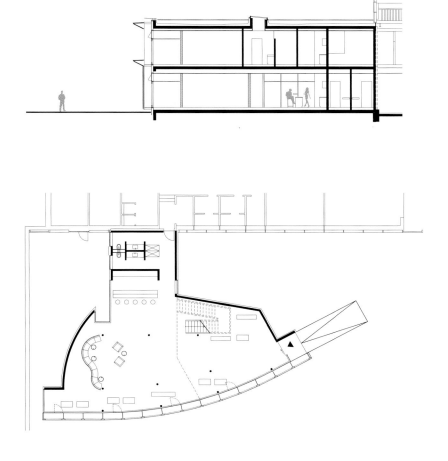

Ben van Berkel / UNStudio

↑ | View from street at night

Galleria Centercity

Choongchungnamdo

A wave-like appearance, which changes with the position of the viewer, is created through two layers of customized aluminum extrusion profiles on top of a back layer of composite aluminum cladding. The vertical profiles of the top layer are straight; but those of the back layer are angled. The lighting design was developed in parallel with the architecture and capitalizes on the double-layered façade structure. The media surface consists of custom-produced fixtures that are integrated within the mullions of the outer façade layer. At the corners of the building the low-resolution media walls fluidly turn into a high-resolution zone, capable of displaying information with more detail.

CONSTRUCTION FACTS
Structure: new building. **Construction type:** double-layered façade. **Material:** aluminum, laminated glass. **Fixing:** customized aluminum triangle profiles. **Insulation:** noise protection, sun screen. **Special functions:** media façade, integrated media walls.

PROJECT FACTS

Address: 521-3 Buldangdong, Seobukgu, Cheonan, Choongchungnamdo, Korea. **Client:** Hanwha Galleria Co. LTD. **Completion:** 2010. **Building type:** retail. **Other creatives:** Gansam Architects & Partners, Seoul, Korea (executive architect/site supervision/landscape architect). **Construction engineer façade:** KBM Co. LTD (consultants).

↑ | Entrance area
↓ | Concept diagram façade

↑ | Detail aluminum structure

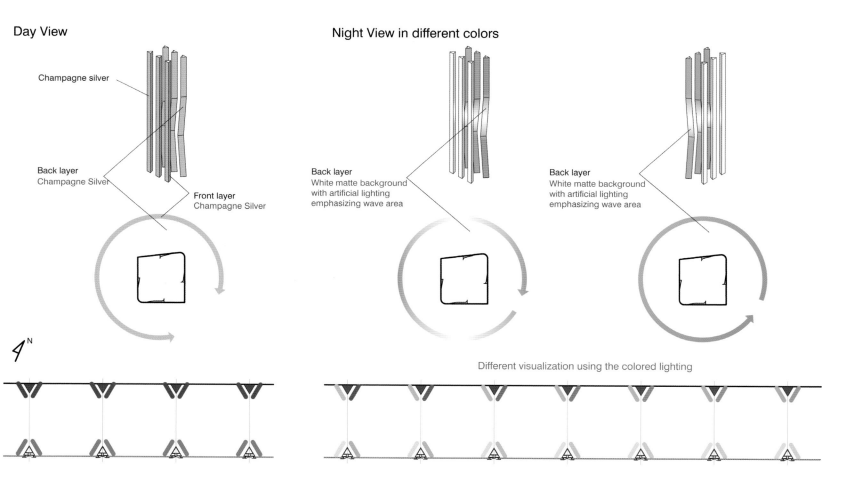

Day View

Champagne silver

Back layer
Champagne Silver

Front layer
Champagne Silver

Night View in different colors

Back layer
White matte background
with artificial lighting
emphasizing wave area

Back layer
White matte background
with artificial lighting
emphasizing wave area

Different visualization using the colored lighting

↑ | Entrance area
→ | The building's façade acts as canvas at night

Greenpix Zero Energy Wall

Beijing

Polycrystalline photovoltaic cells are laminated within the glass of a curtain wall and placed with changing densities on the entire building's skin. GreenPix is a large-scale display comprising 2,292 colored (RGB) LED light points featuring the first photovoltaic system integrated into a glass curtain wall in China. The building performs as a self-sufficient organic system, harvesting solar energy by day and using it to illuminate the screen after dark, mirroring a day's climatic cycle. The very large scale and the characteristic low resolution of the screen enhances the abstract visual qualities, providing an art-specific communication form in contrast to commercial applications of high-resolution screens in conventional media façades. Its "intelligent skin" interacts with the building interior and the outer public spaces using embedded, custom-designed software, transforming the building façade into a responsive environment for entertainment and public engagement.

CONSTRUCTION FACTS
Structure: new building. **Construction type:** curtain wall. **Material:** glass with integrated photovoltaics, LEDs. **Fixing:** punctuated fixing. **Special functions:** media façade generates solar energy by day and displays light installations at night.

PROJECT FACTS

Address: Xicui Road, Beijing, China. **Client:** Jingya Corporation. **Completion:** 2008. **Building type:** entertainment complex. **Lighting and structural advice:** Arup. **Façade design:** Simone Giostra & Partners. **Solar technology R&D:** Schüco International KG, Sunways AG. **Artist in residence:** Jeremy Rotsztain.

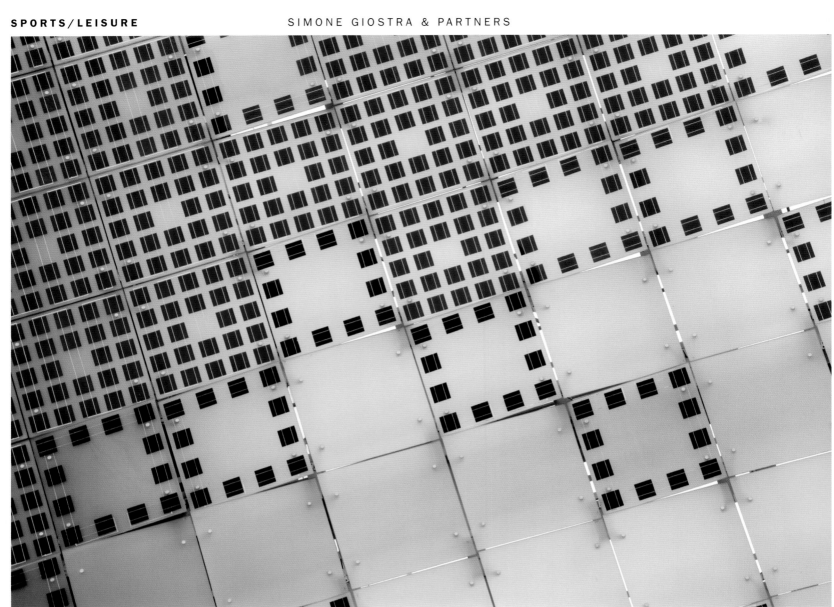

↑ | Detail integrated photovoltaics
↙ | Detail drawing façade element
↓ | Section façade

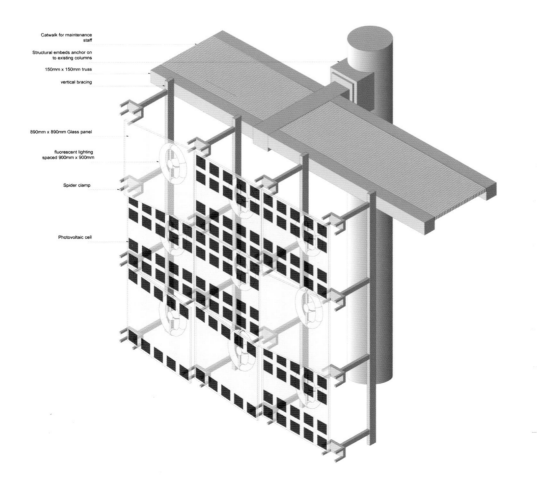

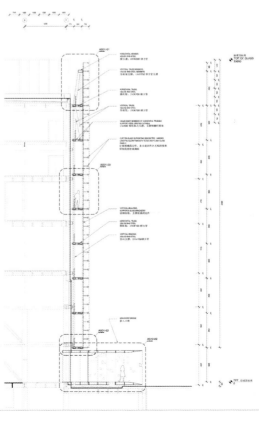

↑ | Media wall at night
↙ | Energy diagram during the day
↓ | Energy diagram at night

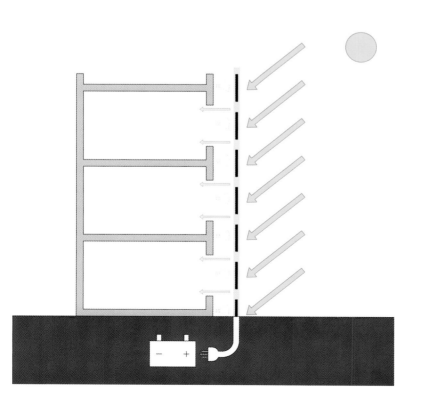

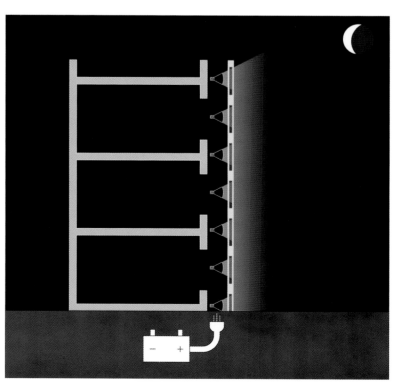

LIKEarchitects

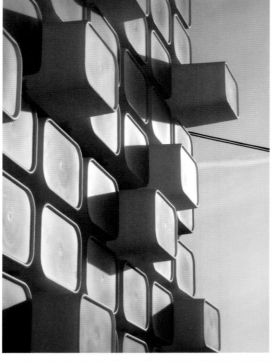

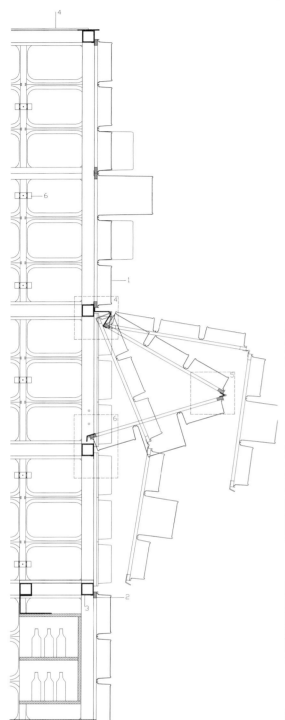

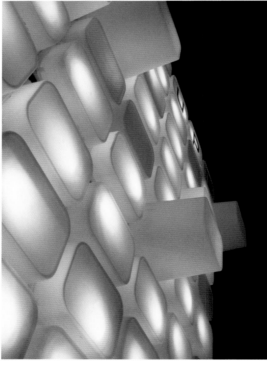

← | Section
↑↖ | Detail plastic boxes by day
↑↑ | Illuminated bar at night
↖ | Detail illuminated boxes
↑ | Bar by day

Temporary Bar

Porto

This bar is a winning entry of an academic competition of the Faculty of Architecture in Oporto. It was built in one week. The design was affected by such issues as budget constraints and short construction duration. Based on Ikea's concept of 'build-it-yourself', the project consists of a modular building made of different depth storage boxes that stands as a visual reference capable of dramatically changing its appearance – by day as white abstract and closed volume; and by night a box of changing light following the DJs. Night after night drinks were sold out in the popular bar.

CONSTRUCTION FACTS
Structure: temporary building. Construction type: system façade elements. Material: plastic boxes. Fixing: punctuated fixing. Special functions: lighting.

PROJECT FACTS
Address: Parque da Cidade, Porto, Portugal. Client: Associação de Estudantes da Faculdade do Porto. Completion: 2008. Building type: temporary construction.

↑↑ | Ski Jump
↑ | Detail façade
↗ | Elevation tower

New Holmenkollen Ski Jump

Oslo

CONSTRUCTION FACTS

Structure: new building. **Construction type:** steel span and cantilever. **Material:** stainless steel mesh. **Fixing:** tension fixing. **Insulation:** wind screen.

The façade is perceived as one continuous band. It begins at the top of the slope and runs alongside the landing hill and the spectator stands, encapsulating the whole arena in a white framing glow. This glowing band serves as a permanent wind screen from the top inrun to the landing hill. The façade at the inrun is lit up from within, between the structure and the glass to create a diffused misty image. From afar the color will melt into one image greatly depending on the seasons of the year and the difference in day and night, but up close a gradient of transparent, translucent and opaque zones will reveal the different depths of the design and construction; a diverged programmatic x-ray.

PROJECT FACTS

Address: Kongeveien 5, 0787 Oslo, Norway. **Client:** Oslo Kommune, Idrettsetaten. **Completion:** 2011. **Building type:** ski jump and stadium. **Other creatives:** Norconsult, Bygganalyse, Grindaker AS, ÅF Hansen & Henneberg Intra, Metallplan. **Construction engineer façade:** Metallplan.

Elliott + Associates
Architects

↑ | West view

Car Park Two at Chesapeake

Oklahoma City

The exterior of the building features staggered metal panels that screen the view of the vehicles but also provide the airflow necessary to make it an open parking structure. The internal ramps and the screening feature establish a harmony between this building and the adjacent structures. The metal panels match details on the adjoining office building, and the brise soleil on the west side of the garage connects to it visually. The horizontal panels vary in size, changing from a width of 15 centimeters at ground level to 30, 60 and 120 centimeters as they rotate around the façade and add texture. While there is no exterior lighting on the building, the glow from the internal lighting permeates the horizontal panels.

CONSTRUCTION FACTS
Structure: new building. **Construction type:** curtain wall. **Material:** staggered metal panels, glass. **Fixing:** part of construction.

Address: 6300 N. Classen Boulevard, Oklahoma City, OK 73118, USA. **Client:** Chesapeake Energy Corporation. **Completion:** 2011. **Building type:** parking. **Other creatives:** Walker Parking Consultants (structural engineering).

↑ | **Detail brise soleil**
↓ | **Façade structure**
↓↓ | **West elevation and section**

↑ | **Brise soleil connection**
↓ | **Detail east elevation**

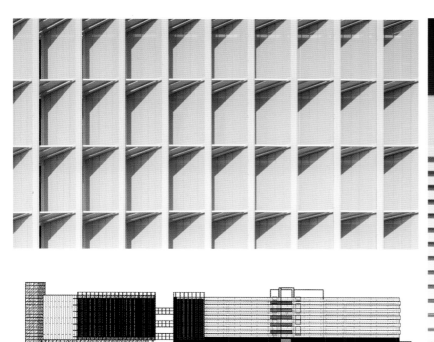

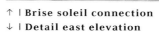

Building 13   Car Park II

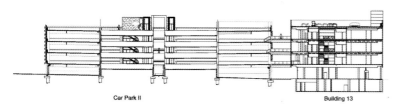

Car Park II   Building 13

Moore Ruble Yudell
Architects & Planners

↑ | Façade on 4th Street

Santa Monica Civic Center Parking Structure

Santa Monica

The design creates a gateway and an easily identifiable landmark for the Santa Monica Civic Center, while affording spectacular views of the Pacific Ocean and the city. Pre-cast white, ribbed concrete panels are set in a rhythmic, variegated pattern on all façades, capturing and enhancing the rich play of shadows provided by the brilliant sunlight while screening the presence of parked cars. A series of bays made of channeled colored glass of varying sizes are set at angles to bring a luminous and ever-changing quality to the building. They are lit up in the evening, appearing like a shimmering curtain to passing pedestrians and motorists. The parking structure is one of the first LEED certified buildings of its kind in the USA.

CONSTRUCTION FACTS

Structure: new building in context. **Construction type:** curtain wall. **Material:** structural metal outriggers, colored laminated glass channels, ribbed pre-cast panels, steel mesh panels. **Fixing:** self-supporting, suspension, structural metal outriggers. **Special functions:** illumination.

Address: 333 Civic Center Drive, Santa Monica, CA 90401, USA. **Client:** City of Santa Monica, California. **Completion:** 2007. **Building type:** public parking. **Other creatives:** International Parking Design (executive architect). **Construction engineer façade:** Woodbridge Glass Inc. (curtain wall installer), Werner Systems (curtain wall engineer).

↑ | Illumination at night
↓ | Detail materials
↓↓ | Diagram sustainability
→ | Section façade

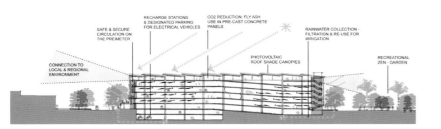

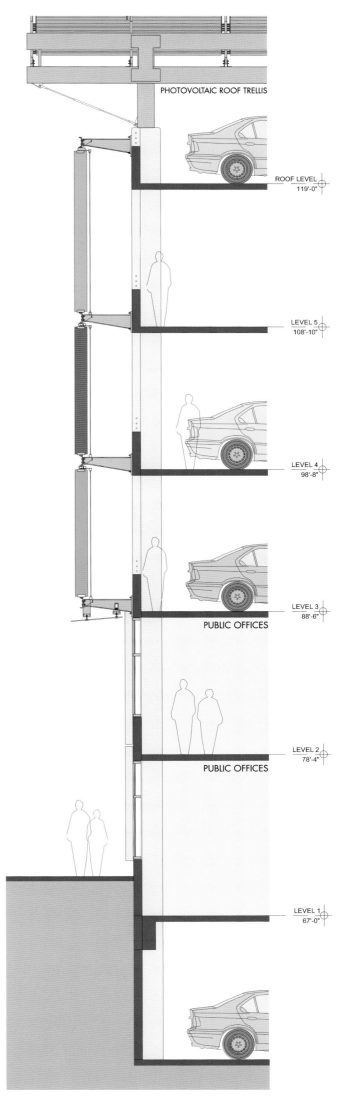

PHOTOVOLTAIC ROOF TRELLIS

ROOF LEVEL
119'-0"

LEVEL 5
108'-10"

LEVEL 4
98'-8"

LEVEL 3
88'-6"

PUBLIC OFFICES

LEVEL 2
78'-4"

PUBLIC OFFICES

LEVEL 1
67'-0"

Inbo

↑ | View from the street

Parking Garage

's Hertogenbosch

The new public parking garage for visitors was designed as a landmark. The free-standing position of the building, big enough to hold some 700 cars, called for a sculptural approach and a dynamic shape that differs from every viewing angle. The solution was found in developing a veil façade, fixed by a substructure at a distance from the main structure, thus making an unpredictable geometry feasible without compromising the efficiency of the primary structure. The striking façade design is based on a repetitive pattern of slanted and shaped panels. The flush-mounting panels create the impression of a polished monolithic volume, while the anodized hue and perforations reveal the wide variety of embedded elements.

CONSTRUCTION FACTS
Structure: new building, solitaire. Construction type: post-and-beam construction, perforated veil façade. Material: galvanized and powder-coated steel. Fixing: flush-mounted with corrosion-free pin-and-slot fittings and anchors. Special functions: natural ventilation through perforation.

Address: Voorplein Jeroen Bosch Ziekenhuis, s'-Hertogenbosch, The Netherlands. **Client:** VOF Wilems-poort. **Completion:** 2011. **Building type:** parking. **Other creatives:** Jaques Prins, Kevin Battarbee, Jaco Troost (team), Har Hollands (lighting designer). **Construction engineer façade:** Pieters Bouwtechniek.

↑ | **Night view**
↓ | **Longitudinal section**

↑ | **Entrance area**
↓ | **Cross section**

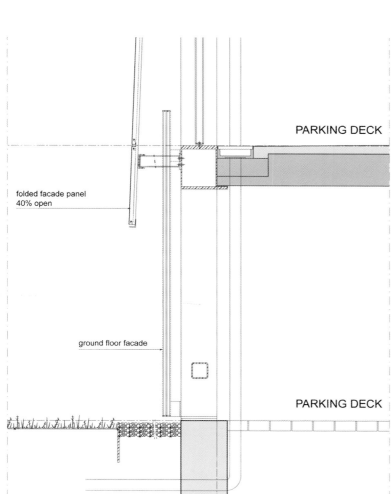

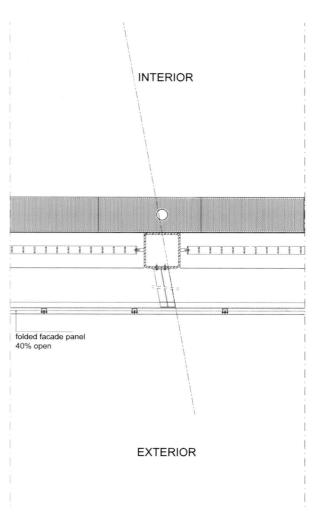

Elliott + Associates Architects

↑ | Detail east façade

Car Park One at Chesapeake

Oklahoma City

The building covers a city block and accommodates 791 vehicles. The façade is a structure of stainless steel mesh. The reflective quality of the mesh allows the surface to "dissolve" into the sky from reflections. The edges disappear and the surface provides a daily report on the weather. During sunset, the western elevation captures the magic moment when the yellow becomes orange and finally becomes purple just before turning black. A unique feature of the exterior is the aluminum outriggers on the east and south elevations. These create changing linear shadows that match the line of the parking stripe hidden inside. To connect the car park to the existing campus across the street the architects incorporated masonry, a clay-fired solar block in a matching color to the campus' king-sized bricks.

CONSTRUCTION FACTS
Structure: new building. **Construction type:** curtain wall. **Material:** woven stainless steel panels. **Fixing:** part of construction.

Address: 6100 N. Western Avenue, Oklahoma City, OK 73118, USA. **Client:** Chesapeake Energy Corporation. **Completion:** 2008. **Building type:** parking. **Other creatives:** Walker Parking Consultants (structural engineering).

↑ | **South side with outrigger array shadows**
↓ | **Section**

↑ | **Detail black mesh panel**
↓ | **Detail structure/mesh**

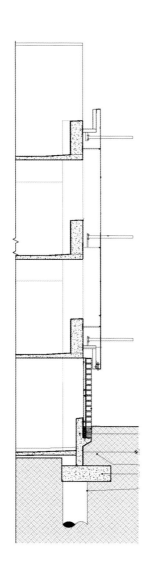

↑ | Entrance and exit

HTCE Parking Lot

Eindhoven

The concrete-covered landscape of this former industrial area has been completely transformed. The campus acts as a social space while cars disappear out of sight into the parking lot. Located at the center of the High Tech Campus Eindhoven, the parking lot provides 1,200 parking spaces and room for 550 bicycles. The construction itself marks the entrance to the campus. The 160-meter façade rises above the main body of the building, increasing the height of the construction in relation to its width. The façade is made out of aluminum sections and suspended glass panels with different colors and transparencies. The aquamarine color of the façade is decorated with fish in a rolling pattern that represents the coming and going of cars.

CONSTRUCTION FACTS
Structure: new building, solitaire. **Construction type:** curtain wall. **Material:** galvanized and powder-coated steel. **Fixing:** punctuated fixing (aluminum structure with glass).

Address: High Tech Campus 1, 5656 AE Eindhoven, The Netherlands. **Client:** Philips Real Estate. **Completion:** 2007. **Building type:** parking. **Other creatives:** Ellen Brouwers atelier voor kunst vormgeving (glass art).

↑ | Side view
↓ | View of printed glass panels on top floor

↑ | Detail aluminum structure

Mei architecten en
stedenbouwers

↑ | View from the street

Gnome Garage Almere

Almere

The development of the Kaboutergarage, a parking garage with 413 parking spaces, is part of the expansion of the city centre of Almere-Buiten. The unique façade of the garage contains natural elements, like integrated plant containers with specific plants related to the orientation of the façade. By using a stretch-forming technique – commonly utilized in the automotive industry – the perforated façade panels show characteristic images of the province of Flevoland, like birds, windmills, garden gnomes, and bird houses. The perforation supplies natural ventilation to the parking garage and creates an open atmosphere, especially at night.

CONSTRUCTION FACTS
Structure: new building. **Construction type:** perforated, ventilated façade. **Material:** perforated stainless steel stretch-formed panels. **Fixing:** punctuated fixing.

Address: Straat van Florida, 1334 PA Almere, The Netherlands. **Client:** Stadsbeheer Gemeente Almere. **Completion:** 2010. **Building type:** parking. **Other creatives:** Robert Winkel, Menno van der Woude, Hennie Dankers, Robert Platje, Pepijn Berghout, Maurice de Ruijter, Nars Broekharst.

↑ | **Detail façade with plant containers**
↓ | **Façade motif**

↑ | **Impression of the façade**
↓ | **View from inside**

itects Index

3deluxe in/exterior

Schwalbacher Straße 74
65183 Wiesbaden (Germany)
T +49.611.9522050
F +49.611.95220522
inexterior@3deluxe.de
www.3deluxe.de

→ 262, 270

4a Architekten GmbH

Hallstraße 25
70376 Stuttgart (Germany)
T +49.711.38930000
F +49.711.389300099
kontakt@4a-architekten.de
www.4a-architekten.de

→ 90

a3lab

Kaiserstraße 68
60330 Frankfurt/Main (Germany)
T +49.69.15612463
mail@a3lab.org
www.a3lab.org

→ 176

adam architekten GbR

Dreimühlenstraße 33
80469 Munich (Germany)
T +49.89.21029430
F +49.89.210294320
info@adam-architekten.de
www.adam-architekten.de

→ 84

ANGELIS & PARTNER, Architekten GbR
Alexis Angelis, Joachim Finke, Onno Folkerts,
Horst Gumprecht

Peterstraße 38
26121 Oldenburg (Germany)
T +49.441.2656541
F +49.441.26550
mail@angelis-partner.de
www.angelis-partner.de

→ 256

Jun Aoki & Associates

107-0062 Tokyo (Japan)
F +81.3.54683821
www.aokijun.com

→ 54

Aranguren & Gallegos

Calle Otero y Delage 118
28035 Madrid (Spain)
T +34.917.341901
F +34.913.160811
arquitectos@arangurengallegos.com
www.arangurengallegos.com

→ 32

Architectkidd

1/6 Soi Pasana 1, Sukhumvit 63
North Prakhanong, Wattana, Bangkok (Thailand)
T +66.2714.3468
F +66.2390.0497
hello@architectkidd.com
www.architectkidd.com

→ 274

Arndt Geiger Herrmann
René Arndt, Thomas Geiger

Mythenquai 355
8038 Zurich (Switzerland)
T +41.44.4886060
F +41.44.4886061
mail@agh.ch
www.agh.ch

→ 158

Baar-Baarenfels Architekten

Rudolfsplatz 6/3
1010 Vienna (Austria)
T +43.1.5329432
F +43.1.5329433
office@baar-baarenfels.com
www.baar-baarenfels.com

→ 278

BIG – Bjarke Ingels Group
Bjarke Ingels, Thomas Christoffersen

Nørrebrogade 66D, 2nd floor
2200 Copenhagen N (Denmark)
T +45.7221.7227
big@big.dk
www.big.dk

→ 167

Architekten BKSP
Grabau Leiber Obermann und Partner

Freundallee 13
30173 Hanover (Germany)
T +49.511.2888203
F +49.511.2888101
info@bksp.de
www.bksp.de

→ 238

C. F. Møller Architects

Europaplads 2
11 8000 Aarhus C (Denmark)
T +45.87.305300
cfmoller@cfmoller.com
www.cfmoller.com

→ 20

Santiago Carroquino architects

Arquitecto de La Figuera 4
50015 Zaragoza (Spain)
T +34.976.526813
F +34.976.526813
info@carroquinoarquitectos.com
www.carroquinoarquitectos.com

→ 75, 76

Chaix & Morel et Associés
Philippe Chaix, Jean-Paul Morel, Remi Nieuwenhove,
Walter Grasmug

16, Rue des Haies
75020 Paris (France)
T +33.1.43706924
F +33.1.43706765
aacma@chaixetmorel.com
www.chaixetmorel.com

→ 124, 230

Claesson Koivisto Rune Architects

Östgötagatan 50
116 64 Stockholm (Sweden)
T +46.8.6445863
F +46.8.6445883
all@ckr.se
www.claessonkoivistorune.se

→ 48

Clavel Arquitectos
Manuel Clavel Rojo

C. Peligros, nº3, 3ºA
30001 Murcia (Spain)
T +34.968.212314
F +34.968.970119
clavel-arquitectos@clavel-arquitectos.com
www.clavel-arquitectos.com

→ 52

CODE UNIQUE Architekten BDA

Katharinenstraße 5
01099 Dresden (Germany)
T +49.351.8107880
F +49.351.81078825
contact@codeunique.de
www.codeunique.de

→ 44

Coop Himmelb(l)au
Wolf D. Prix / W. Dreibholz & Partner ZT GmbH

Spengergasse 37
1050 Vienna (Austria)
T +43.1.546600
F +43.1.54660600
office@coop-himmelblau.at
www.coop-himmelblau.at

→ 56

Mario Cucinella Architects Srl

via Matteotti 21
40129 Bologna (Italy)
T +39.051.6313381
F +39.051.6313316
mca@mcarchitects.it
www.mcarchitectsgate.it

→ 58

Dietrich | Untertrifaller Architekten ZT GmbH

Arlbergstraße 117
6900 Bregenz (Austria)
T +43.6991.788880
F +43.5574.7888820
arch@dietrich.untertrifaller.com
www.dietrich.untertrifaller.com

→ 280

dIONISO LAB
José Cadilhe

T +351.966.418823
mail@dionisolab.com
www.dionisolab.com

→ 132

DITTEL | ARCHITEKTEN
Frank Dittel

Rotenwaldstraße 100/1
70197 Stuttgart (Germany)
T +49.711.46906550
F +49.711.46906551
info@d-arch.de
www.d-arch.de

→ 282

Ehrlich Architects

10865 Washington Boulevard
Culver City, CA 90232 (USA)
T +1.310.8389700
F +1.310.8389737
info@ehrlicharchitects.com
www.ehrlicharchitects.com

→ 70

Elliott + Associates Architects

35 Harrison Avenue
Oklahoma City, OK 73104 (USA)
T +1.405.2329554
F +1.405.2329997
design@e-a-a.com
www.e-a-a.com

→ 296, 302

Enota

Poljanska cesta 6
1000 Ljubljana (Slovenia)
T +386.438.6740
F +386.438.6745
enota@enota.si
www.enota.si

→ 127, 150, 266

estudio.entresitio

Gran Vía 33
28013 Madrid (Spain)
T +34.91.7010330
F +34.91.7010331
estudio@entresitio.com
www.entresitio.com

→ 66

Farshid Moussavi Architecture

66 Warwick Square
London, SW1V 2AP (United Kingdom)
T +44.20.70336490
office@farshidmoussavi.com
www.farshidmoussavi.com

→ 258

Faulders Studio
Thom Faulders

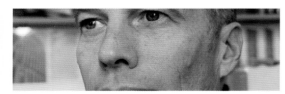

1571 Ninth Street
Berkeley, CA 94710 (USA)
T +1.510.6930013
info@faulders-studio.com
www.faulders-studio.com

→ 182

fischer berkhan architekten
Markus Fischer, Julia Berkhan

Stavanger Straße 21
10439 Berlin (Germany)
T +49.30.25358098
F +49.30.25358099
info@fischer-berkhan.de
www.fischer-berkhan.de

→ 138

Fránek Architects

Kamenná 13
639 00 Brno (Czech Republic)
T +420.725.392238
franek.arch@email.cz
www.franekarchitects.cz

→ 21

FXFowle Architects

22 West 19th Street
New York, NY 10011 (USA)
T +1.212.6271700
F +1.212.4638716
info@fxfowle.com
www.fxfowle.com

→ 250

Massimiliano and Doriana Fuksas

Piazza del Monte di Pieta', 30
00186 Rome (Italy)
T +39.06.68807871
F +39.06.68807872
office@fuksas.com
www.fuksas.it

→ 12

GATERMANN + SCHOSSIG,
Architekten Generalplaner

Richartzstraße 10
50667 Cologne (Germany)
T +49.221.9258210
F +49.221.92582170
info@gatermann-schossig.de
www.gatermann-schossig.de

→ 218, 236, 244

Manuelle Gautrand Architecture

36, Boulevard de la Bastille
75003 Paris (France)
T + 33.156.950646
contact@manuelle-gautrand.com
www.manuelle-gautrand.com

→ 14, 206

Gewers & Pudewill
architects designers engineers
Georg Gewers, Henry Pudewill

Schlesische Straße 27
10997 Berlin (Germany)
T +49.30.69598800
F +49.30.695988015
info@gewers-pudewill.com
www.gewers-pudewill.com

→ 154

Ernst Giselbrecht + Partner
Architektur ZT GmbH

Brockmanngasse 48
8010 Graz (Austria)
T +43.316.817050
F +43.316.8170509
office@giselbrecht.at
www.giselbrecht.at

→ 284

GKS Architekten+Partner AG

Winkelriedstrasse 56
6003 Luzern (Switzerland)
T +41.41.2499999
F +41.41.2499998
mail@gks.ch
www.gks.ch

→ 170

Gravalos Di Monte architects

c/ San Vicente de Paúl 4 pral. izda.
50001 Zaragoza (Spain)
T +34.976.296692
gravalosdimonte@terra.es
www.gravalosdimonte.wordpress.com

→ 75

Group A

Pelgrimsstraat 3
3029 BH, Rotterdam (The Netherlands)
T +31.10.2440193
F +31.10.2449990
mail@groupa.nl
www.groupa.nl,
www.groupalive.com

→ 110

Halle 58 Architekten

Marzilistrasse 8a
3008 Bern (Switzerland)
T +41.31.3021030
F +41.31.30219889
info@halle58.ch
www.halle58.ch

→ 122

hammeskrause architekten
freie architekten bda

Krefelder Straße 32
70376 Stuttgart (Germany)
T +49.711.6017480
F +49.711.60174850
info@hammeskrause.de
www.hammeskrause.de

→ 94

Ferdinand Heide Architekt BDA

Leinwebergasse 4
60386 Frankfurt/Main (Germany)
T +49.69.4208270
F +49.69.42082729
info@ferdinand-heide.de
www.ferdinand-heide.de

→ 92

Henning Larsen Architects

Vesterbrogade 76
1620 Copenhagen V (Denmark)
T +45.8233.3000
F +45.8233.3099
mail@henninglarsen.com
www.henninglarsen.com

→ 36

HPP Architects
HPP Hentrich-Petschnigg & Partner GmbH + Co. KG

Kaistraße 5
40221 Dusseldorf (Germany)
T +49.211.83840
F +49.211.8384185
duesseldorf@hpp.com
www.hpp.com

→ 16

Inbo

Postbus 57
3930 EB Woudenberg (The Netherlands)
T +31.33.2868211
info@inbo.com
www.inbo.com

→ 300, 304

INNOCAD Architektur ZT GmbH

Grazbachgasse 65a
8010 Graz (Austria)
T +43.316.7103240
F +43.316.71032418
office@innocad.at
www.innocad.at

→ 168

J. MAYER H. Architects

Bleibtreustraße 54
10623 Berlin (Germany)
T +49.30.644907700
F +49.30.644907711
contact@jmayerh.de
www.jmayerh.de

→ 194, 242

Jackson Clements Burrows
Pty Ltd Architects
Tim Jackson, Jon Clements, Graham Burrows

One Harwood Place
Melbourne VIC 3000 (Australia)
T +61.3.96546227
F +61.3.96546195
jacksonclementsburrows@jcba.com.au
www.jcba.com.au

→ 144

Jakob + MacFarlane Architects

13–15 rue des petites écuries
75010, Paris (France)
T +33.1.44790572
F +33.1.48009793
info@jakobmacfarlane.com
www.jakobmacfarlane.com

→ 184

Jarmund/Vigsnæs AS Architects MNAL
Einar Jarmund, Håkon Vigsnæs, Alessandra Kosberg

Hausmanns gate 6
0186 Oslo (Norway)
T +47.22.994343
F +47.22.994353
jva@jva.no
www.jva.no

→ 102

JDS / Julien De Smedt Architects

Vesterbrogade 69D
1620 Copenhagen (Denmark)
T +45.3378.1010
F +45.3378.1029
office@jdsa.eu
www.jdsa.eu

→ 295

Jestico + Whiles

1 Cobourg Street
London NW1 2HP (United Kingdom)
T +44.207.3800382
jw@jesticowhiles.com
www.jesticowhiles.com

→ 116, 134

Jo. Franzke Architekten

Ludwigstraße 2–4
60329 Frankfurt/Main (Germany)
T +49.69.1381200
F +49.69.13812029
info@jofranzke.de
www.jofranzke.de

→ 152

JSWD Architekten
Frederik Jaspert, Konstantin Jaspert, Jürgen Steffens, Olaf Drehsen

Maternusplatz 11
50996 Cologne (Germany)
T +49.221.9355500
F +49.221.93555055
info@jswd-architekten.de
www.jswd-architekten.de

→ 62, 124, 230

Just/Burgeff Architekten GmbH

Kaiserstraße 68
60329 Frankfurt/Main (Germany)
T +49.69.60607320
F +49.69.60607510
mail@just.burgeff.de
www.just.burgeff.de

→ 176

klab Architecture
Konstantinos Labrinopoulos

2 Achaiou str. Kolonaki
106-75 Athens (Greece)
T +30.210.3211139
F +30.210.3211155
info@klab.gr
www.klab.gr

→ 264

Klaiber+Oettle, Architekten und Ingenieure

Kornhausstraße 14
73525 Schwäbisch Gmünd (Germany)
T +49.7171.997920
F +49.7171.9979229
mail@klaiberundoettle.de
www.klaiberundoettle.de

→ 46

Holger Kleine Architekten

Lobeckstraße 30
10969 Berlin (Germany)
T +49.30.322970432
info@kleinemetzarchitekten.de
www.kleinemetzarchitekten.de

→ 198

knerer und lang Architekten GmbH
Prof.-Ing. Thomas Knerer, Dipl.-Ing. Eva-Maria Lang

Werner-Hartmann-Straße 6
01099 Dresden (Germany)
T +49.351.8044000
F +49.351.8024173
architektur@knererlang.de
www.knererlang.de

→ 96

Arhitektura Jure Kotnik

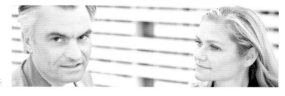

Dobja vas 127
2390 Ravnena Koroškem(Slovenia)
T +386.41.340963
info@jurekotnik.com
www.jurekotnik.com

→ 68, 74

LAb[au], laboratory for architecture and urbanism

104 Lakensestraat
1000 Brussels (Belgium)
T +32.2.2196555
F +32.2.2196555
lab-au@lab-au.com
www.lab-au.com

→ 224, 235

Leuppi & Schafroth Architekten AG

Zurlindenstrasse 134
8003 Zurich (Switzerland)
T +41.44.4504400
F +41.44.4504707
info@leuppischafroth.ch
www.leuppischafroth.ch

→ 22

LIKEarchitects
Teresa Otto, Diogo Aguiar

info@likearchitects.com
www.likearchitects.com

→ 294

MAD

3rd floor West Tower, no.7 Banqiao Nanxiang,
Beixinqiao Beijing, 100007 (China)
T +86.10.64026632
F +86.10.64023940
office@i-mad.com
www.i-mad.com

→ 42

+ arquitectos

Av. Providencia 2318, Of. 44
Providencia, Santiago (Chile)
T +56.2.2331323
F +56.2.3218802
correo@masarquitectos.cl
www.masarquitectos.cl

→ 234

Renato & Reto Maurizio

Cad Castell
7516 Maloja (Switzerland)
T +41.81.8382010
F +41.81.8382011
info@studiomaurizio.ch
www.studiomaurizio.ch

→ 248

Mei Architecten en stedenbouwers
Robert Winkel

Schiehavenkade 202
3024 EZ Rotterdam (The Netherlands)
+31.10.4252222
info@mei-arch.nl
www.mei-arch.nl

→ 160, 306

Dirk Melzer Landschaftsarchitekt & Umweltingenieur

Marktplatz 15
56349 Kaub (Germany)
T +49.6774.8239
F +49.6774.8163
mail@dirk-melzer.de
www.dirk-melzer.de

→ 108

Mestura Architects
Humbert Costas, Manuel Gómez, Jaime Blanco,
Carlos Durán, Josep M. Estapè

Calle Valencia 287 1º 1ª
08009 Barcelona (Spain)
T +34.93.4578072
F +34.93.4573207
mestura@mestura.es
www.mestura.com

→ 72

Miniwiz Co. Ltd.

14F No.102 Guang Fu South Rd.
Da An District, Taipei 106, R.O.C. (Taiwan)
T +886.(2).27310502
F +886.(2).27310512
contact@miniwiz.com
www.miniwiz.com

→ 49

Moore Ruble Yudell Architects & Planners

933 Pico Boulevard
Santa Monica, CA 90405 (USA)
T +1.310.4501400
F +1.310.4501403
info@mryarchitects.com
www.mryarchitects.com

→ 298

MVRDV

Dunantstraat 10
3002 JC, Rotterdam (The Netherlands)
T +31.10.4772860
F +31.10.4773627
office@mvrdv.nl
www.mvrdv.nl

→ 174

Nalbach + Nalbach Architekten
Hon.Prof. Johanne Nalbach

Rheinstraße 45
12161 Berlin (Germany)
T +49.30.8590830
F +49.30.8511210
buero@nalbach-architekten.de
www.nalbach-architekten.de

→ 172

Neutelings Riedijk Architects

P.O. Box 527
3000 AM Rotterdam (The Netherlands)
T +31.10.4046677
F +31.10.4142712
info@neutelings-riedijk.com
www.neutelings-riedijk.com

→ 27, 166

Nickl & Partner Architekten AG

Lindberghstraße 19
80939 Munich (Germany)
T +49.89.3605140
F +49.89.36051499
mail@nickl-architekten.de
www.nickl-architekten.de

→ 78, 104

NORD

3 Aird's Lane
Glasgow G15HU (United Kingdom)
T +44.141.5529996
glasgow@nordarchitecture.com
www.nordarchitecture.com

→ 111

Ateliers Jean Nouvel

10, cité d'Angoulême
75011 Paris (France)
T +33.1.49238383
F +33.1.43148110
info@jeannouvel.fr
www.jeannouvel.com

→ 40, 136

Petzinka Pink Architekten

Thomas Pink

Cecilienallee 17
40474 Dusseldorf (Germany)
T +49.211.4787142
F +49.211.4787110
info@petzinka-pink.de
www.petzinka-pink.de

→ 190, 202, 216

Progress Eco

Dobrów 7
28-142 Tuczępy (Poland)
T +48 15 864 62 70
F +48.15.8646278
arch@progressarch.com
www.progressarch.com

→ 268

Promontorio

R. Fabrica Material de Guerra, 10
CP1950-128 Lisbon (Portugal)
T +351.218.620970
F +351.218.620971
ana@promontorio.net
www.promontorio.net

→ 28

Sanjay Puri

20 Famous Studio Lane, Off. Dr. E.Moses Road
Mahalaxmi, Mumbai 400011 (India)
T +91.22.24965840
F +91.22.24965896
spstudio@sanjaypuri.in
www.sanjaypuriarchitects.com

→ 135

RARE Architecture

Studio 110, 10 Great Russell Street
London WC1B 3BQ (United Kingdom)
T +44.20.32399332
mail@r-are.net
www.r-are.net

→ 140

René van Zuuk Architekten bv

De Fantasie 9
1324 HZ Almere (The Netherlands)
T +31.36.5379139
info@renevanzuuk.nl
www.renevanzuuk.nl

→ 148

Renzo Piano Building Workshop

Via P.P. Rubens, 29
16158 Genova (Italy)
T +39.10.61711
F +39.10.6171350
italy@rpbw.com
www.rpbw.com

→ 180, 250

Architectenbureau Marlies Rohmer

Postbus 2935
1000 CX Amsterdam (The Netherlands)
T +31.20.4190086
F +31.20.4190096
info@rohmer.nl
www.rohmer.nl

→ 82

SALTO Architects

Kalaranna 6
10415 Tallinn (Estonia)
T +372.6.825222
info@salto.ee
www.salto.ee

→ 50

Philippe Samyn and Partners sprl, architects & engineer

Chaussée de Waterloo, 1537
1180 Brussels (Belgium)
T +32.2.3749060
F +32.2.3747550
sai@samynandpartners.be
www.samynandpartners.be

→ **196, 208**

schmidt hammer lassen architects

Åboulevarden 37, Postboks 5117
8000 Aarhus C (Denmark)
T +45.86.201900
F +45.86.184513
info@shl.dk
www.shl.dk

→ **226**

Schmucker und Partner Planungsgesellschaft mbH

P3, 14 Planken
68161 Mannheim (Germany)
T +49.621.1070272
F +49.621.1070248
schmucker@schmucker-partner.de
www.schmucker-partner.de

→ **64**

Schulz & Schulz Architekten GmbH

Lampestraße 6
04107 Leipzig (Germany)
T +49.341.487130
F +49.341.4871345
schulz@schulzarchitekten.de
www.schulz-und-schulz.com

→ **100**

Shim Sutcliffe Architects Inc.
Brigitte Shim, Howard Sutcliffe

441 Queen Street East
Toronto, Ontario M5A 1T5 (Canada)
T +1.416.3683892
F +1.416.3689468
studio@shimsut.com
www.shim-sutcliffe.com

→ **126, 145**

Simone Giostra & Partners

55 Washington Street, Suite 454
New York, NY 11201 (USA)
T +1.212.9208180
F +1.212.9208180
info@sgp-architects.com
www.sgp-architects.com

→ **290**

Prof. Han Slawik Architekt

Fischerstraße 1-A
30167 Hanover (Germany)
T +49.511.1696101
F +49.511.1696102
mail@slawik.net
www.slawik.net

→ **214**

Soeters Van Eldonk architecten BV

Postbus 15550
1001 NB Amsterdam (The Netherlands)
T +31.20.6242939
F +31.20.6246928
arch@soetersvaneldonk.nl
www.soetersvaneldonk.nl

→ **26**

SPEECH Tchoban/Kuznetsov
Sergey Tchoban, Sergey Kuznetsov

Krasnoproletarskaya ulitsa, 16
Moscow, 127473 (Russia)
T +7.495.7417893
F +7.495.7417892
info@speech.su
www.speech.su

→ **114, 188**

Squire and Partners

77 Wicklow Street
London, WC1X 9JY (United Kingdom)
T +44.20.72785555
F +44.20.72390495
info@squireandpartners.com
www.squireandpartners.com

→ **225**

Studio Bellecour architectes

4, boulevard de Strasbourg
75010 Paris (France)
T +33.1.40400707
F +33.1.40400788
contact@studiobellecour.com
www.studiobellecour.com

→ **210**

Studio M
Hajime Masubuchi

1-23-1-C Kitamagome Ota-ku
Tokyo, 143-0021 (Japan)
T +81.3.57188017
masubuchi@s-t-m.jp
www.s-t-m.jp

→ **182**

Tham & Videgård Arkitekter

Blekingegatan 46
116 62 Stockholm (Sweden)
T +46.08.7020046
info@tvark.se
www.tvark.se

→ **24**

Patrick T I G H E Architecture

1632 Ocean Park Blvd
Santa Monica, CA 90405 (USA)
T +1.310.4508823
F +1.310.4508273
info@tighearchitecture.com
www.tighearchitecture.com

→ 162

Toyo Ito & Associates, Architects

Fujiya Bldg., 1-19-4,Shibuya
Shibuya-ku, Tokyo, 150-0002 (Japan)
T +81.3.34095822
F +81.3.34095969
www.toyo-ito.co.jp

→ 120

U. D. A. Arquitectos

Ronda General Mitre 13
Barcelona 08017 (Spain)

→ 120

UNStudio
Ben van Berkel

Stadhouderskade 113
1073 AX Amsterdam (The Netherlands)
T +31.20.5702040
F +31.20.5702041
info@unstudio.com
www.unstudio.com

→ 276, 288

v-architekten gmbh

Huhnsgasse 42
50676 Cologne (Germany)
T +49.221.6699930
F +49.221.66999333
mail@v-architekten.com
www.v-architekten.com

→ 108

Vaíllo & Irigaray

Antonio Vaíllo i Daniel, Juan L. Irigaray

Huartec/Tafalla 31 Bajo
31003 Pamplona (Spain)
T +34.948.290054
F +34.948.290303
estudio@vailloirigaray.com
www.vailloirigaray.com

→ 80, 112, 128, 164

Valode & Pistre architectes

115, rue du Bac
75007 Paris (France)
T +33.1.53632200
F +33.1.53632209
info@v-p.com
www.v-p.com

→ 222

Vicens + Ramos

Ignacio Vicens y Hualde, José Antonio Ramos Abengózar

C/ Barquillo No. 29
28004 Madrid (Spain)
T +34.915.210004
info@vicens-ramos.com
www.vicens-ramos.com

→ 30

Wingårdh Arkitektkontor AB

Kungsgatan 10A
41119 Gothenburg (Sweden)
T +46.31.7437000
F +46.31.7119838
wingardhs@wingardhs.se
www.wingardhs.se

→ 254

Zechner & Zechner ZT GmbH

Martin Zechner, Christoph Zechner

Stumpergasse 14/23
1060 Vienna (Austria)
T +43.1.59703360
F +43.1.597033699
email@zechner.com
www.zechner.com

→ 146

Zinterl Architekten ZT GmbH

St. Georgengasse 1
8020 Graz (Austria)
T +43.316.720242
F +43.316.72024210
office@zinterl.at
www.zinterl.at

→ 86

3deluxe — 262 (portrait), 263, 270
Hervé Abbadie — 125
Diogo Aguiar — 294 a.l.
Daici Ano — 54–55
Art Grey Photography — 162–163
Michael Bader — 44–45
Sue Barr — 140, 142, 143 a.
Geordie Barrie — 225 (portrait)
Vincent Basler — 148 (portrait)
Beeidsmaak Fotografie — 205 (portrait), 300 (portrait)
Boris Beja — 68 (portrait), 74 (portrait)
Adolf Bereuter — 280 (portrait)
Michael Berkhan — 138
Helene Binet — 259, 260
Christine Blaser — 122–123
Sarah Blee — 27
Marco Boella — 295
Nicolas Borel — 185–186, 187 l., 211, 213 a.
courtesy of Breuninger, Stuttgart — 282–283
Ivan Brodey — 102–103
Lene Brüggemeier — 214 (portrait)
Lluis Casals — 76–77
Antonin Chaix — 124
Calvin Chua — 141, 143 b.
Claesson Koivista Rune — 48 a.r., 48 m.
COOP HIMMELB(L)AU — 57 m.r., 57 b.
Tim Crocker — 116–119
Emma Cross — 144
Jose Manuel Cutillas — 112–113, 128–131, 164–165
Conné van d'Grachten — 95 a.l.
Michel Denancé — 180–181, 222, 223 b.r., 250–253
Digidaan — 110
Daniele Domenicali — 58–61
James Dow — 145
Eberle&Eisfeld — 155, 157
HG Esch — 94, 95 a.r., 244–247
Torben Eskerod — 20
Clemens Fabry — 56 (portrait)
Faulders Studio — 183 a.
Fellenberg — 242, 243 a.
Vincent Fillon — 15 a., 206–207
Foto und Bilderwerk Oldenburg — 256 (portrait)
David Franck — 194–195
Roger Frei — 22, 23 b.
Frener + Reifer, Günter Wett — 232
Vera Friedrich — 152 (portrait)
Brigitte Friedrichs — 62 (portrait)
David Frutos — 52–53
Philip Gaedke — 65 a.
Gamma — 14 (portrait), 206 (portrait)
Giancarlo Gardin — 248–249
Denis Gliksman — 210 (portrait)
Jesus Granada — 32–35, 75
Fernando Guerra — 132–133
Roland Halbe/arturimages — 66–67, 136–137, 184, 187 r.

Thilo Härdtlein — 146–147
Ester Havlova — 21 m.l.
DJ Hoogerdijk — 149 a.l.
Inbo — 301 a.l., 305 a.r.
Inbo/Sonia Arrepia — 300, 301 a.r., 305 a.l.
Ingenieurbüro Franke, Glienicke — 217 b.
Michael Ives — 296 (portrait), 302 (portrait)
Quentin Jeandel — 210, 212
Peter Jeffree — 258
Hanns Joosten — 198–201
Jose Santos Julião — 28–29
Reiner Kaltenbach — 18, 19 a.
Miran Kambič — 68–69, 74, 127, 150–151, 266–267
Guido Kasper — 90–91
Taufik Kenan, Berlin — 190–193, 216–217
Jens Kirchner — 17, 19 b.
Bruno Klomfar — 280–281
Felix Krumbholz — 62, 63 m., 63 b.
La Fibre Comm. — 197 a.r.
Andrew Lee — 111 l.
Nic Lehoux — 36–39
Max Lerouge — 14
Thomas Lewandowski — 63 a.
Patrick Lindell — 48 a.l.
John Linden — 298, 299
Jens Lindhe — 167
Åke E:son Lindman — 24–25, 254–255
Lindner Group KG — 204 b., 205 b.r.
Karli Luik — 51 a.l.
Moreno Maggi — 13
Olaf Mahlstedt — 256–257
Duccio Malagamba — 56–57
Maurizio Marcato — 12 (portrait)
Robert Marksteiner — 146 (portrait)
mawpix — 47 m.
Scott McDonald — 296–297, 302–303
MEW — 20 (portrait)
Constantin Meyer — 108–109
Satoru Mishima — 261
moderne stadt — 218, 221 a.
Ricky Molloy — 226 (portrait)
Adam Mørk — 226–229
R. Mosler — 214–215
Stefan Müller-Naumann — 78–79, 84–85, 100–101, 104–107
Stefan Müller — 172–173
Jeroen Musch — 160–161, 306–307
Alexei Naroditsky — 223 a.
Sandro Neto — 294 a.r., b.
James Newton — 134
Akzo Nobel — 82–83
João Ó — 294 (portrait)
Mikael Olsson — 24 (portrait)
Olympic Delivery Authority, London — 111 r.
Paul Ott — 86–89, 168–169, 284–287

Erik-Jan Ouwerkerk — 100 (portrait)
Pedro Pegenaute — 72–73
Marie-Françoise Plissart — 196, 197 a.l., 208–209
Inga Powilleit — 276 (portrait), 288 (portrait)
Daniel Priester — 139
Will Pryce — 225
Emanuel Raab — 262, 263 a.r., 271–273
Jesper Ray — 254 (portrait)
Rainer Rehfeld — 236, 237 b.l.
Christoph Reichelt — 96 (portrait)
Sebastian Reuter — 154, 156
Ralph Richter — 16
Christian Richters — 276, 277, 288, 231, 233 a.
Tomas Riehle, Bergisch-Gladbach — 202–205
Nikkol Roth, Holcim — 194 (portrait), 242 (portrait)
Mark Röthlisberger, Building Dept. Canton Zurich — 23 a.
Philippe Ruault — 12, 15 b., 40–41, 174–175
Piia Ruber — 50
Daria Scagliola, Stijn Brakkee — 26, 166
Schraubverschluss — 243 b.
ShuHe, courtesy of MAD — 42–43
Martin Siplane — 50, 51 a.r., 51 m.
Eibe Sönnecken — 176–179
SPEECH — 114–115, 188–189
Lupi Spuma — 284
Staatliches Bauamt Regensburg — 92
Christian Steinmetz — 16 (portrait)
Studio Bellecour — 213 b.
Studio M/Faulders Studio — 182, 183 b.
Studio Petrohrad — 21 a.l., m.r.
SVein — 36 (portrait)
Ingmar Timmer — 26 (portrait)
Bill Timmerman — 70–71
Yoshiaki Tsutsui — 54 (portrait)
Jean-Luc Valentin — 152–153
Chris van Uffelen — 11
Barbra Verbij — 82 (portrait)
Pablo Vicens y Hualde — 30–31
Petr Vokal — 278–279
Norbert von Onna — 304, 305 b.
Jens Weber — 96–99
Guy Wenborne — 234
Wikimedia Commons: Dori — 9
Wikimedia Commons: Raggatt2000 — 8
Michael Wolff — 230
Frank Wurzer — 190 (portrait), 202 (portrait), 216 (portrait)
Luke Yeung — 274–275
Kim Yong-Kwan — 288
Nicole Zimmermann — 218 (portrait), 236 (portrait), 244 (portrait)
Thomas Züger — 158–159

Cover front: — Roland Halbe/arturimages
Cover back left: — Faulders Studio
Cover back right: — Åke E:son Lindman

IMPRINT

The Deutsche Nationalbibliothek lists this publication in the
Deutsche Nationalbibliografie; detailed bibliographic data
are available in the Internet at http://dnb.d-nb.de.
ISBN 978-3-03768-110-7

© 2012 by Braun Publishing AG
www.braun-publishing.ch

1st edition 2012

Editorial staff: Manuela Roth, Jan Schneider,
Chris van Uffelen
Translation: Cosima Talhouni
Graphic concept: ON Grafik | Tom Wibberenz
Layout: Michaela Prinz
Reproduction: Bild1Druck GmbH, Berlin